The Threshold of Democracy

Athens in 403 BCE

FOURTH EDITION

REACTING CONSORTIUM

OTHER TITLES IN THIS SERIES

Greenwich Village, 1913: Suffrage, Labor, and the New Woman
Mary Jane Treacy
Patriots, Loyalists, and Revolution in New York City, 1775–1776, Second Edition
Bill Offutt
Rousseau, Burke, and Revolution in France, 1791, Second Edition
Jennifer Popiel, Mark C. Carnes, and Gary Kates

Also available

Charles Darwin, the Copley Medal and the Rise of Naturalism, 1862–64
Marsha Driscoll, Elizabeth E. Dunn, Dann P. Siems, and B. Kamran Swanson
Confucianism and the Succession Crisis of the Wanli Emperor, 1587
Daniel K. Gardner and Mark C. Carnes
Defining a Nation: India on the Eve of Independence, 1945
Ainslie T. Embree and Mark C. Carnes
Henry VIII and the Reformation Parliament
John Patrick Coby
The Trial of Anne Hutchinson: Liberty, Law, and Intolerance in Puritan New England
Michael P. Winship and Mark C. Carnes
The Trial of Galileo: Aristotelianism, the "New Cosmology," and the Catholic Church, 1616–33
Frederick Purnell Jr., Michael S. Pettersen, and Mark C. Carnes

CONTRIBUTING ADVISORS

Lisa Cox, Greenfield Community College

Rebecca Kennedy, Denison University

Kenny Morrell, Rhodes College

Bret Mulligan, Haverford College

The Threshold of Democracy

Athens in 403 BCE

FOURTH EDITION

Josiah Ober Stanford University
Naomi J. Norman University of Georgia
Mark C. Carnes Barnard College

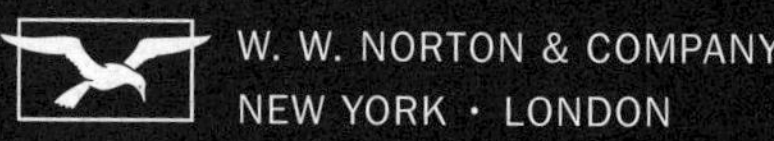

W. W. Norton & Company has been independent since its founding in 1923, when William Warder Norton and Mary D. Herter Norton first published lectures delivered at the People's Institute, the adult education division of New York City's Cooper Union. The firm soon expanded its program beyond the Institute, publishing books by celebrated academics from America and abroad. By midcentury, the two major pillars of Norton's publishing program—trade books and college texts—were firmly established. In the 1950s, the Norton family transferred control of the company to its employees, and today—with a staff of four hundred and a comparable number of trade, college, and professional titles published each year—W. W. Norton & Company stands as the largest and oldest publishing house owned wholly by its employees.

Printed in the United States of America

Associate Editor: Justin Cahill
Project Editor: Jennifer Barnhardt
Editorial Assistants: Travis Carr and Penelope Lin
Managing Editor, College: Marian Johnson
Managing Editor, College Digital Media: Kim Yi
Production Manager: Ashley Horna
Marketing Manager, History: Sarah England
Design Director: Rubina Yeh
Book Design: Alexandra Charitan
Permissions Manager: Megan Jackson
Composition: Jouve International
Illustrations: Malcolm Swanston
Manufacturing: Sheridan Books, Inc.

Library of Congress Cataloging-in-Publication Data

Ober, Josiah.
The threshold of democracy: Athens in 403 B.C. / Josiah Ober, Naomi J. Norman, Mark C. Carnes. — Fourth edition.
pages cm. — (Reacting to the past)
Includes bibliographical references.
Summary: "In this updated addition to the Reacting to the Past family, the classroom is transformed into 5th-century Athens, a city divided in the wake of military defeat and open rebellion. With democratic stability uncertain, students must draw from a wide range of perspectives and original source material to approach issues of citizenship, elections, re-militarization, and dissent. Students also engage directly with history through innovative role-playing games, devised by acclaimed pedagogical experts, which develop leadership, speaking, writing, and critical thinking skills in a fun and unique classroom experience" — Provided by publisher.
ISBN 978-0-393-93887-6 (paperback)
1. Democracy—Greece—Athens—History—To 1500. 2. Democracy—Greece—Athens—History—To 1500—Sources. 3. Athens (Greece)—Politics and government. 4. Athens (Greece)—Politics and government—Sources. I. Norman, Naomi J. II. Carnes, Mark C. (Mark Christopher), 1950- III. Title.
JC75.D36C37 2016
320.938'5—dc23

2015019000

W. W. Norton & Company, Inc., 500 Fifth Avenue, New York, NY 10110-0017
wwnorton.com
W. W. Norton & Company Ltd., 15 Carlisle Street, London W1D 3BS

6 7 8 9 0

ABOUT THE AUTHORS

JOSIAH OBER is Constantine Mitsotakis Professor in the School of Humanities and Sciences at Stanford University, where he holds joint appointments in the departments of political science and classics. He is the author of several books on classical Athenian political and intellectual history, most recently *Political Dissent in Democratic Athens* (Princeton University Press, 2001). He is currently working on a project about the relationship between democratic political culture and the social circulation of knowledge.

NAOMI J. NORMAN is a Josiah Meigs Distinguished Teaching Professor of Classics at the University of Georgia, where she teaches courses in Greek, classical culture, and classical archaeology, and serves as director of the UGA Reacting to the Past program. Her current projects include a book on the archaeology of ancient Carthage, a textbook on classical archaeology, and, with Carl Anderson and T. Keith Dix, a Reacting game that takes place in Rome on the Ides of March, 44 BCE.

MARK C. CARNES is professor of history at Barnard College and creator of Reacting to the Past. He is the author of many books on American history and general editor of the twenty-six-volume *American National Biography*, published by the ACLS and Oxford University Press.

CONTENTS

The Threshold of Democracy

Athens in 403 BCE

FOURTH EDITION

PART 1: INTRODUCTION

BRIEF OVERVIEW OF THE GAME

The Threshold of Democracy: Athens in 403 BCE recreates the intellectual and political dynamics of one of the most formative periods in Western history. After nearly three decades of war, Sparta crushed democratic Athens, destroyed its warships and great walls, and installed a brutal regime, the "Thirty Tyrants." Their bloody excesses led to a brief civil war and, as the game begins, the tyrants have been expelled and democracy restored. But questions remain.

Is direct democracy, as Pericles conceived of it, an effective mode of governance? Should Athens retain a political system in which all decisions are made through open debate by an assembly of six thousand citizens? Should leaders and magistrates continue to be chosen by random lottery? Should citizenship be broadened to include slaves who fought for democracy and foreign-born metics who paid taxes in its support? Should Athens rebuild its defensive walls and warships and again extract tribute from city-states throughout the eastern Mediterranean?

Or should Athenian citizens listen to the critics? These include powerful landowners, who propose to replace the Assembly with a governing council, and the followers of Socrates, who advocate a governing elite chosen for its intellectual merit and philosophical disposition. Should Athens eschew imperialism and naval expansion and instead focus on agricultural pursuits?

After a few class sessions to set up the game, the instructor/Gamemaster will assign every player a role in the game. Most will be assigned to one of several political factions, ranging from the Thrasybulans, the radical democratic followers of Thrasybulus, to the more moderate Periclean democrats, to the conservative Solonian aristocrats (oligarchs), and, lastly, to the followers of Socrates. Each player will also be assigned to a position in the government by random lottery, some serving as Assembly President, others as magistrates (archons) in the court system, and still others as practitioners of various religious rites. Players win by achieving some or most of their victory objectives, which sometimes include secret goals and strategies. But the most reliable path to victory is to persuade others—especially "undecided" figures—to vote in support of your positions. Although "undecided" or "indeterminate" players are free to be persuaded on many issues, they will also "represent" Athenian constituencies and positions.

The debates are informed by Plato's *Republic*, as well as excerpts from the speeches of Pericles, an important democratic leader, the texts of Thucydides and Xenophon (who, though they may appear as figures in the game, have also provided written accounts of the recent history of Athens), and other contemporary sources. By examining democracy at its threshold, the game provides a profound basis for considerations of its subsequent evolution.

PROLOGUE

In the Footsteps of Theseus

In the dark you stumble. Your heart pounds. The Spartan ambush was on a night like this. Iron swords ripping into leather and flesh. A piercing scream. Arms frozen in terror. By the time you raised your sword they were gone. Was it one attacker, or ten? And then you stumbled, a body at your feet. A warm, sticky fluid oozed through your sandals. And then a soft, desperate panting. It was Euromachus, a childhood friend, a member of your patrol. By morning, the panting had stopped. There was a deep gash in his neck. He was dead.

But that was then, during the war. You force yourself to breathe. The war is over. The Spartans have gone home. You have tripped on a loose stone, not a body. The roads have probably not been repaired since the slaves ran off, when the Spartans occupied this part of Attica. With the city so poor, many citizens now perform tasks suited only for slaves. Think of it! Free women serving as wet nurses, your own mother selling trifles in the agora.

You get your bearings: Castor and Pollux remain high in the sky, but Taurus has begun to slide toward the western horizon. Taurus, the bull! Was the constellation named after the Minotaur, the monster that dwelt beneath the palace of King Minos of Crete and devoured the Athenian children? That was when Crete was a great power and Athens a mere vassal state, obliged each year to send a boatload of children for sacrifice. In your lifetime, though, it's been the other way around: Athens has collected annual tribute—great piles of silver—from other city-states. It built the glorious Parthenon, high atop the Acropolis, and other impressive temples. And the Long Walls. And mighty fleets of triremes, filling the harbor of Piraeus. (See the map on page 34.)

But the fleets are gone. The triremes have been sunk and the Long Walls dismantled. Spartan soldiers control the city, including the temples on the Acropolis. Will Athens now become a vassal of Sparta?

Back in ancient times, Theseus emerged to slay the Minotaur. Then he brought the many tribes of Attica together so that they became one: the *demos*—the people—of Athens. You remember, too, that Theseus walked along the very road on which you now tread. Perhaps it was where you stumbled that Theseus came upon the half-beast who murdered wayfarers for the fun of it. But Theseus was a demigod and threw the beast over a cliff, the first of his many deeds to rid Athens of its enemies. And that was long, long ago, when the gods mingled with human flesh and begat people of divine proportions. Nowadays people are smaller, and the gods pay them less heed. Perhaps that's why things have gone so wrong.

The sun smolders in the east, below Mount Hymettus, and a faint haze extinguishes the nearest stars. Darkness loosens its grip on earth, and you can see the outline of the hills and valleys of Attica. You breathe more easily. The fields should soon be coming to life. It is the season of *Boedromion*—"the time to harvest olives," as Hesiod wrote so many generations ago. Last night after dinner you unrolled your volume of his treatise on farming and showed it to your cousins and uncles. "Better to study things as they are, and not the symbols of them," they teased you. But as you described his advice, they listened. "Leave the fields fallow every other year," you read aloud, and saw that they were nodding in agreement. "Be sure to have a sharp-toothed dog to keep away thieves," you read, and as you intoned Hesiod's words you stared at the shaggy mutt by the fire. Everyone laughed. "No matter," your uncle replied. "Thieves won't bother anyone. Nothing left to steal. Spartans burned the barley and ripped up most of the grapevines and fig trees. Even the sacred olive trees."

His words weighed upon you. They still do. Athens needs leadership. Leaders like you—and you wince. *You* led your platoon into an ambush. You will never forget Euromachus's lifeless eyes, staring at you. You carried his body back to Athens, his blood drenching your cloak. You worried that his head, severed at the neck, might fall off.

You still carry that burden as you walk to Athens—and to the Pnyx. (See the map on page 34.)

Now you can see the Dipylon Gate—at least what's left of it. Within Athens, thousands are awakening. They, too, will soon be hurrying to the Pnyx, carrying bags of figs and bread dipped in olive oil to tide them through the afternoon. Usually the city people get the best seats. You hasten along, but the road has become clogged with farmers, all pressing toward the Dipylon Gate. You know that similar throngs are streaming through the other dozen or so gates of Athens. The road from Piraeus will be choked with perhaps a thousand citizens, mostly oarsmen who used to be paid by the state to row the triremes, the immense warships that for decades defended Athens and ensured its superiority throughout the Aegean. But now that the triremes are gone, how will the sailor-citizens make a living?

At the Dipylon Gate

As you walk through the gate, a shaft of light strikes the Parthenon atop the Acropolis, the citadel of Athens. For centuries the Acropolis was invulnerable. In the time of Theseus, the wild warrior-women—Amazons—swept down from the Black Sea and nearly forced their way up and into the fortress. But they failed. Many decades ago the Persian horde under King Xerxes seized the Acropolis. Your great grandfather was among those who served in the navy that destroyed the Persian fleet in the Gulf of Salamis in 480 BCE, forcing the Persians to withdraw. It was after more Athenian victories two decades later that Pericles called for construction of the Parthenon, begun in 447 BCE, which houses an enormous golden statue of Athena. Many said that the temple, though dedicated to a goddess, was really a monument to Pericles and Athenian democracy.

Some say that if Pericles had not died so early in the war Athens would not have been defeated. Like so many Athenians, he was taken by the Great Plague—twenty-six years ago, in 429 BCE, when you were still a child. That you survived was something of a miracle, or so your relatives claimed. Pericles erred, many said, in abandoning the countryside to the Spartans and crowding the citizens within the gates of Athens. Pericles thought the people of Attica would be secure behind its Long Walls, a fortification that stretched for miles to Piraeus, protecting both cities and creating a safe corridor between them. No one would go hungry: grain ships from the Black Sea and Egypt could unload at Piraeus and transport food and other necessities by cart through the protected corridor to Athens. The Athenian navy, with hundreds of triremes, was invincible; it would ensure the safe arrival of grain ships. Everyone knew that. But the city became overcrowded, with tens of thousands of people inhabiting rude huts along the inside of the Long Walls. Then came the plague. Many thousands died, more than could be buried properly.

Athens did not surrender then, and the war continued, interrupted by a few brief truces. Nor did it surrender ten years ago, after the disaster in Sicily, when the Athenian invasion force of fifty thousand men was wiped out. The better part of an entire generation—the young men of Athens—never returned from the other side of the world. Sparta then set up permanent camps beyond the walls, and thousands of slaves fled Athens and slipped into the countryside. Yet even then Sparta could not breach the walls of Athens. Many pointed to this as proof of the wisdom of Pericles' strategy.

Until last year, 405 BCE. Then the Athenian generals committed the horrible blunder at Aegospotami. They allowed the Spartan navy to capture or destroy nearly a hundred triremes, many of them sitting helpless on the beach. Most of the Athenian sailors were butchered. With the Spartan navy free to blockade Piraeus, the grain ships could not get through. The Spartan army then tightened its siege outside the Long Walls. Last year the people of Athens and Piraeus went without food. For months they held out. Better starve, most reasoned, than be slaughtered by the Spartans. Spartan mercy, the saying went, was an oxymoron. (You recall the stony faces when the Athenian Assembly voted to execute all of the men of Mytilene and sell their women and children as slaves; Mytilene had sided with Sparta during the war.)

Last spring, with many dying of hunger, Athens at last surrendered. And Spartan troops marched through the Dipylon Gate and set up camp in the Acropolis, from which vantage point they could keep an eye on everyone.

You notice that the crowd has funneled into a bottleneck at the gate. You see that some avoid it simply by climbing over the rubble of the ancient walls, great squares of cut stone. You take the shortcut, too, hurrying past the boulders where Spartan soldiers stood, stiffly and silently, supervising the work as half-starved Athenian laborers dismantled the walls. Young girls played the flute while soldiers from Thebes and Corinth—Sparta's allies—wore garlands of flowers and gestured obscenely at the vanquished Athenians. At you. You looked down. For as long as you can remember, Athens ruled much of the Aegean. Now must it become a vassal state to Sparta—and to Thebes and Corinth as well? Are Athenians to be little more than slaves, subject to the will of others?

At the Agora

You arrive at the Agora, the lifeblood of Athens where all roads converge. Vendors are setting up stands and merchants are opening their shops. Many of the merchants are metics, foreign-born residents who pay a fee to live in Athens. There are fewer than in the past, and some of the shops are gone. How can you run a business when few have the money to buy your wares? You check the sun. You will be at the Pnyx within twenty minutes—plenty of time—and you cannot resist taking a stroll. You walk across the racetrack toward the monument to the Ten Tribal Heroes. A group has crowded around it, but only a single message is posted: "Assembly Today."

After the Spartans had occupied Athens and destroyed its Long Walls, a similar notice was posted. You got up early that day, too. Critias was the first to speak—and the last. He explained that democracy had failed Athens—that democracy was a pestilential form of government that endangered all of Greece. He added that the Spartans had no desire to destroy the Athenian people, but only to rid Athens of its democracy and its pretensions of empire. Thus the survival of Athens required the elimination of the democratic empire. The people of Athens would be spared, he declared, if they followed his counsel.

He suggested appointing thirty prominent citizens—he read their names—who would determine the ancient "constitution" of Athens. They would temporarily rule the city. Eventually, Critias added, the Council of Thirty would be guided by an Assembly limited to three thousand substantial citizens—those who would do what was best for the city without looking for state handouts or the fees paid to rowers on triremes. Some shouted objections, but Critias gestured toward the Spartan troops ringed along the top of the Pnyx, spears at the ready. "If we do not do as I propose," he added, "Athens will be turned into a pasture." This brought more shouts, but most people could not take their eyes off the Spartans. The man next to you muttered, "It's a done deal." Critias's plan was endorsed. The Council of Thirty would govern Athens; the democracy was dead.

You pause as you walk past the lawcourts. That's where the evil began. The evening after Critias's takeover, he ordered the arrest of several prominent democrats, including Dionysodorus, who had opposed surrender. They were secretly tried for treason and executed. "The city must be purged of unjust men," Critias declared, and "the rest of the citizens must be inclined to virtue and justice." Critias then hired a police force of three hundred young men who carried whips, seized weapons from democrats, and otherwise intimidated them. The thugs singled out metics for harassment and arrest, especially those who were rich and possessed large fortunes. Then still more democrats were arrested. Whenever an arrest turned into a riot, Critias's soldiers ran to fetch the Spartans. Many democrats fled Athens. A few vowed to destroy Critias and the Thirty Tyrants, as they were now called.

Thrasybulus emerged as leader of the democratic insurgents. He set up camp at the old fort at Phyle, north of Athens, and declared war on the Thirty Tyrants. Several hundred democrats joined his band. He put out word that metics and even slaves who fought with him would be given the rights of Athenian citizens. Several hundred metics enlisted in his army, as did perhaps a hundred slaves. Within several weeks he had an army of nearly 750.

The Thirty cracked down harder on the remaining democrats in Athens. In all, about 1,500 were executed, most without trials. Then Critias and his supporters, backed by the Spartan garrison, marched out to Phyle to crush Thrasybulus. But Thrasybulus attacked first, catching Critias by surprise, and inflicted heavy casualties. That night the Thirty set up camp in the field. Snow began to fall that night and continued throughout the next day. The Spartans, cold and unnerved by the stiff opposition, trudged back to Athens. Word of Thrasybulus's astonishing victory spread throughout Attica, and more democrats joined him in Phyle. A few nights later his army slipped around Athens and into Piraeus, where he took a strong position at the ancient fort atop the hill at Munichia, within the city. The Thirty attacked the next day, backed by seven hundred Spartans, but again were thrown back. Over one hundred Spartans were killed, and Critias lay dead, too. The democrats controlled Piraeus.

There were more battles last year. For a time Thrasybulus and his ragtag army seized the initiative. But the civil war descended into a stalemate. Eventually Pausanias, one of the two kings of Sparta, met with Thrasybulus and the moderate

Athenian oligarchs—those who disapproved of the Thirty. The two sides—democrats and oligarchs—agreed to settle their differences and establish a government based on the ancient constitution of Athens. (What that meant was anyone's guess.) Then Pausanias withdrew the Spartan garrison. This was just last week. Within hours, the Thirty Tyrants were gone, too, having fled. Yesterday, Thrasybulus and his men marched triumphantly back into Athens. And word was posted that the Assembly meetings would resume. Today.

At the Cobbler's Shop: With the Followers of Thrasybulus

As you hasten through the Agora, you spot Thrasybulus at the cobbler's shop. His arm remains bandaged from the wound he received at Piraeus. You wonder if he killed Critias by his own hand.

You notice that Thrasybulus is gesturing forcefully as he speaks with Anytus, wealthy owner of a tannery. Huddled with them are several metics; one slave is also talking and gesturing animatedly. You know a number of slaves, as well as metics, joined democrats in Piraeus and fought bravely against the Thirty Tyrants. They acted then as if they were citizens; doubtless Thrasybulus intends to propose that they be granted actual citizenship.

A friend, one of Thrasybulus's followers, beckons. You gesture to the swords and wicker shields that have been heaped next to the pile of unfinished leather. "What," you ask, "will happen at the Assembly today?" "We shall see," your friend replies. "The forces of oligarchy are tenacious. We all thought they had been finished off eight years ago, when we put down the oligarchical coup [of 411 BCE]. But they came back, and with a bloody vengeance. Now the Thirty are once again rumored to be gone and oligarchy disgraced for good. But the only time you can deal with them is when they're dead. We must root out all of the enemies of democracy once and for all."

He offers some barley cakes, but you shrug your shoulders and wave your hand toward the Pnyx. "Got to go," you say. He tugs at your tunic: "We're trying something new, you see? The kings of Persia and Sparta, the tyrants of Syracuse and Carthage, the oligarchs of Corinth—the whole world hates and fears democracy. But we know it works. It gives people a say in their destiny, so they work and fight harder. When the Persians herded their huge army into Greece, driving them forward with whips and spears, they were amazed when the Athenian soldiers charged to meet them at Marathon, ready to die for their state. A few months ago, when we ambushed Critias and the Spartans at Phyle, screaming with fury, some of them ran, piss dripping down their legs. Spartans!

I tell you, democracy is the way of the future. But it won't happen by itself. Democracy will prevail only when the enemies of democracy have been crushed. I saw them butcher Phrenycus, hacking him down like a dog. Right in the middle of the street. And I know who was behind it. My god, he must pay for his crime!"

His words send a shiver down your spine. As you leave, somewhat hastily, you beg his forgiveness.

At the Moneylenders' Tables: The Socratic School

Just beyond the bankers' tables, you spot Socrates, a notably ugly and ill-kempt old man. He is famous—even infamous—for his startling views and irrepressible wit. He says that the Athenian people are like sheep; that they are easily swayed by powerful orators, whether in the Assembly, the lawcourts, or the theater; that they make fools of themselves in pondering—collectively!—complicated issues of jurisprudence or affairs of diplomacy and warfare; that they are more concerned with pilfering drachmas from the public treasury than with establishing justice and promoting virtue; that they do not think much, or often, or well. The more he indicts the people and institutions of Athens, the more his students applaud him, or so some say.

You recall that Socrates was the subject of the first play you ever saw, *Clouds*. It was by Aristophanes, in the new style—a comedy. Why, you wonder, did Aristophanes and comedy become all the rage during the nearly three decades Athens was continually at war? In *Clouds*, Aristophanes portrayed Socrates as keeper of a "think-shop" that floats among the clouds: "Never could I have discerned matters celestial, if I did not mingle my intellect with its kindred air." One Strepsiades, beleaguered by debts, approaches Socrates to learn "Wrong Logic" so as to confuse and evade his creditors. In your favorite scene, Socrates inquires as to Strepsiades' aptitude for logic.

> SOCRATES: Is your memory good?
> STREPSIADES: It all depends. Good if someone owes me; if I owe someone, alas, it is very bad.
> SOCRATES: Have you a gift for speaking?
> STREPSIADES: For speaking, no. For cheating, yes.
> SOCRATES: What do you do if someone hits you?
> STREPSIADES: I wait a bit and get witnesses. Then I file suit.

Like everyone else, you laughed. But now Socrates is regarded differently. You notice the grim expressions of the young men gathered about him by the tables. You spot Aristocles and Xenophon, young men of good families who have always been among

Socrates' gabby gathering. They look worried. There were whispers about Socrates and Critias when the Tyrant held absolute power. Now that Critias is dead and gone, many remark that he was once one of Socrates' most faithful students. Socrates also taught Alcibiades, who betrayed Athens eleven years ago and then helped Thrasybulus during the oligarchical coup of 411 BCE. Some ask whether Socrates taught Critias and Alcibiades the Wrong Logic, thus instigating the crimes of the Thirty.

Socrates apparently envisions a society in which philosophers (such as him and his students? you wonder) serve as rulers while eschewing the pleasures of wealth and power. The "guardians," as they would be called, are to lead simple, chaste lives, dedicated solely to the welfare of everyone else. Even women, if adjudged intellectually superior, will join the ruling elite of this utopia. There will be no Assembly meetings or *dikasteria* (lawcourts), which Socrates says encourage the ignorant to discuss matters beyond their comprehension. Nor will there be publicly sponsored plays, which teach people the arts of manipulation and encourage falseness. (And where people go to laugh at philosophers like him!) The ultimate goal of Socrates and his supporters is to purify thought, and thus to help thinkers arrive at a deeper understanding of ultimate truths. Words must be defined with precision, and ideas must fit together according to the rules of logic, devoid of the human passions and cravings that impair the operation of reason. Thought must be reflective, not intuitive. His is an ambitious notion.

Socrates' students now take their leave and head toward the Pnyx, carrying no weapons but their wits. Socrates himself holds back. This most garrulous of Athenians refuses to take part in meetings of the Assembly—or so it is rumored. But you think you remember seeing him there, lurking in the shadows toward the back.

At the Barber's Shop: The Solonian Aristocrats

As you cross near the racetrack, you spot several prominent landowners huddled inside a barbershop. Some are wealthy—you recognize one whose father owns an enormous vineyard near Phyle that was worked, before the war, by scores of slaves. But most oligarchs are simple farming folk much like your relatives. One voice rises above the others: "We don't need—Athens doesn't need—any more tyrants, like Critias and his thugs." Several nod in agreement. "Our city should be ruled by a large group of the best men, those who care about Athens and know what is best for it." More nods. "That's what we stand for. We spit on Critias and those of his ilk. But the fact that he was evil does not prove that his enemies were blameless, or that their views are good ones." A man next to the speaker lifts a goblet of wine in a toast, and the others do likewise; they lower their voices, and then burst out in laughter.

Now the others join in. Almost to a man, they denounce Pericles' strategy for the war, which allowed enemy soldiers to pour into Attica unmolested while Athenian farmers, most of them well-trained and well-armed as foot soldiers (hoplites) and everyone else scampered to safety behind the Long Walls. Occasionally, hoplite patrols or a handful of countrymen sneaked out and ambushed small Spartan detachments. "Oh, yes," you say, thinking of Euromachus. "But sometimes they got us, too."

And so it was, as everyone knows, that Athenians fought with their best weapons (the formidable triremes) and on water, where they were invulnerable, rather than on land. While the Spartans were despoiling the fields of Attica, Athenian sailors and hoplites were boarding triremes and conducting lightning raids along the Peloponnesian coast and elsewhere. Whatever the merits of this type of warfare, the cost to the Athenian farmers and landholders was staggering. In addition to the destruction of their homes and fields, the periodic disruptions of the countryside—the Spartans would usually attack during harvest season—encouraged thousands of slaves to run away. Scores of moneylenders were ruined, and trade collapsed.

During the war, too, landowners large and small paid the heaviest taxes. The richest citizens had to build and maintain triremes. It was an honor, of course, but also an unspeakably expensive obligation. Most of the state revenue, moreover, went to pay the rowers of the triremes—the thetes, poorer citizens of Athens and Piraeus who reported for military service with no weapons save their oars. Your uncles complained that when such men could not find work, they crowded into the Assembly and voted for new expeditions or demanded that they be paid merely for showing up there or at the lawcourts. Pericles obliged them and they became his staunchest supporters, while those who owned land became his fiercest foes.

The supporters of oligarchy eye the wine bowl, but the steward, on signal from the owner of the shop, begins to gather up the drinking implements. To bring the session to an end, he declares that patriotism, virtue, and self-restraint are the basic principles of oligarchy. Critias and his ilk conformed to none of these principles. "We want order, stability, and prosperity. People must acknowledge that society is fragile. Its needs must take precedence over the desires of the individual. Society works smoothly, if at all, only when everyone accepts the limits placed on his own behavior. Pericles' great fault was his hubris: his excessive confidence and overweening pride in himself. He imagined that all Athenians could become whatever they desired. That conceit is at odds with the hard realities of the world, foremost among them the defects of human nature." The others nod. "We can wish that every shoemaker has the potential to become a statesman," he adds, "but that kind of wishful thinking is why we lost the war."

"It's time for a change," another declares, thumping his fist upon the table, his face red from exertion—or perhaps the wine.

"Well, yes and no," the owner interrupts. "Plenty will say that our humiliation is reason to try anything. Let metics who were born all over the Mediterranean become citizens! Or slaves, who would as soon cut our throats as their meat. Others will propose that we let woolly-headed sophists decide how to conduct future wars. But you and I know that time is the best test of all ideas, and that traditional beliefs have endured for good reason. Those who sail into the unknown may imagine that they will find boundless treasure; probably, though, their bones will end up on the floor of the ocean. In this time of crisis, Athenians must exercise discipline—of their polity, and of themselves. Though they may wish to eat their fill, they must accept that gluttony is a vice; though they may wish to drink wine all day and seduce their neighbor's wife"—he frowns at the red-faced friend, and the others burst into laughter—"they must learn to work and have self-control; though they may want to live to a ripe old age, they must be willing to give their life for their country. We must do so, too. Men, we must go."

As you leave the colonnade, you notice a pile of weapons stacked outside, watched over by stewards. The oligarchs and democrats had agreed yesterday not to bring their weapons to the Pnyx, but you wonder.

At the Potter's Shop: The Periclean Democrats

You leave, too, but can't resist looking in at the pottery shop, a beehive of activity. The workers are an interesting mix. Some are free while others are skilled slaves, most of whom are paid wages and allowed to keep a portion for themselves. Some were imported from truly savage regions, such as Thrace and Scythia. Some have risen rapidly in their professions. Some became managers. A few became rich. Nearby you notice women slaves gathered at a fountain. Most of them spend their days housekeeping, or are weavers, maids, wet nurses, or prostitutes.

You know the owner of the shop, a leader of the followers of Pericles. When you ask why he didn't flee Athens and join Thrasybulus and the Exiles, he explains that he thought it better to stay and help his city as best he could.

His friends long for the days of Pericles, and hope that someone like him will emerge during the current crisis. They say that if Pericles had lived, Athens would never have lost to Sparta. Another declares that he was the great leader of that or any age. Another adds that his sentences were like chiseled marble. To prove his point, he recites a few stirring lines from the speech Pericles delivered in honor of the men killed during the first year of the war (430 BCE, Core Texts, p. 89): "Our political system does not compete with institutions which are elsewhere in force. We do not copy our neighbors, but try to be an example. Our administration favors the many instead of the few: this is why it is called a democracy."

Pericles' genius, another declares, was leadership. "He knew how to make Athenians put aside their differences and work for a common goal. Like at the Olympics. Athenians learned to cooperate, whether singing in choral competitions, rowing a trireme, or acting in a play." "When Athenians work together," he adds, "they are invincible. We lost to Sparta because madmen on both sides drove a wedge through the polity and broke it apart."

The moderates say that Athens must return to the golden age that Pericles inaugurated a half century ago. They want to see the Assembly filled with earnest citizens, debating, talking, thinking, and educating themselves and the world. They want to elevate the common people to serve even as presidents and magistrates. Athens has become great due to the contributions of even the humblest citizens to its glory. The moderates long to restore the Athenian empire, to build more glorious temples and government buildings, to hold more festivals with more theatrical productions, and to reestablish Athens as the center of the civilized world.

Their vision, too, is an impressive one.

To the Pnyx

The voice of the herald rings out, calling the citizens to hurry to the Pnyx. Soon the *peristarchos* will sacrifice a pig, as was done at the time of Theseus, to ensure that the gods bestow their favor on the deliberations. You begin to run, and your thoughts race ahead, too.

What you say and do at this Assembly session, and the ones in the months ahead, will affect your life, and surely the lives of your children and grandchildren. The survival of Athens depends on you and your fellow citizens.

You hurry past the entrance to the Pnyx—this time no one is handing out the customary obols in payment—and hurry toward an open space on a stone bench toward the front. Today, you will speak. There may be no more mythic heroes of old like Theseus; today the heroes are those Athenian citizens who come together in Assembly to solve their problems.

The Pnyx swiftly fills. The herald calls on those standing in the aisles to take their seats. As they do so, you look out, past the speaker's platform, and see the shimmering Bay of Salamis. There the Athenian navy destroyed the Persians and scored the greatest victory in the history of all mankind. Your reverie is interrupted by the herald's booming voice: "Those who wish to speak should now come forward." You walk down to the rostrum and take a place in the line of speakers. You look up and try to find your neighbors, and cannot.

But you are prepared. For years you have observed closely what others have said during the Assembly, and how they have said it. You have taken notes on who has prevailed at the lawcourts and why, and which actors have won the theater contests. You have studied their words and mannerisms. You have learned about rhetoric, preferring especially the intricate strategies of Gorgias. "Break your argument into little pieces," he wrote, "and list the objections to each; then refute them, one by one." He was a brilliant rhetorician, all the more impressive for being a foreigner.

And you listened to Androcles, a good teacher despite his perverse insistence that you refrain from analogies. "A weasel's way of arguing," he insisted.

The restlessness of the crowd has unnerved the first speaker, and he has stopped in mid-sentence. There are some jeers, and he ends his talk hastily, without any peroration at all. You take a deep breath. Then the herald nods to you. You stride to the rostrum and gaze at the sea of faces. A lout jeers, "Wait 'til you've grown a beard, dearie," and others near him laugh. Androcles' words come to you: "Pause, but not too long, lest the hecklers fill the void."

You plunge ahead and concentrate on your list of points, one for each finger of your left hand (another trick). At first your words tumble out, but then you recalled Androcles' advice: "Speak slowly and clearly. Find a friendly face, or imagine one, and speak to it." As you slow down, you concentrate on what you are saying. Your words flow. Finally, you unclench the final finger, deliver the peroration with suitable emphasis, and blink. It is over. "Well done!" a bearded man in the front calls out.

Your knees tremble as you make your way back to your seat. Strangers reach out to clap you on the back and grab your hand. You recall that several people near the front, the ones who customarily write out the speeches of the best orators, were scribbling away during yours. You look for your friends, seeking affirmation in their eyes. But then you recall those of Euromachus, your childhood friend. This is not about you, but about Athens.

Your work is not finished. It has just begun.

HOW TO REACT

Reacting to the Past is a series of historical role-playing games. After a few preparatory lectures, the game begins and the students are in charge. Set in moments of heightened historical tension, the games place students in the roles of historical figures. By reading the game book and their individual role sheets, students discover their objectives, potential allies, and the forces that stand between them and victory. They must then attempt to achieve victory through formal speeches, informal debate, negotiations, and (sometimes) conspiracy. Outcomes sometimes part from actual history; a postmortem session sets the record straight.

The following is an outline of what you will encounter in Reacting and what you will be expected to do.

Game Setup

Your instructor will spend some time before the beginning of the game helping you to understand the historical context for the game. During the setup period, you will use several different kinds of material:

- You have received the game book (from which you are reading now), which includes historical information, rules and elements of the game, and essential documents.
- Your instructor will provide you with a role sheet, which provides a short biography of the historical figure you will model in the game as well as that person's ideology, objectives, responsibilities, and resources. Your role may be an actual historical figure or a composite.

In addition to the game book, you may also be required to read historical documents or books written by historians. These provide additional information and arguments for use during the game.

Read all of this contextual material and all of these documents and sources before the game begins. And just as important, go back and reread these materials throughout the game. A second and third reading while *in role* will deepen your understanding and alter your perspective, for ideas take on a different aspect when seen through the eyes of a partisan actor.

Students who have carefully read the materials and who know the rules of the game will invariably do better than those who rely on general impressions and uncertain memories.

Game Play

Once the game begins, class sessions are presided over by students. In most cases, a single student serves as a kind of presiding officer. The instructor then becomes the Gamemaster (GM) and takes a seat in the back of the room. Though they do not lead the class sessions, GMs may do any of the following:

- Pass notes
- Announce important events (e.g. Sparta is invading!). Some of these events are the result of student actions; others are instigated by the GM
- Redirect proceedings that have gone off track

The presiding officer is expected to observe basic standards of fairness, but as a fail-safe device, most Reacting to the Past games employ the "Podium Rule," which allows a student who has not been recognized to approach the podium and wait for a chance to speak. Once at the podium, the student has the floor and must be heard.

Role sheets contain private, secret information which students are expected to guard. You are advised, therefore, to exercise caution when discussing your role with others. Your role sheet probably identifies likely allies, but even they may not always be trustworthy. However, keeping your own counsel, or saying nothing to anyone, is not an option. In order to achieve your objectives, you *must* speak with others. You will never muster the voting strength to prevail without allies. Collaboration and coalition building are at the heart of every game.

These discussions must lead to action, which often means proposing, debating, and passing legislation. Someone therefore must be responsible for introducing the measure and explaining its particulars. And always remember that a Reacting game is only a game—resistance, attack, and betrayal are not to be taken personally, since game opponents are merely acting as their roles direct.

Some games feature strong alliances called *factions*: these are tight-knit groups with fixed objectives. Games with factions all include roles called Indeterminates, who operate outside of the established factions. Not all Indeterminates are entirely neutral; some are biased on certain issues. If you are in a faction, cultivating Indeterminates is in your interest, since they can be convinced to support your position. If you are lucky enough to have drawn the role of an Indeterminate you should be pleased; you will likely play a pivotal role in the outcome of the game.

Game Requirements

Students in Reacting practice persuasive writing, public speaking, critical thinking, teamwork, negotiation, problem solving, collaboration, adapting to changing circumstances, and working under pressure to meet deadlines. Your instructor will explain the specific requirements for your class. In general, though, a Reacting game asks you to perform three distinct activities:

Reading and Writing. This standard academic work is carried on more purposefully in a Reacting course, since what you read is put to immediate use, and what you write is meant to persuade others to act the way you want them to. The reading load may have slight variations from role to role; the writing requirement depends on your particular course. Papers are often policy statements, but they can also be autobiographies, battle plans, spy reports, newspapers, poems, or after-game reflections. Papers provide the foundation for the speeches delivered in class.

Public Speaking and Debate. In the course of a game, almost everyone is expected to deliver at least one formal speech from the podium (the length of the game and the size of the class will determine the number of speeches). Debate follows. It can be impromptu, raucous, and fast-paced, and results in decisions voted on by the body. Gamemasters may stipulate that students must deliver their papers from memory when at the podium, or may insist that students wean themselves from dependency on written notes as the game progresses.

Wherever the game imaginatively puts you, it will surely not put you in the classroom of a twenty-first-century American college. Accordingly, the colloquialisms and familiarities of today's college life are out of place. Never open your speech with a salutation like "Hi guys" when something like "Fellow citizens!" would be more appropriate.

Never be friendless when standing at the podium. Do your best to have at least one supporter second your proposal, come to your defense, or admonish inattentive members of the body. Note-passing and side conversations, while common occurrences, will likely spoil the effect of your speech; so you and your supporters should insist upon order before such behavior becomes too disruptive. Ask the presiding officer to assist you, if necessary, and the Gamemaster as a last resort.

Strategizing. Communication among students is an essential feature of Reacting games. You will find yourself writing emails, texting, attending out-of-class meetings, or gathering for meals on a fairly regular basis. The purpose of frequent communication is to lay out a strategy for advancing your agenda and thwarting the agenda of your opponents, and to hatch plots to ensnare individuals troubling to your cause. When communicating with a fellow student in or out of class, always assume that he or she is speaking to you in role. If you want to talk about the "real world," make that clear.

Counterfactuals

In several respects, this game departs from the actual history of Athens. These departures are "counterfactual"—they do not accord with the known facts. The counterfactual elements bring out additional ideas and enhance game play.

For one, the game assumes that Plato's *Republic,* a central text, contains the actual words spoken by Socrates. Most scholars believe that while Plato was a conscientious student of Socrates, his dialogues were imaginative reconstructions that probably do not reflect his teacher's exact words. For the purposes of the game, however, players can cite Socrates' words in the *Republic* as actual quotations from that great teacher. For example, critics of Socrates, such as those who may wish to place him on trial, can use quotations from the *Republic* as evidence of what he has said, as can those who support him.

A second counterfactual premise concerns the absence of Socrates as a figure in the game. Socrates was a highly visible figure in the Agora, often surrounded by young followers. But no player in the game is assigned the role of Socrates. If he is placed on trial, "he" will speak only through quotations from Plato's *Republic*.

Some role sheets, furthermore, include facts and details that have been created for the game. For example, the game assumes that Xenophon is 30 years old in 403 BCE, and thus eligible to attend the Assembly. Records show that he was in fact younger.

Athenian democracy at this time provided the Assembly with the power to debate policies and determine laws; the *boule,* a small group of advisers, merely set the agenda. The game does not provide for a boule, or council, when the game begins. The agenda for the Assembly sessions has been partially predetermined, although the President is usually free to add one or more agenda items. This is to simplify game play.

Another counterfactual concerns the passage of time. The game itself will unfold over six sessions occupying nearly a month of class time. But for purposes of the game, the time that elapses between or even during class sessions is of much greater duration, perhaps even encompassing an entire year. Thus the Assembly may vote to build a fleet of triremes during the fifth session, with ships ready to be rowed by the sixth. The Gamemaster will decide how much time has elapsed in all instances.

But remember: although Reacting time is elastic, it is not reversible. The game takes place from the fall of 403 BCE through the year or so after it. No one can refer as "facts" to things that have not yet occurred. If you speak of the United States of America, the people in the Athenian Assembly will assume you have lost your mental faculties. They may even ostracize you as someone whose rants offend the gods.

PART 2: HISTORICAL BACKGROUND

CHRONOLOGY

Ancient Athens

700–500 BCE Archaic Period

- Cross-cultural contacts formed (e.g., with Egypt); tyranny in many Greek city-states; a flourishing of art, architecture, and literature

500–323 Classical Period

- Cross-cultural contacts expanded; various experiments conducted in politics, including Athenian democracy; advances in art, architecture and literature

490–479 Persian War

- September 490: Battle of Marathon
- August 480: Battles of Thermopylae and Artemisium
- September 480: Battle of Salamis
- June 479: Battle of Plataea

431–404 Peloponnesian War

- 431–421: Archidamian War. Pericles' funeral oration (see Core Texts, pp. 89–94) (431/30); plague at Athens (430/29); Mytilene unsuccessfully tries to withdraw from empire and Athenians debate fate of men, women, and children of city (428); Spartan troops surrender to Athenians at Sphacteria on the island of Pylos (425/24); peace of Nicias (421).
- 416–413: Sicilian Campaign. Athenian assembly votes to send a huge force to Sicily (416); mutilation of the Herms; fleet sails to Sicily under command of Alcibiades, Lamachos, and Nicias (June 415); Nicias asks Athens to send more troops to Sicily (Winter 414/13); Athenian expedition to Sicily obliterated (413)
- 412–404: Final Phase (Ionian War). Ionia in revolt against tribute payments to Athens (412); oligarchic coup of the Four Hundred temporarily rules Athens; Aristophanes' play *Lysistrata* performed in Athens (411); Alcibiades (who had fled Sicily for Sparta first and then fled Sparta) recalled to Athens (409) (he flees again in 408); 20,000 slaves who had been working in the silver mines escape to Decelea (which was occupied by Spartan troops) (407); Athens cobbles together a new fleet and scores a victory at Arginusae; generals fail to rescue shipwrecked Athenian sailors and this scandal clouds the victory (406);

- 412–404, continued: Athenian fleet destroyed by Lysander and the Spartan fleet off Aegospotami (405); Sparta blockades Athens by sea and land—thousands of men, women, and children die of starvation (Winter 404); Athens surrenders to Sparta (Spring 404).
- 404–403: Reign of the Thirty, eventually deposed by Athenians under command of Thrasybulus

---

THE FOUNDATIONS OF ATHENIAN DEMOCRACY

The Threshold of Democracy takes place in 403 BCE, but to prevail, players (and all people!) must understand the deeper historical context of the times in which they live. Your character brings to the game a personal history, a family history, and a cultural history. These histories shape your place in the world, your personal ideas, and your motivations—all of which will affect the actions you take. This part of the game book offers an overview of Athenian history so you can understand how you fit in—and provides some suggestions on how you should approach unanticipated developments.

Greek City-States

It is common for modern historians to speak of "ancient Greece," but this term is not appropriate: "Greece" is a modern political concept, not an ancient one. In antiquity, the territory that we now call Greece was never politically unified. Indeed the mountainous and rocky terrain, the isolated valleys, and the many islands dotting the Aegean Sea encouraged the formation of many local centers of power instead of a single unified state. These local centers are now called city-states—"city" because of their size, and "state" because of their independent political, societal, economic, and military systems. The Greeks called this kind of independent city-state a *polis* (plural: *poleis*), from which we get the word *politics*.

> It generally took two or more days to traverse the fifty miles from Athens to Corinth. Ancient roads were deeply rutted at best and mere tracks at worst. Overland travel was accomplished by wagon or cart, drawn by donkeys or oxen and averaging only about fifteen to twenty miles per day over flat stretches. Sea travel was similarly protracted: the twenty-mile journey from the island of Naxos to the island of Paros, for example, took a full day.

Among Greek city-states Athens was one of the most important, controlling the region known as Attica (see the map on page 24). Athens's main rivals in the fifth century BCE were Thebes, Corinth, and Sparta.

In spite of many distinct differences among the poleis, the Hellenes (the term used by the Greeks) thought of themselves as an identifiable people distinct from their neighbors, whom they called the *barbaroi*. Indeed, Herodotus, a fifth-century BCE Greek historian, praised "the kinship of all Greeks in blood and speech, the shrines of the gods and sacrifices held in common, and common customs too" (8.144). The ancient Greeks all spoke the same language, practiced the same religion, and followed the same cultural practices. Yet they were a fractious people; political upheaval and wars were common. Although all of the Hellenes spoke Greek, they were divided by the development of regional dialects and localized cultural peculiarities. Any Spartan who visited Athens, for example, would be instantly recognized as soon as he opened his mouth because he spoke a distinctive dialect of Greek. Any Athenian who visited Sparta would have been confused (at best) and horrified (at worst) by the whipping of young boys that was part of the Spartan ritual to the goddess Artemis Orthia.

Geography and Climate

The territory of Greece is mountainous and has a very long coastline (about nine thousand miles) with many natural harbors. This distinctive geography—especially the mountain ranges—not only hindered political unification but was also, and continues to be, unsuitable for large scale agriculture; only 20 percent of the entire area is capable of growing grains, olives, and grapevines (the three main staples of the ancient Greek diet). In addition, the small rivers that feed the crops tend to dry up in the summer. Indeed, the winter rainy season (October through May) is followed by a summer drought in July and August. Even in a good year, the average rainfall is barely sufficient to support the major crops; in a bad year, a lack of sufficient rainfall can prove devastating. Thus the individual city-states of ancient Greece were frequently teetering on the edge of famine, and city-states with large or growing populations were always looking for external food supplies.

Attica, the region surrounding Athens, comprised a large triangular promontory with the Aegean Sea on two sides and mountains along the third. (In area, ancient Attica was only slightly larger than contemporary Rhode Island.) Although not especially fertile, ancient Attica possessed rich deposits of clay, silver, and lead. Athens lay just over four miles inland from the ports at Piraeus. This distance was traversed by the so-called Long Walls that created a safe corridor linking the city of Athens to its port at the sea. There was also a cart road that ran from Piraeus to Athens; it followed the course of the northern Long Wall for much of the distance and then swung farther north to enter the city at its main entrance, the Diplyon Gate.

Athens is quite hilly. The most important hill is the Acropolis, an outcrop of limestone 394 feet high that became the city's religious center long before the period during which this game takes place. Below and to the west of the Acropolis are the Areopagus hill (or Hill of Ares) where the oldest courts in Athens convened, the Hill of the Nymphs, and the Pnyx where the Assembly met for public debate. The city sits in a dry plain watered by small rivers. In the fourth century BCE, the ancient geographer Dicaearchus summed it up nicely when he described visiting

Note the locations of the mountains within Attica, as well as the cities of Eleusis, Marathon, and the fort at Phyle.

Athens, remarking that a visitor "comes to the city of the Athenians; the road is pleasant; the ground is cultivated all the way, and has a kindly look. The city is all dry, not well-watered; the streets are badly laid out because of their antiquity. The houses are mostly mean; few are spacious. Strangers visiting the city might be struck with doubt, whether this is really the renowned city of the Athenians, but after a little while one might well believe it."

Ancient Greek life was dominated by the land and by the sea. Most Greeks followed an agrarian lifestyle, living in the countryside and working the fields there, but the sea also lay at the heart of their world. For the Hellenes the Mediterranean was a natural resource, a formative neighbor, a hostile opponent, and a conduit—albeit a dangerous one—for the exchange of materials and ideas. The centrality of the Mediterranean to Greek culture is perhaps best summed up by Plato's likening of the Greeks to "frogs around the pond" (*Phaedo* 109b).

ATHENS IN THE FIFTH CENTURY: POLITICS

The events in Athens that unfold in 403 BCE are, in many respects, the culmination of events, ideas, and customs that dominated the entire fifth century. In 403, Athens is—or, rather, is once again—at the threshold of democracy. In this critical year at the end of the fifth century, the people of Athens were made to reconsider and rehash many of the issues that had been under debate 97 years earlier. It is therefore useful to go back to that first threshold of democracy, in order to put this second threshold in perspective.

Solon and the Solonian Constitution

That first step toward democracy was taken in 594 BCE when Solon, an Athenian aristocrat, was given special authority by the Athenian Assembly to institute economic, legal, and political reforms. At this time, a very large proportion of the population of Athens was in debt to a much smaller group of wealthy landowners. As a result, many debtors lost what little property they had possessed; others became slaves to the landowners; and still others were sold abroad as payment for their debts. In short, Athens was wracked by both economic and social instability and turned to Solon for a remedy.

Only imperfect accounts survive of Solon and his reforms, but the broad strokes of his work are clear: the one-time cancellation of debts, the institution of a new lawcourt to which all citizens were subject, and the creation of the so-called Solonian constitution that was based on a new system for classifying citizens according to wealth instead of birth. This system divided Athenian citizens into four categories: the wealthiest Athenians (known as the five-hundred-bushel men), the Knights (three-hundred-bushel men), the Yeomen (two-hundred-bushel men) and

Once Athens had deposed its king, the city was governed by nine **archons**, the most important of whom were the royal archon (the *archon basileus*), the war archon (the *polemarch*), and the eponymous archon. The royal archon inherited the king's duties concerning religion (such as organizing the Eleusinian Mysteries) and legal matters (such as adjudicating homicide and impiety trials); the polemarch headed the military; and the eponymous archon gave his name to the year he held office and presided over the Council and the Assembly. Athenians dated events in their own history by referring to the "year that so and so was archon." To help them keep track of the years, they displayed in the Agora a large stone inscribed with a running list of the eponymous archons.

The word *tyrannos*, meaning **tyrant**, appears to have been a Lydian word (Lydia is an ancient region located in the western part of modern-day Turkey). In Greek literature, the word is not nearly as freighted with negative connotations as it is in English. Indeed, Sophocles titled his play "Oedipus Tyrannos," not "Oedipus Rex" (the Latin word for king). Greek authors generally use *tyrannos* to describe someone who governs extra-constitutionally—often a usurper who has seized power—or someone who exercises an inordinate amount of power either malevolently or benevolently.

the Thetes (everyone else). The Assembly was open to citizens from all four categories; only the Thetes were excluded from election to the Council (the Boule). But the nine all-important **archonships** were open only to citizens belonging to the two wealthiest categories. These first tentative steps toward a government in which every citizen, to some degree, had a voice were undertaken, according to our ancient sources, to prevent Athens from succumbing to tyranny.

Athenian Tyranny and Democracy

Around 546 BCE Pisistratus, who had twice failed to seize control of Athens, finally succeeded in grabbing power. He governed more or less without dispute until his death in 527 BCE, and governed well, keeping in place the traditional nine archonships and the system of government established by the great lawgiver Solon. In addition, Pisistratus cut taxes, instituted a system of traveling judges, patronized the arts, sponsored ambitious building projects in Athens, and reorganized the Panathenaic festival to include recitations from Homer's *Iliad* and *Odyssey*. He also reduced the power of the aristocrats and thus helped create a political environment that would ultimately lead to democracy.

Upon the death of the **tyrant** Pisistratus, however, power devolved to his sons Hippias and Hipparchus, neither of whom was a particularly astute ruler. Sources suggest that in 514 two private citizens, Harmodius and Aristogeiton, attacked both sons, killing Hipparchus. A descendant of Aristogeiton may be a player in the game. Hippias survived the assassination attempt but his behavior as a leader became cruel, even despotic. In 510 BCE, with help from Sparta, the Athenians expelled Hippias, who took refuge with Darius, the king of mighty Persia. Harmodius and Aristogeiton were captured and executed by Hippias. They eventually became revered as the Tyrant Slayers (*tyrannicides*), and statues were erected in their honor in the middle of the Athenian agora.

Anarchy, Cleisthenes, and the Rise of Democracy

With the expulsion of Hippias, few men in Athens were in an obvious position to step forward and lead the city. Different groupings of aristocratic families tended to fill the political vacuum. Into this situation stepped Cleisthenes, a member of a venerable and powerful aristocratic family whose ancestors supposedly included the Tyrant Slayers. Cleisthenes sought to gain an edge on other powerful rivals by enlisting the support of the numerous "lesser" people of Athens (in Greek, the demos). Some scholars argue that Cleisthenes decided to do this on his own; others contend that the people rose up and demanded it. Whatever the case, it is clear that by 501 BCE, Cleisthenes was firmly in control and Athens had established a form of democracy whose central feature was the Assembly (*Ekklesia* in Greek), where male citizens discussed issues and proposed laws. Subsequent generations of Athenians referred to Cleisthenes as the "father of democracy."

Cleisthenes' Reforms. Cleisthenes re-ordered Athenian society, revitalized institutions for governing the city, and hardened the boundaries between citizens and noncitizens. He sought to weaken the power of the influential families and their larger kinship groups (or tribes). To that end, he created ten new tribes that replaced the four traditional Ionian tribes. This ensured that no single tribe could dominate debate; the new tribes, moreover, were based on residence—not on ancestry. This fundamental change was also reflected in a new naming tradition that emphasized a man's *deme*, or neighborhood name, rather than his parentage. For example, Thucydides, the son of Sophillos, came to be known as Thucydides of (the deme of) Halimus. In this way, a man's aristocratic background—or lack thereof—was not apparent from his official name.

Under Cleisthenes, too, the ten new tribes formed the backbone of the Council, the body that was charged with drawing up the agenda for the Assembly. Under Cleisthenes' reforms, Solon's Council of 400 (100 men from each of the four Ionian tribes) became the Council of 500 (50 men selected by lot from each of the ten new tribes). A president who served for one day was chosen by random lottery from the 500 council members.

The use of sortition (selection by lot), an important component of these reforms, was instrumental in breaking up the power of the old aristocratic families. During the next century sortition was applied to more and more government positions. By the year that the game begins (403 BCE), every public office was assigned by random lottery; the sole exception was the position of general, which was elected. Slaves, women, and children were not citizens and therefore were excluded from this radical form of democracy.

In the 420s BCE, the so-called Monument of the Ten Eponymous Heroes was set up in the agora. This long (about fifty-four feet) monument displayed statues of the ten heroes; under the statue of each hero would be placed information about military conscriptions, public honors, court hearings, upcoming legislation, and the like for members of the tribe. Thus it served as a kind of message board for tribe members when they were in town.

Ostracism and Democracy. Cleisthenes is also credited with introducing the practice of ostracism. This rather odd and cumbersome procedure was used to prevent any individual from gaining too much power and eventually setting himself up as tyrant—or worse. The rules were as follows: each year citizens gathered in the Agora and voted on whether or not they believed there was someone in the city (no names were mentioned at this point) who was becoming so popular as to threaten the democracy. If a majority voted yes, the Athenians would gather again two months later for the ostracism vote, in which they selected one man to exile from the city for ten years. The man would retain his citizenship and property, but would be banned from returning to the city in person—though he could certainly remain in touch with friends and allies and no doubt exert some influence from afar. For this final vote, citizens would scratch the name of the person to be exiled on a broken piece of pottery, *ostrakon* in Greek, or purchase prepared ballots from vendors in the Agora. The word *ostrakon* gives its name to the process. As an institution ostracism is unique and dangerous—or at least uncontrollable—as no one can guarantee who will be ostracized once the Athenians decide to have an ostracism vote.

THE FIFTH CENTURY: WAR AND PEACE

These democratic institutions led fifth-century Athens into a period of peace and prosperity dominated by the statesmanship and vision of Pericles. But this period was bookended by two wars: the Persian War (490–479 BCE) and the Peloponnesian Wars (431–421 and 414–404 BCE).

The Persian War

At the dawn of the fifth century Persia was ruled by King Darius I, also known as Darius the Great (ca. 550–487 BCE). His empire, including some 30–35 million inhabitants, extended from the Aegean Sea in the south to northern Africa and east to the Indus River (now Pakistan). As one territory after another fell under the control of Darius, the expansion of his empire into Greek territory must have seemed inevitable—at least to him. When the Ionian cities (in what is now western Turkey) tried to break away from Persia, they naturally turned to their fellow Ionian cities in Greece for help. Athens sent a small fleet of soldiers and joined an attack on Sardis, the seat of Persian power in the area. Though the attack failed, the Greeks burned the temples at Sardis.

After being removed from Athens, Hippias journeyed to Darius's court; no doubt he encouraged Darius to attack Athens in revenge for his father's death. In later periods, other Greeks would approach the Persian king—despite a long history of enmity—for money, ships, or alliances.

War soon broke out between Persia and the Greeks; and Athens was the major player on the Greek side. In the summer of 490 BCE, Darius sent about thirty thousand men—an enormous force by Greek standards—to invade Greece. Hippias, the son of Peisistratus, sailed with Darius and the Persians.

Marathon. On or around September 8, 490 BCE, the Persian fleet landed on the coast at Marathon, a mere twenty-seven miles from Athens itself. When the Athenians learned of the landing, the ten generals (one elected per tribe) mustered nine thousand **hoplites** and rushed to Marathon. Knowing that the Persian king had sent an overwhelming number of forces against Greece, the Athenians sent one runner,

Pheidippides, to Sparta and another to Plataea to ask for soldiers. The Plataeans sent one thousand hoplites. The Spartans held back, claiming that they could not depart until the full moon perhaps for religious reasons, or perhaps because of their growing enmity toward Athens. Whatever the reason, nine thousand Athenians and one thousand Plataeans faced the Persians alone. Miltiades, the Athenian commander, ordered the Greeks to charge the Persian line—a tactic that surprised the Persians and caused them to turn and run. The Greeks chased the Persians to their ships, cutting down the men and trying to set fire to several vessels. According to Herodotus (6.117), the Greeks killed 6,400 Persians (probably just a guess) against enormous odds and the Athenians lost only 192 men (probably an accurate count) that day at Marathon. The Persian fleet sailed back to Persia.

Hoplite soldiers wore bronze greaves (shin- and ankle-guards) on their legs, a bronze cuirass (chest protector), and a bronze helmet and carried a bronze spear and shield (*hoplon*, in Greek). Such soldiers were citizens of the polis and had to be wealthy enough to purchase their own set of armor and weapons. Hoplite warfare was grueling and brutal (see Hanson 1991). Soldiers lined up in close ranks in a formation known as a phalanx. The hoplites would lock their shields together, which meant that each soldier depended on the soldiers next to him both for protection and to create the shield wall and mass of spear points that made the phalanx effective. It was a formation that bound citizen to citizen in the fight, not for personal glory, but for the protection of the polis.

It is impossible to overestimate the impact of the Athenian victory at Marathon. Soon Athenians commemorated the battle as a victory of a small group of men fighting for freedom against a much larger force intent on enslaving them. Over the course of the fifth century and well beyond, songs were sung in praise of the Marathonomachoi (the men who fought at Marathon), paintings of the battle adorned public buildings (e.g., the Painted Stoa in the Agora), orators referred to it over and over again, and monuments commemorating the battle were erected at Athens, Delphi, and Olympia. As for the 192 Athenians who died at Marathon, they were cremated and buried on the field of battle; a huge mound (almost 30 feet high and 160 feet across) was heaped over them to commemorate their valor and mark the place where they had given their lives fighting for freedom. The Plataeans who perished were also buried where they fell, but the remains of the 6,400 Persians have not been found.

Xerxes Attacks Hellas. After the unexpected defeat at Marathon, Darius was more determined than ever to punish the Athenians and subjugate all of Greece. He began by summoning an even greater number of troops, warships, horses, and transports (Hdt. 7.1), but died in 486 before he could march against Greece a second time. He was succeeded by his son Xerxes, who ruled until his own death in 465. Xerxes inherited both his father's empire and his hatred of the Greeks. By 483, he too was summoning an immense force for an attack against Greece.

Around the same time, Themistocles, an Athenian politician, recognized that Athens would need a strong fleet to survive another Persian invasion. Therefore, when a large vein of silver was discovered at Laurium in southeast Attica and the Athenians suddenly found themselves with a surplus of about 200 **talents**, Themistocles stood up in Assembly and convinced his fellow citizens to use this money to build two hundred warships. This decision would prove to be a decisive factor in saving Athens and Greece from the Persian king (Hdt. 7.144)—and, later, in the creation of the Athenian empire.

A **talent** was a unit of measure equal to more than fifty pounds, as well as a mode of silver currency.

While the Athenians were building their fleet, Xerxes collected a force that might have numbered as many as 500,000 soldiers—arguably the largest army ever mustered up to that time. Sparta invited the Greek cities to a summit at Corinth to figure out how to protect Greece. Aside from Sparta and Athens only twenty-nine other cities attended; all agreed to follow Sparta's lead. When Xerxes' envoys arrived in Greece in October 481, the Pythia, spokeswoman for the oracle at Delphi, advised the Greek cities to "medize" (i.e., to yield to Persia by handing over "earth and water," a sign of submission). She also advised Athens to "trust its wooden walls" against a Persian attack. This ambiguous counsel was interpreted by many Athenians to refer to the fortification walls around the Acropolis in Athens, while Themistocles argued that the "wooden walls" were the wooden hulls of the Athenian fleet. Taking his advice, the Athenians decided to evacuate the city and move the women, children, elderly, and metics to Troezen (Hdt. 8.4–41, 51). Almost before the Greeks could take action, however, Xerxes and his army had crossed the Hellespont into Greece and begun their inexorable march south, intending first to burn Athens in revenge for both Sardis and Marathon. Then the Persians would enter the Peloponnesian peninsula and destroy Sparta. With such an immense army, Persian defeat was inconceivable.

The first decisive encounters were at Thermopylae (a land battle) and Artemisium (a sea battle). The battle at Thermopylae (the "hot gates") is as famous and important as Marathon, as three hundred Spartan soldiers under the leadership of their king Leonidas held a narrow pass for nearly a week, blocking a land route leading south toward Attica. But when the Greek traitor Ephialtes showed them a "back door," the Persians attacked the Spartans from the rear. In the resulting bloodbath, all three hundred Spartans and Leonidas were killed, and the Persian army continued its march south toward Athens. But Spartan heroism at Thermopylae became the stuff of legend, and the Spartan valor at Thermopylae was matched by Athenian valor at Artemisium. Athens's reputation as prime defender of Greek freedom against Persian tyranny was burnished, at least in the eyes of later generations of Athenians. After the Persians moved into Attica, the Greek fleet withdrew to the narrows around the island of Salamis, directly opposite Athens.

Defeat for Both Sides. Xerxes soon arrived in Athens with his massive army. The treasurers of the temple of Athena and a few other Athenians had barricaded themselves behind the wooden walls of the Acropolis. The Persians killed everyone there, sacked the temples, and burned everything on the citadel and in the lower city. Athens was in ruins. Themistocles, however, remained committed to his strategy of luring Xerxes into a naval battle in the narrow straits around the island of Salamis. In these tight quarters, superior Persian numbers would once again be neutralized. Themistocles threatened and cajoled the other Greeks into accepting his strategy; he also sent a slave to Xerxes saying that the Greeks were in disarray and about to slip away. Xerxes, believing the message, ordered his fleet to advance immediately. From atop a hill in Athens, the great Persian king watched in horror as the Athenian fleet sank hundreds of his warships (see Aeschylus "Persians" 408–32 and Hdt. 8.86, 89). Fearing that the Greeks would sail from Salamis and cut his bridge across the Hellespont, Xerxes abandoned Athens and began the long trek back to Asia. The retreat took forty-five days; most of his soldiers starved to death along the way.

When Xerxes abandoned Greece, however, he left behind his general Mardonius and, according to Herodotus, 300,000 soldiers. In 479 Mardonius attacked the Spartans at Plataea; but Pausanias, the Spartan commander, broke the Persian phalanx and killed Mardonius. The Persian forces were routed, with only three thousand left alive. With the defeat at Plataea, Xerxes—who had dreamed of an empire coterminous with the sun—never again sent troops against Greece. In Athens's recollections of the war, Athenian democracy had defeated Persian tyranny and ushered in a period of extraordinary intellectual and artistic achievement.

Between the Persian and Peloponnesian Wars

Athens and other Greek cities rushed to rebuild their defense walls, fearing that the Persian king might once again decide to attack Greece. In addition to rebuilding walls, several of the Greek cities (but not Sparta) created a mutual defense league. Member poleis (city-states) could contribute either money or manned ships that would be used to keep tabs on Persian activity by patrolling the Aegean, which the Persian king would have to cross in order to attack Greece. The money that member city-states contributed was kept under the protection of the god Apollo on the island of Delos; modern historians therefore refer to the alliance as the Delian League. The League was the brainchild of three prominent Athenian politicians: Themistocles, Aristides, and Cimon. (Cimon was the grandfather of Thucydides, possibly a player in the game.) In time, more and more city-states opted to contribute money, relying on Athens to provide the warships (triremes) and the men (the thetes, who were recruited from the lowest ranks of Athenian citizens) to row them. In addition to monitoring Persian activity in the Aegean, the League's ships eventually came to be used to protect Athenian trade routes (especially those used for grain transport) and other Athenian interests. In this way, the Delian League eventually became synonymous with Athenian naval power and dominance over the other member states. (See the map on page 32.) By 476, all pretense of collective self-defense against a possible Persian attack had disappeared and Cimon was using the fleet solely to further Athenian interests. He attacked many of the poleis that refused to join the League and punished those that tried to withdraw from it. When Naxos stopped paying, for example, Cimon used force to restart their payments. As the Athenian navy grew stronger, allies turned into tribute-paying subjects.

While Athens extorted more money from the city-states of the Delian League, Sparta was assiduously strengthening the Peloponnesian League and positioning itself as its leader. The two powers were quickly becoming more influential than

Note the vast area that comprises the Delian League, the expansion of Athenian power and influence before the Peloponnesian War, and the tax/tribute districts.

any others in Greece—and heading toward conflict. Into this charged atmosphere stepped Pericles, who, by the middle of the fifth century, would become the most important public figure in Athens.

Pericles (ca. 495–429 BCE) was born in the deme of Cholargos just north of Athens. His father was Xanthippus; his mother, Agariste. His father was ostracized in 485–484 but was recalled in 479 to help command Athenian troops at Mycale. His mother belonged to the Alcmeonids, a powerful aristocratic family; her great-grandfather was Cleisthenes, the tyrant of Sicyon, and her uncle was Cleisthenes, the so-called father of Athenian democracy. She herself had no real political power, but her family connections were tremendously helpful to the political career of her husband.

Pericles

In the 460s, **Pericles** was a young and wealthy Athenian politician with vast ambition. In the spring of 472, he paid to produce Aeschylus's play *Persians* at the Greater Dionysia festival; this kind of public service (called *liturgy* by the Greeks) was expected from prominent men of wealth for the good of the city. In the 450s, Pericles may have been instrumental (historical sources are not clear on this point) in helping to convince the Athenians to build the Long Walls, the system of fortifications that connected Athens to the Piraeus. (See the map on page 34.) With these walls in place, Athenians would always have access to the sea and to sources of imported grain to feed its growing population. In 469, Pericles and his mentor Ephialtes were recognized as leaders of the most democratic faction in Athens, in opposition to the aristocrat Cimon. Ephialtes was murdered soon after 461, and over the course of the next several years, Pericles introduced the following reforms: payment for jury service, free admission to the theater for the poor, lower property requirements for selection to an archonship, and restriction of Athenian citizenship to those of Athenian parentage on both sides.

The practice of filling government positions by random lottery (sortition) became increasingly popular under Pericles; eventually, it was used to fill all of the public offices within the Athenian political system. The one exception was the position of general (*strategos*), to which one person from each of the ten tribes of Athens was elected. Generals often became the most important officials in the Athenian democracy. The office attracted men of talent; Pericles, for example, was elected general every year from 443 until his death in 429. Although generals primarily were charged only with military matters, some became so powerful that their authority spilled over into other areas. Pericles was one of those generals. He used his position to encourage the creation of new buildings, new statues, new paintings, and the like; this explosion of artistic culture also fostered an outpouring of new literature. For many, the Periclean era was the "golden age" of Athens, and Pericles its "most important citizen" (Thu. 2.65).

TIP

Any player interested in restoring the Athenian Empire should try to be elected General during the game.

Pericles also used his powerful position to transform Athens into an empire. After the defeat of Persia, many Athenians sought to maintain strong ties with Sparta; others, including Pericles, believed that Athens should pursue its own foreign policy and assert its natural hegemony over other Greek poleis. Pericles maintained that Athens should continue to collect tribute from members of the League and exercise control over them. This came to a head in 454 when Athens and her

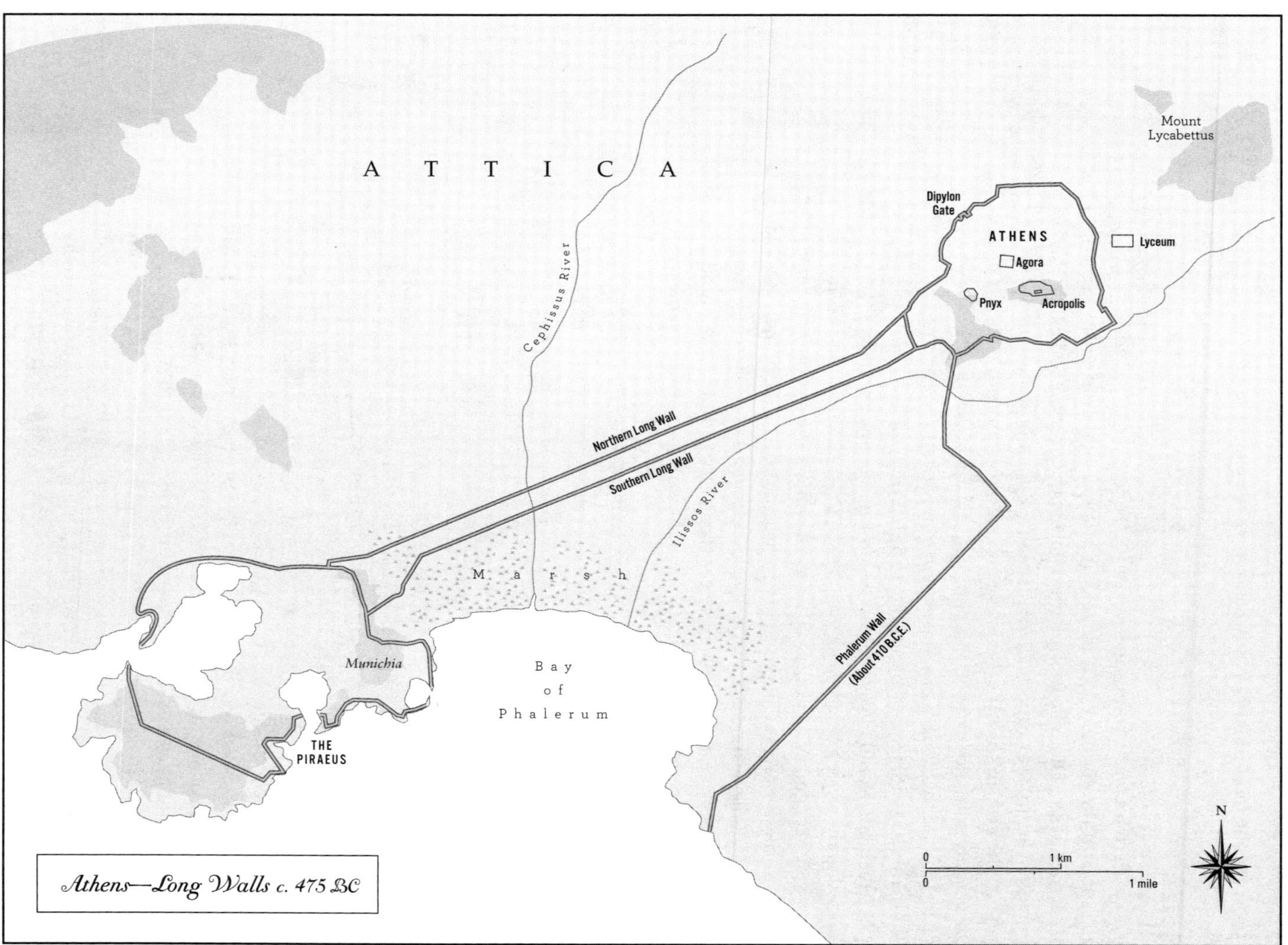

Note how the northern and southern Long Walls connect the fortification system of the ports at Piraeus with that of the polis of Athens.

allies lost a large number of ships (roughly 250) and men (roughly 50,000) who had been sent to assist the Egyptians in their revolt against the Persian king. This loss threatened the League; without ships it could not effectively patrol and protect the Aegean, nor could it guarantee the security of the treasury on the island of Delos. In response, Pericles moved the League treasury from Apollo's sanctuary on Delos to Athena's sanctuary on the Acropolis of Athens—a decision that, under the guise of security, proclaimed Athens's new identity as the (extremely) wealthy leading city of the League. What had once been a league of independent and essentially equal city-states had become an Athenian empire.

Pericles earmarked five thousand talents from the treasury for the construction and restoration of Athens's sacred buildings. The crowning jewel of this program was the Parthenon, which was more of a victory monument than a religious temple. It was adorned with more sculpture than almost any other temple in the Greek world and housed within its central room a magnificent statue of Athena Parthenos (Athena the Maiden) by Phidias. This gold and ivory statue was about forty feet high and cost forty-four talents. The skill and artistry of both the statue and the building that housed it made the Parthenon the epitome of the artistic, architectural, and cultural explosion that characterized mid-fifth-century Athens. Clearly Pericles was an important catalyst for this cultural awakening, but the Athenian democracy itself also played a significant role.

THE PELOPONNESIAN WAR

As Athenian power grew, especially in the Aegean and Ionia, tensions with Sparta and the Peloponnesian League intensified. Indeed, between 460 and 445, there was only one five-year period during which the Athenians were not engaged in open hostilities with the Spartans and their allies in the Peloponnesian League. Athenian naval power—and the economic benefits it delivered to the city—made Sparta (whose power was based on a traditional infantry) anxious and fearful. In turn, the Athenians were fearful, not of Spartan power, but of Athenian vulnerability. The city relied on its navy to secure grain, most of which came from the Black Sea area, to feed its population, while the fleet relied on the importation of timber from Macedonia and Thrace to repair existing ships and build new ones.

In the face of these fears, Athens, Sparta, and their allies agreed to a thirty-year peace in 445. (See the map on page 36.) But in 431, a number of minor episodes involving Thebes, a Spartan ally, and Plataea, an Athenian ally, led to the Peloponnesian War. It is useful to think of the Peloponnesian War in three phases: the Archidamian War (431–421), the Sicilian Campaign (416–13), and the final phase, sometimes called the Ionian War (412–404), which culminated in the unconditional surrender of Athens to Sparta.

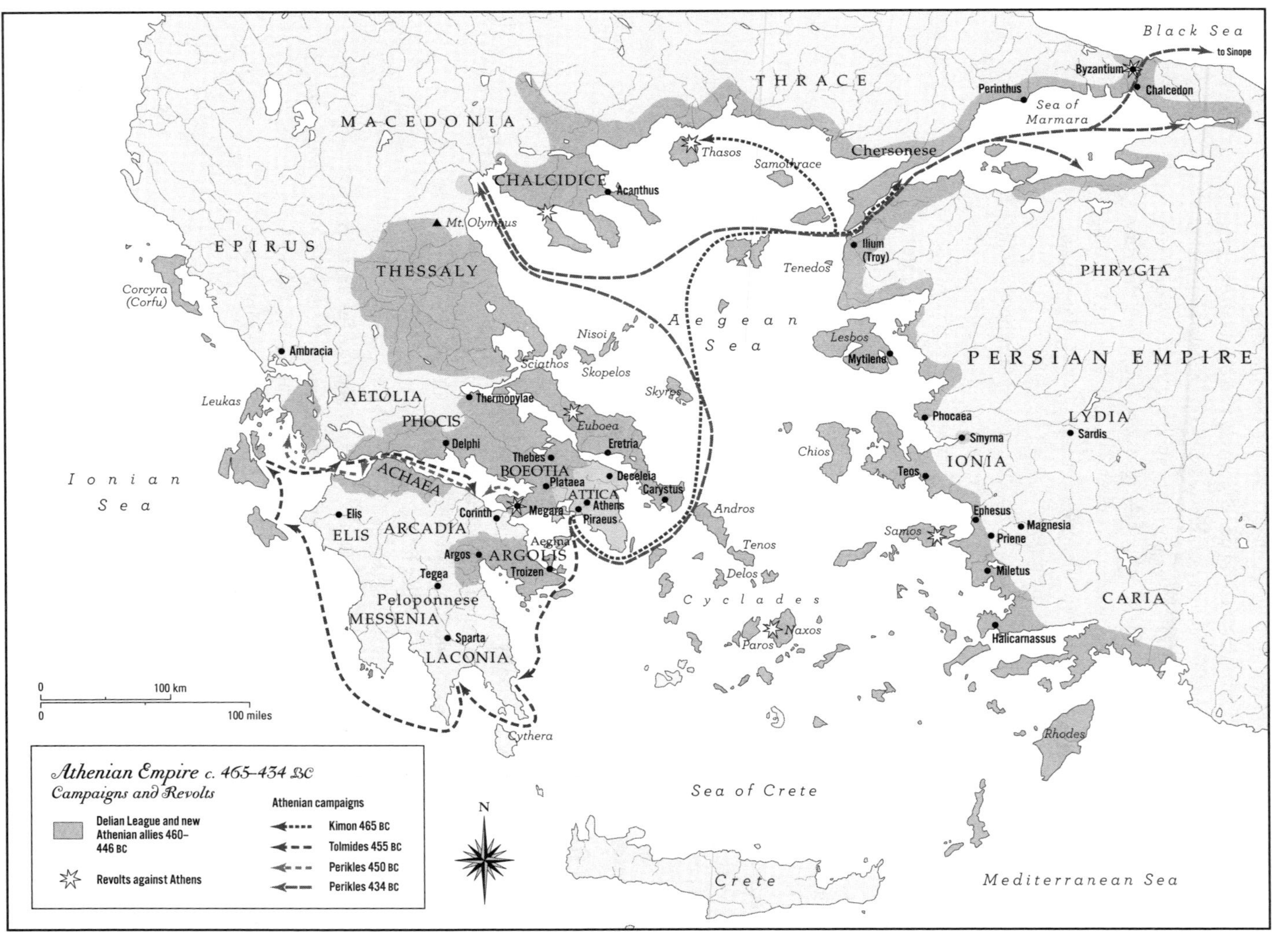

Note how the Athenian Empire has grown and is collecting tribute payments from an ever increasing number of cities. Locate the places that attempt to revolt from Athenian tribute.

The Archidamian War, 431–421

As war erupted in 431, Archidamus, a Spartan king, masterminded Spartan strategy, while Pericles developed the Athenians' plan of action. Archidamus apparently invaded Attica at harvest time (midsummer) in the expectation that he would disrupt the harvest and the Athenian food supply; he expected Athens to surrender quickly. But Pericles abandoned the countryside and its ripening grain and instead relied on the fleet to bring food into Piraeus to feed Athens. He moved everyone inside the walls of Athens and sent the animals across to the island of Euboea. In the first eight years of the war, Sparta invaded Attica five times with no effect on the Athenians, who had already abandoned their property and crops. Just as Archidamus's strategy was designed both to increase Spartan morale and to break the Athenians' spirit, Pericles' goal was also psychological when he sent ships to ravage the Peloponnesian coast. The two sides were following their standard attack plans, with Sparta focusing on land and infantry forces and Athens on sea and naval forces. The two sides quickly reached a stalemate, and neither could make much headway. They were, in essence, fighting two very different wars.

One particularly important event during the first year of the war was Pericles' famous funeral oration. Some Athenians had lost their lives in skirmishes with the Spartans that year, and were brought home to the public burial ground. This was in keeping with the Athenian practice in place since 464 of burying, at state expense, those who had died each year in defense of the city. Thucydides (2.35ff) records the funeral oration that Pericles gave that year. (This is one of Thucydides' most famous speeches and may well have been the inspiration for Lincoln's Gettysburg address.) It is perhaps the most eloquent defense of democracy ever delivered. In it, Pericles summarizes the core values of Athenian democracy: freedom, tolerance, generosity, intelligence, hopefulness, and bravery. In one of the most moving metaphors of the speech, he tells Athenians that they should "gaze on Athens and become her lover." (See Core Texts, pp. 89–94.)

Pericles' strategy of moving everyone inside the city walls and turning Athens into an island was in some ways brilliant, but had one serious unintended consequence: a plague. This was the first great disaster of the war and is described in detail by Thucydides. The disease (which modern scholars continue to try to diagnose, their suggestions running the gamut from bubonic plague to measles) seems to have arrived on the grain ships from Egypt; it first struck the population in the Piraeus and then quickly spread to Athens, killing thousands. People felt abandoned by the gods; because the disease was contagious, the sick went untended and all too often were left to die alone. Thucydides (who also fell victim to the disease but survived it) describes the gruesome conditions that prevailed in the city as the casualties mounted: the moral fabric of the citizens disintegrated; no one was willing to care for the sick; the dead were heaped in piles and left to rot or were tossed unceremoniously onto already burning funeral pyres. Modern historians estimate that 30,000 people—or about a quarter of the population—died in the epidemic, including Pericles.

These casualties stripped Athens of experienced leadership. Into this vacuum stepped the demagogues, newly wealthy men who gained and kept political power by paying off and pandering to the people. Foremost among them was Cleon, a powerful speaker motivated by an extreme hatred of Sparta. He was in command in 425 when 120 Spartan hoplites surrendered to Athenian forces on the island of Sphacteria—something no Spartan soldier had ever done (Thuc. 4.27–28). After the Spartan soldiers were imprisoned in Athens, Sparta offered peace terms; Cleon, out of hatred of Sparta, convinced the Athenians to reject them. Cleon's character is perhaps best exemplified by his actions three years earlier, in 428, when the people of Mytilene on the island of Lesbos withdrew from the Athenian empire and then, subjected to a display of Athenian power, were forced once again to pay tribute. As the Athenians were debating what to do about Mytilene, Cleon stood up in the Assembly and argued for the execution of the every single man and the enslavement of all women and children. Enthralled by the skillful orator, the Assembly voted to accept his proposal and a ship was dispatched with this order. The next day, cooler heads insisted that the decision be reconsidered by the Assembly. Diodotus took the floor and argued that only the leaders of the revolt should be executed. The Assembly concurred and dispatched another ship with new orders, just barely arriving in time to save the Mytilenians (Thuc. 3.36–50).

Athenians and Spartans fought with mixed results at different places over the next few years. Whenever the subject of peace was broached, Cleon's was the most significant voice in the Assembly arguing against it. The Spartan commander Brasidas was equally adamant about pursuing the war against Athens. Finally, in 422, both Cleon and Brasidas were killed during a battle at Amphipolis. This opened the road to peace, and in 421 Nicias (a wealthy conservative Athenian who was an ardent opponent of Cleon) and the Spartan king Pleistoanax reached an agreement known as the Peace of Nicias (Thuc. 5.18). The Peace of Nicias was supposed to last thirty years, but, in reality, was merely a pause in hostilities. It gave each side some breathing space.

Nicias and Alcibiades

Two new influential voices entered the Assembly at this point: Nicias and Alcibiades. Nicias was a member of the Athenian aristocracy. (Diognetus, the half-brother of Nicias, may be a player in your game.) His father left Nicias with a large fortune derived chiefly from the silver mines at Laurium and as many as a thousand slaves to work them. His political views were fairly moderate, especially when compared to those of Cleon and even Pericles before his death. He was not a gifted public speaker, instead rising to prominence by funding choruses for Athenian dramas, sponsoring and funding religious festivals, and performing various acts of piety.

He had a reputation for being devout and is often referred to, in our sources, as "lucky." He was physically brave, but not bold.

Alcibiades, on the other hand, was bold—perhaps even too bold. Like Nicias he was very wealthy, but whereas Nicias used his wealth to honor the gods and the city, Alcibiades used his to satisfy his extravagant tastes. As a result, he seems always to have been in need of money. He was a follower and admirer of Socrates (see Plato's *Symposium*) and a skilled public speaker. He was by birth an aristocrat from a prominent family but allied himself with the demos following the example of Pericles, his guardian. Many Athenians disapproved of Alcibiades because he had Spartan relatives, others because of what they considered his low morals and lack of self-discipline (Thuc. 6.15). Nevertheless he was elected general for the first time in 419; from this position he would play a major role in the Sicilian Campaign (416–413).

The Sicilian Campaign

The Sicilian Campaign, which would be the greatest disaster of the war for the Athenians, began when the small city of Segesta sent ambassadors to its ally Athens asking for help against its Dorian neighbor, Selinus. Thucydides sets the stage for us with a debate in the Assembly between Nicias (who argues against helping Segesta) and Alcibiades (who argues fervently in favor of it). Pericles had consistently warned against expanding the war, but he was long dead; the decision was thus left to others who had forgotten his advice and had personal motives. Some sought personal glory and wealth, a camp that, no doubt, included Alcibiades himself. Others may have been attracted by the fertile grain-producing fields of Sicily. Still others may have been tempted by the thought of conquering all of Sicily and thus securing the complete collapse of Spartan power. Thucydides' text describes Alcibiades urging the Athenians to send an expedition to achieve glory and expand the empire, while Nicias (54 years old to Alcibiades' 34 years) cautions that Selinus is far away and unknown. The charismatic Alcibiades won the debate, and the Assembly voted to send sixty ships. In a last-ditch effort to convince the Athenians to reconsider, Nicias argued that such an expedition was much too small to succeed and needed many more troops to achieve its goal. He assumed that the scope of the campaign he described would scare off the Athenians. Instead the Assembly voted to send exactly what Nicias had proposed: 100 ships, 5000 hoplites, 1300 archers, 30 cavalry (an unusually small number), and a veritable "city" of hangers-on (Thuc. 6.31). To add insult to injury, the Assembly voted that Nicias, Alcibiades, and Lamachus, an older veteran, share command of the expedition.

The force was collected and readied for sailing. But on the evening of June 6th, almost all of the herms in the city—images of the god Hermes in the shape of a pillar with an erect phallus and the head of the god, often placed at property boundaries and at thresholds to buildings and houses—were mutilated. Fear gripped the city when, at daybreak, this sacrilege became known; no one was more upset than the devout Nicias. Many believed the destruction had been a concerted plot against the democracy, while others thought it merely drunken hooliganism perpetrated by young men, including Alcibiades. Despite this powerful omen, the fleet sailed for Sicily on the next day, as originally planned. Thucydides describes it as the largest and most expensive force ever assembled.

After the fleet sailed, many young men were accused, arrested, and put on trial for being the "Herm Cutters." Alcibiades was recalled from his position as general in order to be put on trial, accused both of mutilating the Herms and of profaning the Eleusinian Mysteries—a much more serious charge. A ship was dispatched to bring him to Athens for punishment. Rather than face the wrath of the Athenians, Alcibiades jumped ship on the journey home and eventually fled to Sparta. An Athenian jury convicted him in absentia and sentenced him to death. Alcibiades told the Spartans of Athens's plan for conquering Sicily and, perhaps, all of Italy. He advised them to renew the war in Greece so that Athens would be forced to fight on two fronts and to send troops commanded by a Spartan general directly to Syracuse in Sicily. This advice would prove to be the undoing of the Athenians' Sicilian Campaign.

Moreover, none of the remaining commanders of the campaign believed in the fundamental mission of the expedition. With the decision to recall Alcibiades, the Athenian Assembly essentially doomed the Sicilian venture to failure. And fail it did, spectacularly. In 414, Lamachus was killed in action, leaving Nicias in sole command. That winter, Nicias, sick and despondent, sent a dispatch to Athens requesting that the city either recall the expedition (his preference) or send reinforcements and a fleet as large as the first one. Presumably he expected the Athenians to balk at the size of the force he was requesting, but, just as before, they voted for his request and sent seventy-three ships, five thousand hoplites and many other soldiers all under the command of Demosthenes (not the famous orator). Athens had now committed even more resources to the campaign despite having little reason to expect a better outcome. Meanwhile the Spartans followed Alcibiades' advice and sent troops to Sicily under the command of Gylippos.

With the arrival of the Spartans, both Demosthenes and Nicias realized that the tide had turned, that they might lose, and that it was time to withdraw. On the evening of August 27, 413, as the Athenians prepared to board their ships, there was an eclipse of the moon. This omen frightened both the soldiers and the religious Nicias, who decided that they must wait for the new moon before withdrawing. By the time of the new moon, however, the Athenian fleet had been destroyed in battle in the harbor of Syracuse. Nicias had no recourse but to withdraw by land—a very tricky and dangerous operation. On September 11, the Athenian army finally abandoned its campsite outside of Syracuse, leaving the dead unburied and abandoning the sick and wounded. The fleeing Athenians were easy prey for the Spartans and Syracusans, who killed or captured the entire force (with all of the gruesome details recorded by Thucydides, 7.72–87). Both Demosthenes and Nicias were executed, and of the approximately forty thousand Athenian and allied troops who fought in Sicily (most of whom were experienced oarsmen and not hoplites), only seven thousand survived. These unlucky souls were imprisoned in the deep quarries in and around Syracuse under the most miserable conditions; most were eventually sold into slavery. The remaining Athenians were left to die slowly; some (in particular those who could entertain their captors by reciting passages from the plays of Euripides) were released or managed to escape. These eventually found their way back to Athens and brought firsthand news of the disaster to their fellow Athenians. Alcibiades' audacious plan had ended in utter defeat for Athens. And Alcibiades had witnessed none of it.

The Last Phase of the War

When news of the Sicilian disaster first reached Athens, the people refused to believe it. But as other survivors trickled into the city and told the same story, the Athenians panicked, especially when the Spartans—following Alcibiades' advice to renew the war at home and force the Athenians to fight on two fronts simultaneously—fortified the site of Decelea, only about ten miles from Athens. This was the very thing that many Athenians most feared, as it cut them off from their homes and crops and from the revenue of the nearby silver mines.

Almost immediately, the Assembly voted to build new ships; by 412 they had cobbled together a navy to match the Peloponnesian fleet. After huge numbers of oarsmen had perished in Sicily, Athens was newly dependent on rowers who were slaves, rather than free citizens. This was no doubt distasteful to the Athenians but allowed them to fight nine more years. Most of the action took place in Ionia, and Alcibiades—who had fled Sparta by now and taken up residence at the court of the Persian governor in Ionia—was in the thick of it, lending his support first to Sparta, then Persia, and finally Athens.

Indeed, as early as 411, Alcibiades, who had wanted to be recalled to Athens, began exchanging messages with the Athenian leaders on the island of Samos. He claimed that if they would install an oligarchy in Athens that was friendly to him, he would bring them Persian gold and perhaps even a Persian fleet of 147 triremes. Although he was not able to deliver on his grandiose promises, the oligarchs still staged a coup in Athens. The oligarchy of the Four Hundred vowed to create a citizen body restricted to the Five Thousand: men who could afford their own arms and would not need to be paid for serving on juries and performing other civic duties. While drawing up this list of prominent citizens, the Four Hundred killed many democrats and confiscated their property. As these events were unfolding in Athens, Thrasybulus (a key figure in the game and the leader of the Thrasybulans) first enters our story. He persuaded Athenian troops in Ionia to vote to recall Alcibiades. When they did, Thrasybulus himself retrieved Alcibiades and brought him to Samos, where he was welcomed and took part in naval skirmishes in the Hellespont. By 409, two factions (extremists and moderates) had fomented dissension within the Four Hundred, which soon collapsed. Democracy was restored, but only briefly.

As a result of Alcibiades' naval successes in the Hellespont, the Athenians elected him general in absentia in 407/6 and invited him to return to Athens. He spoke in his defense in the Assembly, whereupon the Athenians voted to clear him of the charges of impiety in the mutilation of the Herms. He was once again in the citizens' favor—but his luck was short-lived. The very next year he suffered a naval loss and, fearing once again for his life, fled to his property in the Chersonese, never again to return to Athens.

In 406, the Athenians once again managed to put together a fleet of 150 ships, this time paying for it by melting down the gold and silver dedications in their sanctuaries. To man the ships, the Athenians used slaves—who were promised freedom—and metics—who were promised citizenship. With this fleet, the Athenians defeated the Peloponnesian navy off the coast of Arginusae near Mytilene. (See the map on page 32.) But rather than rescue those Athenians whose ships had sunk, the Athenian generals chased the fleeing Spartan ships. When a storm swept across the sea, the generals ordered their ships to shore. Most of the abandoned Athenians perished, and their bodies were never recovered. This was a violation of both practice and religious custom. In response, Athens put the generals on trial en masse (another violation of practice) and executed most of them. Socrates, who was serving in the Council at that time, refused to participate, a heroic act that enraged many of his fellow citizens and would affect Athenians' perceptions of him for many years.

After Arginusae, Athenian defeats mounted, culminating the following year in a defeat at Aegospotami (see the map on page 32). Late in 405 BCE, the Spartan admiral Lysander sailed his fleet to the Hellespont and anchored at Lampsacus on the eastern side of the straits. There was no place nearby with adequate food and water where the Athenians could set up their base, so they were forced to beach their ships at Aegospotami on the western side. There, food and water supplies were equally poor. Taking a lesson from Salamis, the Athenians tried to lure Lysander into battle in the narrow straits. Rather than take the bait, however, Lysander watched and waited for four days as the Athenians beached their ships and foraged for supplies. On the fifth day, when the Athenians scattered to look for food, Lysander attacked. He captured 171 ships on the beach and killed at least three thousand Athenians as they returned with supplies.

News of the disaster soon reached Athens. According to Xenophon's account, that night "a sound of wailing ran from Piraeus through the long walls to the city, one man passing on the news to another; and during that night no one slept, all were mourning, not only for the dead, but far more for themselves," fearing they might receive the same treatment they had earlier meted out to others (Xen. *Hell.*

2.2.3). The next day the Athenians met in Assembly and voted to block up all the harbors except one, to repair the walls, to station guards, and to ready the city for a siege. After Aegospotami, there was nothing but its great walls separating Lysander and the city of Athens.

The Final Siege

Word soon leaked out that Lysander would kill any Athenian found outside the walls of Athens. More people flooded back into the city, which meant more mouths to feed. Within days, Lysander had arrived and anchored 150 ships at Piraeus, closing the entrance to the harbor. At about the same time, the Spartan kings marched to Athens and set up camp in the Academy on the outskirts of the city. Athens was besieged by land and sea with no ships, allies, or provisions. Not knowing what to do, they reinstated political rights for those who had been disenfranchised but—oddly—refused to ask for peace. Indeed, when a citizen stood up in the Assembly and proposed that Athens accept the Spartan demand to dismantle a stretch of the Long Walls, his fellow Athenians threw him into prison and passed a decree forbidding anyone from making such a proposal again. By winter, the siege of Athens had begun.

The situation was dire, as deaths from starvation began to climb. After some time, as food became scarcer and scarcer and casualties mounted, Theramanes (an oligarch who had participated in the rule of the Four Hundred) offered to contact Lysander and discuss peace. The Athenians waited through the winter for his return; by the spring of that year, people were dying in the streets, with disease and starvation rampant. When Theramenes finally arrived with terms from Sparta, Athens had no choice but to accept them: they were force to cede control of their foreign policy and agree to "join the Spartan alliance, destroy the Long Walls and the fortifications of Piraeus, recall the exiled oligarchs, and surrender all but 12 ships" (Xen. *Hellenica* 2.2.23). Harsh terms, yes, but not as harsh as some had advocated: Corinth and Thebes had argued that Athens should be completely destroyed, the men killed, and the women and children enslaved. All the same, the terms of the agreement were carried out with gusto by the victors: according to our sources, Spartan flute girls played music as the Athenians dismantled the walls that had ensured their security for decades. With the destruction of the remnants of their fleet, the Athenian empire was gone. Athens was devastated. The golden age was over.

Post-War Destruction by the Thirty

Lysander put in place a council of thirty oligarchs personally loyal to him to rule Athens. This body became known as the Thirty. They had no interest in the rule of law and asked for Spartan troops to support them while they purged the city.

Sparta sent them seven hundred soldiers who were also loyal to Lysander. What followed was nothing short of a reign of terror as the Thirty executed their enemies (especially democrats) and confiscated their property. Modern historians suggest that in a few short months, they had killed as many as 1,500 Athenians. Two voices stand out among the Thirty: Theramenes, the relative moderate who had earlier gone to Lysander and Sparta looking for peace terms, and Critias, a radicalized former friend of Socrates. Theramenes proposed drawing up a list of three thousand wealthy men (approximately 10 percent of the population) who would enjoy full citizenship; Critias proposed that anyone not on this list be killed or tortured. When the two could not come to a compromise, Theramenes was prosecuted and poisoned. Critias was left in charge.

Thousands decided that the only way to survive was to leave Athens. Many fled to Thebes, which had been an ardent opponent of Athens but at this particular moment offered asylum against the excesses of the Thirty. In January 403, a small force of seven hundred Athenian democrats set up a small fort at Phyle on the border between Attica and Boeotia and on a hill overlooking the Piraeus (see the map on page 24). Critias stormed the latter but was killed. The surviving members of the Thirty asked Lysander for protection, but the Spartan king, suspicious of Lysander's growing power, recalled the general instead. Most members of the Thirty fled; the Athenians were left to their own devices to craft their own future. This is the moment at which the game begins.

THE OTHER ATHENIANS: WOMEN, METICS, AND SLAVES[1]

Because this game is set either in the Athenian Assembly or the dikasteria (lawcourts), most players are male citizens over the age of 30. Female citizens were not allowed to serve in the Assembly or as jurors in the lawcourts; the same was true of most metics (foreign-born peoples living in Athens) and slaves. (Some exceptions are noted in the following pages.) Similarly, Thucydides and Xenophon (who may figure in the game as players) based their "histories" of the Peloponnesian War and its aftermath largely on speeches delivered in the Assembly as well as interviews and letters with the generals and chief political leaders. Such materials further distort our understanding of the era by neglecting the important roles of women, metics, and slaves in nearly all aspects of Athenian life. Although these figures may not directly figure in the "action," they played major roles in nearly all aspects of Athenian life and policy. In fact, male citizens were able to spend so much time in the Assembly and lawcourts because women, metics, and slaves were doing nearly all of the labor to sustain Athens.

NOTE

For further reading, see the Selected Bibliography, pages 237–39.

The Status of Women

Women in Athens did not have independent legal status. Athenian law required women, both citizen and metic, to have a male relative (the *kurios*) to represent them in legal contexts, whether in the courts, for purposes of inheritance, or for significant financial transactions. For example, if a married woman wanted to sell land or bring charges against someone who assaulted her, she was required to ask her designated kurios to do so on her behalf. While all metics needed a *prostates*, an Athenian citizen to sponsor and represent them in law, metic women needed both a prostates and a kurios, though we know of some metic women who only had a prostates. A woman was not permitted to own land or a home, but she could have moveable property (such as clothing, furniture, and goats or cattle), typically in the form of a dowry, which went with her from her father's home to her husband's but was kept separate from her husband's estate.

Women typically married in Athens before the age of 16, often as young as 13 or 14, and their husbands were typically 25 to 30 years old. If a woman married into a household with some status and income, she would be charged with managing the affairs of the house. This included supervising household servants, stores of food, and finances. She would also weave basic clothes for the members of the household and care for the children. This was considered the norm for women who were citizens. Metic women married to Athenian citizens or without male relatives, however, were often subject to public ridicule. Any women without male relatives in Athens had little to no means of legal recourse without a kurios, and were therefore vulnerable to physical violence and mistreatment by citizens.

Were Women Secluded?

> I should perhaps say something concerning the excellence of women, to those of you who will now be widows, and I shall give one piece of advice only: your fame will be great if you do not act in a way inferior to the nature of your sex, and your glory will be to be the least mentioned among men concerning either your excellence or your faults (Thuc. 2.45)

This statement of Pericles in his funeral oration to the widows of the war dead (see Core Texts, p. 89) has seemed to many to be the clearest description of the ideal woman in classical Athens: hidden away in the domestic sphere, secluded from men and from the public, unmentioned either for good or ill. In oratory, it was considered impolite and even insulting to name the women of your opponent's family. Women are frequently pictured in outdoor scenes veiled or with their heads otherwise covered, the veil serving as a metaphorical substitute, perhaps, for the interior space they have left. While possibly an ideal, this was an unattainable way of life for most women in Athens.

Vase images show women in their homes reading and playing music together, and literary sources suggest that women visited each other regularly. The archaeological record indicates that there was no "female quarter" within the average home and that women did go out into public spaces. Aristocratic women were prominent in the religious sphere, while many women in the lower classes and among the metic population worked outside the home in a variety of occupations. Comedy, tragedy, oratory, and inscriptions depict women, both citizen and metic, working primarily as shopkeepers and sellers in the markets. Metic women had a broader range of occupations than citizens (and slaves participated in many of them as well), but one citizen woman shows up in a list of shoemakers and another among a list of fullers (those who removed impurities from wool to make the resulting cloth thicker). These women could hardly have escaped the public eye while doing their work; the prevalence of such women in our sources suggests that seclusion was more of an elite ideal than a reality for many women in classical Athens. But because of the force of this ideal, women who did work or act in public were at times targeted for public shaming and are sometimes linked to prostitutes in male-produced historical texts. Prostitution was practiced legally in Athens, and there is evidence especially of slave women living and working in brothels.

Women and Religion. Citizen women and girls played a key part in the religious life of the city, despite other political and social limitations. In addition to being central to the performance of funerary rites and the maintenance of family cults and tombs, select girls from elite Athenian families lived in and served as attendants in the temples on the Acropolis. By the fourth century BCE, elite girls lived as "bears" in the sanctuary of Artemis at Brauron as part of a coming-of-age ritual. Girls from citizen families were also central to the Panathenaiac procession and the weaving of the ritual *peplos* for the statue of Athena. Women served as priestesses for major cults in Athens and participated in civic rituals. The priestess of Athena Polias was typically a woman from an elite citizen family; she was the only woman permitted to speak in the Athenian Assembly. The title character in Aristophanes' *Lysistrata* may be based on one of the most well-known priestesses of Athena, Lysimache. Women also played a central role in the cults of Athena Nike and Dionysos in Athens, as well as the cult of Demeter and Kore at Eleusis. The priestess of Athena Nike was chosen by lot from among all citizen women to serve in the fifth-century temple on the Acropolis. Metic women also served in prominent cult roles from the end of the fifth century, some as priestesses in foreign cults such as Bendis from Thrace, Cybele from Anatolia, and Isis from Egypt.

In addition to participating in public festivals and serving in civic cults as attendants and priestesses, women in Athens participated in a number of women-only festivals, many of which focused on the fertility of the city and its people. The Thesmophoria, Anthesteria, and Adonia were especially important and celebrated the gods Demeter (and her daughter Kore), Dionysos, and Aphrodite, all of whom were linked to fertility and the agricultural cycles of Greece. The festivals, especially the Thesmophoria, were objects of much superstition and suspicion and were closed to men; men who interfered with them were believed to incur the wrath of the gods. Miltiades, the leading general at the battle of Marathon who later suffered a major military defeat, was imprisoned for debt, and died in prison of gangrene, was thought to have earned his bad luck by interfering with the Thesmophoria. In Aristophanes' play *Thesmophorizusae*, a male relative of Euripides dresses as a woman and breaks into a festival to try to prevent the women from plotting revenge against the playwright for his on-stage portrayals of women. Common assumptions that women indulged excessively in wine and even sex at their festivals were reflected in myths and images of the maenads, frenzied followers of Dionysos.

Stereotypes relating to women's supposed excessive appetites abounded in both literature and paintings, which depicted them as hypersexual, gluttonous, and incapable of proper Greek moderation. On many tombstones and funerary vases, however, women solemnly fulfilled their duties as mothers, daughters, wives, and priestesses.

Metics in Athens

Legal Status. A metic was a resident of Athens but not a citizen. Metics comprised both freeborn immigrants to Athens and freed slaves; they and their descendants were excluded from the rights of and access to citizenship; even if born in Athens, they were excluded from citizenship because their parents were not Athenians. In some circumstances, the state granted citizenship to individual metic men and their male children, but metic women could be citizens only for the duration of their marriage to an enfranchised metic. Citizenship grants were typically awarded in recognition of extraordinary service to the state and were bestowed on wealthy metics who, for example, funded ships in the fleet or performed other services to the state. Other privileges that could be granted to male metics were exemption from the metic tax, the right to own land, the right to own a house, and honorary status. Metics could not in normal circumstances own permanent property (land or homes) in Athens, although they could, of course, own moveable property. They were also subject to a special tax, the *metoikion*. The tax rates were twelve drachmas per year for men and their households, six drachmas per year for independent metic women.

Metics were under the jurisdiction of the *polemarch*, who determined their status and heard lawsuits in which they were involved. Tax officials were specifically designated to register metics and record their payment of the tax, while men known as the *poletai* sold into slavery any metics who violated one of the laws that applied specifically to them. There were three types of legal prosecution to which metics alone were subject. The first was the *graphe xenias*, the charge of pretending to be a citizen which was sometimes punished by death. Next was the *graphe aprostasiou*, the charge for failure to register and pay one's tax. Metics found guilty of this would be sold into slavery. Finally, metics who were freed slaves could be brought up on a *dike apostasiou*, a term typically translated as "the disregard of one's prostates" or even "escape from one's owner," the penalty for which was a return to slavery under one's former owner. The fact that metics could be liable to this charge in addition to the graphe aprostasiou suggests the tenuousness of the metics' free status in classical Athens, even for those who were freeborn immigrants.

Historians have traditionally assumed that metic status was initiated along with democracy when Cleisthenes reformed the tribes, but there is no ancient evidence for this view. Recent scholarship has suggested, based on ancient inscriptions and literary evidence, that metic status was first created in the decade after the Persian wars as a response to high levels of immigration to the city and as the Athenians attempted to identify themselves more clearly from other Greeks, especially members of the Delian League.

Periclean Citizenship Law. Before 451 BCE, an Athenian citizen was legally defined as anyone born of an Athenian citizen father. That year, however, Pericles proposed legislation to limit citizenship to those born of both an Athenian-born mother and a citizen father, though exceptions to the law were necessary throughout the fifth century because of the pressures of the Peloponnesian War and the plague.

As the game begins in 403 BCE, many Athenians blame the resident foreign population for Athens's defeat in the Peloponnesian War. Common prejudices against metics are found especially in orations from the fourth century where metics are associated with both a lack of patriotism and greed. Antipathy toward metics may further reflect the fact that the metic population has changed over time, being at first predominantly Greek and later comprising freed slaves of generally non-Greek descent. Many Athenians may seek to reenact the Periclean citizenship law of 451 BCE; some zealous citizens may even seek to prohibit marriage between Athenian citizens and metics.

Metic Population. Metics are often believed to have been predominantly non-Athenian Greek merchants and craftsmen who came to Athens to work on the numerous building programs. They were, in fact, found in all walks of life, practiced almost all occupations in Athens, and came from all over the Mediterranean, especially from Asia Minor, the Black Sea, Egypt, and southern Italy. Metics worked in Athens as tavern keepers, shopkeepers, potters, carpenters, blacksmiths, shoemakers, woolworkers, clothing merchants, and perfume makers and sellers, to name a few trades found on inscriptions. Wealthier metics ran banks, shipping companies, and weapon and shield factories. Some operated mines and made their fortunes by leasing out slave labor.

There is no certain way to calculate metic population numbers in Athens, though it is often estimated that the number of metics (including women and children) was roughly 20,000 at the start of the Peloponnesian War and as low as eight to ten thousand by the middle of the fourth century. The restrictions on metics were strictly enforced after the Peloponnesian War and, with the threat of potential enslavement hanging over any metic who was taken to court for violating metic laws, immigrant numbers decreased.

Famous metics in Athens include the speechwriter Lysias (possibly a player in the game), the sophist Gorgias (whose son may be a player in the game), and the philosopher Aristotle. Pericles' beloved Aspasia was a metic from the city of Miletus. Their son was granted citizenship under an exception to the Citizenship Law after Pericles' two citizen sons died in the plague.

Slaves

Population. Athens, like most societies in antiquity, was a slave-owning society. Slavery in Athens, as in Greece generally, was not based on race or ethnicity; although the Athenians were in principle opposed to keeping fellow Greeks as slaves, this did not prevent them from doing so in practice. The majority of slaves in Athens, however, were non-Greeks from Thrace, Scythia, Egypt, and throughout the Near East. There is even some evidence in the fourth century BCE of slaves from sub-Saharan Africa. Not every Athenian owned a slave and many owned only one or two, but there were some, such as Callias, who held as many as a thousand. Scholars have had difficulty assessing the total number of slaves in Athens in the classical period, but estimates range from as few as 20,000 to as high as 150,000 (compared to a citizen population of around 30,000).

Slave Roles and Occupations. Slaves in Athens occupied a great variety of roles and occupations that were also performed by metics and citizens. Slaves in the domestic sphere worked as nurses, personal servants, cooks, tutors, and household managers. A large portion of female slaves engaged in wool-working, either in individual households or in small factories. Slaves with special skills as craftsmen worked in shops alongside their owners or were leased out to the state to work on the many building projects in Athens during the fifth century. Slaves made up a large portion of the workers on the Erechtheum on the Acropolis and were paid the same or, in some cases, a higher wage than citizen workers. Slaves sometimes lived independently from their owners and ran businesses or shops on their behalf. Overseers at mines, large farms, and factories were almost always slaves. We have evidence of slaves running brothels, taverns, perfume shops, and other shops on behalf of but in separate towns from their owners. One important industry in Athens controlled almost exclusively by slaves or freed slaves was banking. Slaves in the banking industry were the most likely to become very wealthy. A handful of slaves are also known to have both operated shipping businesses for their owners and owned ships of their own. Slaves who ran businesses are often called "privileged" slaves; many earned their freedom or were granted it, and then continued their trade in Athens. The same was true of some domestic slaves. Only a small number of slaves or former slaves were awarded citizenship in Athens, typically for extraordinary service to the city such as paying for and manning ships for the fleet, donating shields and weapons to the hoplite forces, or fighting on behalf of the city in a time of great crisis.

Slave Status. Slaves were considered property in law, but the treatment of slaves and their independence from their owners varied greatly, as did their wealth and integration into Athenian society. Because they shared professions with and were often physically indistinct from their Greek owners, one could not always tell at first glance in Athens who was a slave and who was free. In principle, all slaves were subject to violent treatment at the hands of their owners (whipping, rape, and branding, for example). In law, a slave's testimony could only be used if it had been elicited through torture. Further, slaves were protected in law from being killed and from any violence at the hands of someone other than their owner. Some of the slaves who received pay for their work and became wealthy bought their own freedom with their earnings. As mentioned above, a small number became so wealthy (and used that wealth to aid the city) that they earned citizenship, but these were exceptions, not the rule.

There is some debate among scholars as to whether or not freed slaves had residual obligations to their former owners. Freed slaves joined the ranks of metics in Athens if they chose to stay in the city, and it appears to have been expected that a freed slave would take his or her owner as a prostates. There is no evidence from the classical period, however, of a legal category of freedman in Athens comparable to Roman slaves' continuing legal obligations to their former owners as a condition of freedom.

The slaves most likely to be subject to mistreatment were those used for manual labor, primarily in agriculture and in the mines or as rowers on mercantile or military vessels. Female slaves were sometimes set up as prostitutes in their owners' brothels. Modern understandings of slave societies are most closely paralleled in the experiences of these Athenian slaves, who generally labored long hours in physically challenging conditions. They tended to have shorter lives than the more privileged slaves who worked in the domestic sphere, or who lived apart from their owners and ran businesses or farms on their behalf.

Rich and Poor in Ancient Athens[2]

It is clear that women, metics, and slaves played important—albeit sometimes invisible—roles in the Athenian polis, but the most important demographic division was between poor citizens and citizens who were not poor. Athenians would have characterized the thetes (the oarsmen) as the poor; they comprised the approximately nine thousand male Athenian

NOTE

For further reading on money and the financial situation in Athens, see the Selected Bibliography, pages 237–39.

citizens who rowed the ships and thus were excused from all taxation and other financial contributions to the state. About a third of these poor citizens owned land, but it was worth less than two thousand drachmas per year. The non-poor included another roughly nine thousand male Athenian citizens who possessed land worth at least two thousand drachmas and who were responsible for a variety of monetary and material contributions to the state.

The Pnyx had room for only six thousand adult male citizens. Even in 403 BCE, when the number of eligible attendees was greatly diminished by losses from the war, many citizens lived too far from Athens to regularly attend Assembly sessions.

The more money a citizen possessed, the greater were his obligations to the finances of the polis. The wealthiest citizens comprised the "liturgical class"—the three hundred or so men who possessed property worth more than three talents, who could afford to undertake **liturgies**. (A talent was a lump of silver weighing about fifty pounds; a single talent could cover the cost of building a trireme or paying the wages of two hundred oarsmen of a trireme for an entire month.) Next in wealth was the "leisure" or "propertied" class, the roughly nine hundred Athenians who had at least five hundred drachmas of income and at least one talent of property. Although not wealthy enough to fund liturgies by themselves, they often joined with other wealthy individuals to participate in joint liturgies. Next in rank were the "knights," the eighteen hundred Athenians who possessed at least three hundred drachmas of income and one-half talent in property which was subject to an emergency property tax known as the *eisphora*. After the Knights were the hoplites or yeomen, the six thousand Athenians who had one hundred and fifty drachmas of income and property valued at over 1,800 drachmas. They were called hoplites because they could afford to purchase the armor and weapons necessary to serve in the army.

Although Athenians funded their civic institutions by familiar means (agriculture, property taxes, tariffs, rents), they also raised state funds through a distinctive mechanism: the **liturgy**. Liturgies were public services undertaken by wealthy individuals to support a specific state activity, such as a performance at a public festival (*choregia*) or paying to build a trireme (*trierarchy*). Liturgies began as voluntary contributions by which the wealthy could display their civic spirit and cultivate goodwill among the people. Over time, however, liturgies became compulsory for wealthy Athenians and metics.

THE TREASURY OF ATHENA: FINANCE AND ECONOMICS

As the game begins, Athens's economy is in turmoil. The war and its disastrous conclusion followed by the depredations of the Thirty had a profound effect on the economy. Throughout the Peloponnesian War, agricultural production throughout Attica was disrupted—first by Spartan raids during the so-called Archidamian War, then by the Spartan occupation of Deceleia, and finally by the chaos of the Thirty. With the loss of Athens's empire, foreign tribute vanished, trade withered, and overseas possessions were lost. But the situation is not hopeless. In 403 BCE, the Athenians can resume trading around the Aegean and even farther afield—assuming they can build ships and produce goods for export—and the harvest can be gathered without risk for the first time in years. The question before the

Assembly is how to rebuild Athens's economic house and regain its status as one of the most prosperous city-states in Greece.

Agriculture—along with trade—is the lynchpin of the Athenian economy. The primary crops in Attica are the olive, the vine, and grain. Thucydides and other ancient authors tell us that Spartan armies raided the Attic countryside during the war, but questions linger over the extent of the damage to the olive groves, vineyards, and grain fields, and to the houses and farm buildings in the countryside. In other words, the impact of the war on the economy is hard to determine. It seems that the policy of the Spartan raids was not to destroy farmland and crops but to incite the Athenians to come out from behind the city walls and defend their homes against the Spartans. In other words, the goal was to kill Athenian soldiers and not to devastate the fields. Indeed, olive trees and vineyards are difficult to destroy and seem to have survived the war for the most part. If the majority of farms had been thoroughly destroyed, there would have been an enormous agricultural crisis, a crisis that would have taken about fifty years to overcome. But there is ancient literary evidence that farming resumed right after the war ended and that olive trees and vineyards were productive. It seems that rural estates were still functioning, although at a more modest level since an estimated twenty thousand slaves had defected to the enemy during the war.

In other words, in 403, the Assembly can assume that the Attic countryside will produce revenues for the polis. These agricultural revenues will be bolstered by revenues from the silver mines, the tax on metics, an import tariff, standard liturgies, rents on state property, and, eventually, from renewed trade. Indeed, a speech by Demosthenes claims that a certain Phainippos had a modest-sized farm that yielded twelve drachmas a day selling wood, as well as three talents of barley and wine. Although this speech was delivered about 25–30 years after our game begins, it does give us an idea of the amount of wealth represented by an average farm.

The cost of building and maintaining ships—both trading vessels and warships—is another important part of the Athenian economy. From Thucydides' account of the ships the Athenians sent against Sicily in 415 BCE, we learn that it cost about one talent to build a trireme and an additional talent a month to man and maintain that ship and its crew. As ship-building got better and thus less expensive, timber became harder to get and thus more expensive, making it difficult to calculate the precise cost of building and maintaining a ship in 403 BCE.

In addition to building ships, the Athenians had to spend money on religious festivals and cults; indeed, their religious sensibilities would not allow them to ignore their obligations to the gods, and this money was spent no matter how tight money became. They also had to pay a variety of public officials, including jailers, the keepers of the official weights and measures, and the Scythian archers who served as a kind of police force in Athens. These expenditures on state religion and public order would have gobbled up a significant amount of the funds available to the polis.

Athenians could raise additional funds in an emergency, but only with great difficulty (they were just as resistant as modern citizens to paying taxes). The most common ways to raise revenue were either to increase the liturgies paid by the wealthiest citizens or to raise tariffs on trade into the Piraeus or taxes on metics (twelve drachmas per year per metic in the late fifth century). They could also recalculate the *eisphora*, the property tax paid by some citizens and metics (thetes, as the members of the lowest economic class, were traditionally exempt from this tax). Enacting any of these policies would, for example, raise enough money to rebuild a small fleet and send it on a tribute mission to one of the traditional tribute-paying zones (see the map on page 36). If the mission failed, however, many of the taxpayers would be ruined.

TIP

At the start of the game, Athenians can spend no more than seventy-five talents per meeting of the Assembly without raising additional revenues. Extraordinary expenses—such as the 125 talents necessary to rebuild the fleet and launch a tribute mission, or the nearly one hundred talents required to restore pay for those serving on juries—will require additional revenues.

In classical Athens, as in the contemporary United States, political affiliations cut across class lines. Basic self-interest would often lead many property owners to favor a more restricted government, while the landless tended to support a more radical democracy. Some of the most passionate democrats, such as Thrasybulus, had been rich before the war but had lost most of their wealth by 403. Small farmers among the yeomen were often the most supportive of limited government and of curtailing welfare for the thetes.

CONCLUSION

Athenians who gathered in the Assembly or the law courts in 403 BCE were influenced by a number of historical factors: their long and illustrious past, the rise and development of democracy in Athens, the victories and defeats of the Peloponnesian War, the rise and fall of the Athenian empire, and the tumult of the reign of terror instituted by the Thirty. The women who married the Assemblymen, managed their households, and raised their children helped shape their beliefs and actions. And the vast number of slaves and metics who lived among them helped make their way of life possible and exposed them to different cultures and different ways of being and thinking. Their way of life was an agrarian one, centered on the countryside and the farms that produced the crops that fed them and provided their personal and public fortunes. They were dependent on the olive, the vine, the grain, and the ships that plied the Mediterranean, transporting Athenian goods and Athenians ideas. Your character brings all of this knowledge and awareness into the Assembly when he enters that special place to debate the issues of the day with his fellow citizens.

PART 3: THE GAME

MAJOR ISSUES FOR DEBATE

The elements of Athenian democracy—six thousand male citizens debating laws and policies and deciding them collectively in meetings of the Assembly; trials with judges chosen randomly; juries of five hundred—may seem unfamiliar to you. The central texts, Plato's *Republic* and Pericles' funeral oration in support of democracy, are challenging and equally unfamiliar. The circumstances that produced the Peloponnesian War are complex and mystifying.

But the main debates in this game, below, are as familiar as the week's headlines.

Reconciliation. When a group or a nation has suffered grievous harm at the hands of its own people, should those responsible be punished in the name of justice? Or should a society forget the sins—and sinners—of the past and focus on reconciliation for the present and future?

The Political Status of Immigrants and Noncitizens. Does a society benefit from the political participation of foreigners, and the new ideas and concepts they bring? Or does the presence of foreigners rip a society's cohesive fabric? Similarly, what role should female citizens and noncitizens play?

The Merits of Democracy. Is direct democracy, in which everyone has equal input into the systems of governance, preferable to representative democracy, in which voters elect leaders to promote their points of view? Is democracy preferable to monarchy (one ruler)? To oligarchic rule (rule by a few)? To ensure equal participation, should citizens be paid to attend the Assembly? To prevent undue influence by wealthy or charismatic figures, should leaders be chosen randomly?

Free Speech. Most people recognize that, even in a democracy, the right to "free speech" has its limits: one can't yell fire in a crowded theater. Are citizens of a democracy entitled to promote the overthrow of the democracy that guarantees them freedom of speech? Should people be allowed to tell lies, or make remarks that are obviously wrong or scandalous?

Power and Justice. The Athenian empire spread its ideals of democracy to the states it forced into the Athenian empire. Can a powerful democratic state justly impose its will on weaker states ruled by alternative, and even anti-democratic, political systems?

RULES AND PROCEDURES

Winning the Game: Victory Objectives

Players win if, at the end of the game, the historical figures they represent have accomplished their main objectives. Most players are members of one of four factions. Victory for one player in the faction usually means victory for all. If the Thrasybulans have won most of the votes in the Assembly and have succeeded in convicting Socrates of treason, they have essentially assured that their radical democracy will prevail over the Solonian aristocrats and followers of Socrates. Conversely, if the democratic system has been replaced, then the Solonian aristocrats or the followers of Socrates may well have won.

But the final decision may rest on other matters. For example, the Thrasybulan system of democracy will likely require revenues derived from the collection of tributes from city-states subject to Athenian naval power. If Athens fails to rebuild its fleet, or if the fleet is lost in the final Game Session, the radical democratic victory may have gone down with the ships. Conversely, the followers of Socrates may still win even if their mentor, as in history, drinks the fateful hemlock and dies.

Some individual figures, especially the Indeterminates, have special or even unique victory objectives. They may win by asking brilliant questions, by researching a particular historical mind-set and voicing it well, or by otherwise enhancing the game—waiting until the final session to decide which "position" is the best one. For these players, defining victory objectives is more complicated, and may involve meeting privately with the instructor/Gamemaster.

Other Rules

The game will unfold in two separate contexts:

- The Assembly at the Pnyx, where some six thousand Athenian citizens (adult males only) meet every ten days or so to make political decisions; and
- The Dikasteria, the nine lawcourts, where forty-five hundred Athenians (five hundred at each court) determine whether individuals have broken laws or harmed other Athenians and should be punished.

Proceedings of the Assembly

Announcement of Agenda. The game includes five Assembly sessions. For each session, one agenda topic is prescribed as indicated in the following table; the President of the Assembly is free to choose a second topic. There are two exceptions:

During the first Assembly session, the only allowable topic is the Reconciliation Agreement; and during the sixth (and last) Assembly session, the President may choose more than one additional topic and need not announce it in advance of the session. Note that the fourth Game Session is not a meeting of the Assembly but of a lawcourt (*dikasterion*):

Sequence of Assembly Sessions with Prescribed Agenda Topic

GAME SESSION 1: ASSEMBLY	President 1	Reconciliation Agreement: a) Should Athenians forget the "past wrongs" of the supporters of the Thirty? b) Should Athenians be prohibited from filing lawsuits against the supporters of the Thirty?	*No other agenda item allowed*
GAME SESSION 2: ASSEMBLY	President 2	Electorate: Should metics and worthy slaves be admitted and allowed to vote in the Pnyx? To serve as jurors in the lawcourts?	President 2 may choose a second topic, but must announce that topic in time for players to prepare for it in advance
GAME SESSION 3: ASSEMBLY	President 3	Social Welfare: Should Assembly-men and jurors be paid?	President 3 may choose a second topic, but must announce that topic in time for players to prepare for it in advance
GAME SESSION 4: LAW-COURTS	TRIAL DAY	This session is reserved for a trial.	If no archon requests a trial in advance of Trial Day, then the GM will ask President 4 to hold an Assembly session and announce the topic in advance
GAME SESSION 5: ASSEMBLY	President 5	Should laws and major decisions be made by the Assembly, or by a governing council? If the latter, how should the members of the council be chosen?	President 5 may choose a second topic, but must announce that topic in time for players to prepare for it in advance
GAME SESSION 6: ASSEMBLY	President 6	Remilitarization/restoration of the Athenian empire. Should Athens rebuild its fleet, recommence tribute collection, and reconstitute its empire?	President 6 may choose a second topic or more, and may do so without warning

Arriving at the Assembly Session on Time. Prior to the beginning of an Assembly session, Scythian archers (the closest Athens had to police officers) block off the streets leading to the Agora (marketplace) and then, using long ropes dipped in red dye, corral people into the Pnyx, the open-air theater were Assembly sessions are held. Any Athenian citizen with red dye on his clothing can be fined for failing to do his civic duty. (For the purposes of the game, the GM can "fine" late arrivals by reducing their vote tally by 10 percent. Such a decision is entirely under the GM's discretion.)

The Pig Sacrifice. The President of the Assembly begins each session by instructing the herald to sacrifice a pig, deliver a prayer to the gods, and sprinkle the pig's blood around the outside boundary of the Pnyx, making it a sacred space. Once the sacrifice has been completed, the Gamemaster will then deliver the judgment of the goddess Athena by asking the Herald to choose one slip of paper from Pandora's Urn and read it aloud. (See the section on Pandora's Urn, below.)

Pandora's Urn. Whether most Athenians believed in their gods and myths is hard to determine. But we do know that desecration of shrines and religious statues was a serious offense, and that many generals would not initiate military campaigns when the portents were unfavorable. And whatever their beliefs, worship of the gods was an inextricable element of public rituals and private lives. Temples and ancient shrines dedicated to the gods can be found throughout Athens, though the most important religious sites are located atop the Acropolis. There stands the magnificent Parthenon, a temple dedicated to Athena, the daughter of Zeus. The main religious rites are performed on altars just outside the temples, often during festivals honoring particular gods. Other rites occur within the private home. Often religious rituals involve the sacrifice of animals as offerings to the gods.

The game reflects this religious sensibility chiefly through Pandora's Urn, a vessel provided by the Gamemaster which includes slips of paper signifying the will of the gods. Following the pig sacrifice at the outset of each Assembly meeting and/or intermittently throughout the game, the Gamemaster will instruct the Herald for the session to draw from the urn one or more slips of paper that will dictate a course of action or consequence. This process, of course, is not "random," but a decision of the gods or, perhaps more specifically, the goddess Athena. One example: "A load of spoiled fish arrived in the port of Piraeus, and has caused hundreds from Piraeus to become ill. Those players from Piraeus cannot speak today, and their vote totals are cut in half." The Gamemaster will then implement the gods' decision.

> **TIP**
>
> Clever Heralds can use Pandora's Urn to benefit their faction and harm their adversaries.

If the Gamemaster deems the Herald's sacrifice to be especially worthy, then she may allow the Herald to choose two slips of paper and select which of the "judgments" will apply to the class. Individual players and entire factions may improve their chances of a favorable response from the gods in various ways. One is by showing their devotion to Athens by dressing in suitable Athenian garb. Or they can undertake public works, such as building (models of) triremes and temples, or memorizing a speech from a play by Euripides or Aristophanes (or, better, by performing part of a scene in a public space, outside of class time, and capturing it on video). Appreciative gods might even bring more supporters to an especially diligent player or faction and increase their vote count!

The Debates Begin

After the gods have rendered a judgment, the President of the Assembly thanks the Herald and asks him to remain near the podium to assist in counting votes. Then the President will restate the agenda and outline any rules, such as length of initial presentations. Then he will ask, "Who wishes to speak?" [In Greek, *"tis agoreyein bouletai?"*]

Each President has considerable latitude to "preside" over the session as he sees fit, although he is expected to abide by basic standards of fairness. In fact, any Athenian official who abuses his office or shows poor judgment can be censured, at the end of his term, by a vote of the Assembly. Presidents will likely establish time limits for speeches and instruct someone to watch the *klepsydra*—water clock—to enforce this rule.

But Athenians become impatient with overly rigorous restrictions on debate. They are not Spartans, and they may become restless if a President runs the discussions like a military drill. Athenians believe in a free flow of ideas, and Presidents may find it more in keeping with Athenian practices to allow for questions and free discussion.

Any player who wishes to speak should walk to the podium. If someone is already speaking, players may form a line behind it.

Ensuring Clarity of Legislation. Speakers who want the Assembly to "do" something (pass a law, make a decision, etc.) should write their proposed law or decree on the blackboard. All laws or decrees should be simple, direct, and concise, if only because they must be chiseled onto stone tablets once the Assembly approves them. The President may request, for example, that no law exceed fifteen to twenty words in length, and all proposed laws must bear the name of the person proposing it. For example: "All government positions should be selected by lot."—SIGNED, THRASYBULUS; or, "Athens should impose a tax on all property holders and build fifty triremes."—SIGNED, MELETUS. Laws that are approved by the Assembly often become known by the names of their authors: "Meletus's Law," for example.

Supervising Votes. When the President feels that an agenda issue has received a full and fair hearing, he must call for a vote. This is done by asking Athenians to raise their placards, which show their current vote total. The Herald will assist the

President; the Gamemaster may supervise the proceedings to ensure fairness. The President will then announce the vote, which will be ratified by the GM.

Inscribing the Law in Stone. If a law is passed during a President's tenure, that law must be inscribed in stone in a public place. (At the very least, it should be posted on the class website, or written down on a slip of paper and submitted to the GM.) Remember to include the name of the proposer/author of the law.

Overturning Laws. The will of the current Assembly is supreme. It may pass a law during one session and overturn it during the next. Whether a player has achieved his or her victory objectives depends on the laws that are in force at the end of the final Game Session, as determined by the GM.

Constitutional Issues. All laws passed by the Assembly are binding. The only exception is if a law is struck down by a lawcourt. Consider the following hypothetical example: assume that the Assembly has passed Lycon's Law, "No one may Defame the Gods." In a subsequent meeting of the Assembly, Anytus, in a fit of anger, shouts, "Zeus be damned! This is an outrage!" Citizen Aristocles, outraged at this violation of Lycon's Law, persuades an archon to hold a trial, with Aristocles as prosecutor of Anytus. Assume, too, that during the trial Anytus admits that he defamed Zeus but claims that he had a right to do so: "In Athens, we're free to say whatever we want, even curse the gods if we choose." If a majority of the 501 jurors vote to acquit Anytus, the jurors will have effectively repealed Lycon's Law.

Graphe Paranomon. Another way of repealing a law is by initiating a *graphe paranomon* ("suit against a law") and delivering a speech denouncing a particular law. If Anytus wants to repeal Lycon's Law, for example, he can give a speech claiming that it violates other Athenian laws and traditions. If a majority of the Assembly concurs, the law is annulled.

Ostracism. The practice of ostracism (see the Historical Background section, p. 28) was largely abandoned by the Greeks after 418 BCE, but for the purposes of the game it is still a viable option. No ostracism can be proposed before the fifth Assembly session, however, and there can only be one ostracism during the game. If a majority of the Assembly votes to proceed with an ostracism vote, the Gamemaster will distribute slips of paper to all members of the Assembly. Each member will write the name of a person he or she proposes for ostracism. The person whose name appears on the most ballots will be ostracized. The Gamemaster will notify the President of the Assembly of the outcome; the ostracized student will presumably be banished from Athens, obviously incapable of voting

WARNING! *Ostracism is a powerful and unsettling weapon, used rarely by the Athenians. Those who proposed ostracism were sometimes ostracized themselves.*

on any measures before the Assembly or participating in any dikasterion. If he or she holds a position in the Athenian government, the GM will name a substitute to take his or her place; the GM will advise the student on how to proceed after the ostracism.

Retention of Leadership Powers. At the beginning of the game, each student/Leader controls five hundred votes in the Assembly, and forty or so votes in the dikasterion. (The exception is Lysias, a metic, who has no votes in the Assembly or a lawcourt.) This distribution presumes that every student/Leader will speak effectively during class sessions. Students who are members of any of the four factions are expected to speak at least once in each Game Session or meeting of the dikasterion. Any faction member who fails to speak may lose one hundred or more votes in succeeding sessions. (Failure to participate in class, of course, also affects one's overall grade.) The instructor makes all decisions in such matters. The Gamemaster will prod the Assembly President to ensure that everyone at the podium is called on sooner or later. Indeterminates are under less of an obligation to give speeches, at least during the first half of the game. But they are required to ask questions—several a session—until the final session. By the end of the game, but not before the fifth session, all Indeterminates must have taken a clear position and explained it in a speech to the Assembly.

TIP

All students have the right to approach the podium so as to ensure that they will be recognized to speak.

Disqualification for Reading Aloud. Reading aloud is rarely an effective rhetorical strategy. It is often boring and unsuited to an impressive leader such as yourself.

Dikasteria (Lawcourts)

Athens democratizes its trials. To ensure fairness, and to ensure that the collective will of the Athenian citizenry is represented, each jury for a dikasterion consists of 501 citizens. All citizens of Athens over 30 years old are eligible to serve as jurors in trials; traditionally, jurors receive pay of three obols (half a drachma) for each trial day of service. (The normal daily wage for a worker is six obols, or one drachma.) On trial day, when as many as nine separate dikasteria might be held, each citizen puts a ball with his name on it into a machine, which randomly distributes potential jurors to different dikasteria. All jurors are then given a chit, indicating the name and location of the dikasterion to which they have been assigned. They then report for duty and submit the chit, which is necessary to ensure payment for their service as juror. As a good citizen, you will show up on trial days and will likely be assigned to a dikasterion. In the event of a trial, you will take part in the deliberations of the dikasterion as a juror or perhaps as a plaintiff or defendant. All decisions of the dikasterion are made by majority vote.

All trials are presided over by a magistrate (archon); all of the archons are chosen randomly at the outset of the game, as is true of all other government positions (excepting general).

TIP

The fourth Game Session is normally reserved as "Trial Day." The Gamemaster may schedule short trials on other days as well if an archon agrees to hold a trial.

How to Initiate a Trial. If a player wishes to charge any person (Athenian citizen or otherwise, present in Athens or not) with any offense, that player should approach one of the archons. (The names of the archons are public knowledge; ask the Gamemaster if you forget their names.) If any one of the archons agrees that your case has sufficient merit to proceed to trial, then that archon will ask the Gamemaster to schedule one. A trial of Socrates will likely use up all or most of Game Session 4 and might even consume part of the next Game Session. A trial involving a private offense may be as brief as fifteen minutes and require little development.

Players will be notified if and when their trial will be held: time constraints may place limitations on the number of trials held during the game. If an archon declines a player's request for a trial, that player can make a request to any or all of the other archons. If no archon will accept the case, then it is dead.

If the Gamemaster schedules a trial, the person making the charge will function as the lead prosecutor. The prosecutor may invite others to join in this task. The charge should be announced when the trial is scheduled, so that the defendant and his supporters have time to prepare a defense.

If the Gamemaster agrees to a trial, he or she will schedule it on Trial Day (Game Session 4) or by taking away some time from an Assembly session.

Laws and Legal Precedents. Neither the prosecutor(s) nor the archon is obliged to cite a specific law or legal precedent that the defendant has presumably violated. The trial itself functions as a means of setting laws. For example, a prosecutor could charge another person with the "crime" of eating figs during Assembly sessions, though no such statute seems to have existed in ancient Athens. If the dikasterion convicts someone of this offense, then all Athenians will know that chewing figs during Assembly sessions is a violation of Athenian norms, and thus of Athenian law. (In fact, the Greek word *nomos* stood for both custom and law.) In short, Athenian citizens, acting as a jury, set laws through their decisions. Athenians equate the dikasterion with the Athenian citizenry more generally because, with over five hundred jurors, it represents a statistically significant sampling of the citizenry.

The archon will preside over the trial, setting procedural rules. Athenians expect archons to behave in a fair and reasonable manner; those who fail to do so run the risk of being censured. The defendant may speak for himself or ask others to assist in this capacity. If Socrates is placed on trial, however, he will not speak in his own defense.

There is one legal distinction worth considering. Athenian law distinguishes between offenses against the polis (the state) and against other private citizens. Both types of offenses are adjudicated by a dikasterion. But the nature of punishment differs. An offense against a private citizen requires that the fine be paid to the victim of the crime; an offense against the state requires that the fine be paid to the state. If Person X borrows money from Person Y and fails to pay it back, Person X will likely be fined, with the payment going to Person Y. If, however, Person X hits Person Y with a rock, that would be viewed as a crime against the state because it threatens public order. Person X, if convicted, would make a payment to the Athenian treasury. It is significant that verbal attacks against persons are regarded as crimes against the state because they, like a physical assault, imperil public order. The archon, in indicating that a trial is to go forward, should indicate whether it is of a public or private character.

Warning! *Assembly leaders who have been penalized for nonparticipation may lose their ability to cast votes in the dikasterion.*

Selection of the Jury. For game purposes, all Leaders, including the magistrate, will constitute the jury; each Leader will control fifty votes. A vote of 7 to 5 will represent a vote of 350 to 250.

Warning! *Not all votes will be counted. Read these rules for more detail.*

Rendering the Verdict. At the end of the trial, the Gamemaster will distribute two types of marbles (or some other tangible marker) to each Leader. One type will denote innocence, the other guilt. The Gamemaster will then place two urns on the table, hidden behind a screen: a "Counting Urn," which will include each player's vote; and a "Discard Urn," for the other marble. When voting, each juror will deposit a marble in both urns. Only those in the "Counting Urn" will be counted.

But not ALL of the marbles in the "Counting Urn" will be counted: for a class of sixteen students, for example, the Gamemaster will count only the first twelve marbles she (or her designee) withdraws from the Counting Urn. This is because, in ancient Athens, no prospective juror knew which trial they would be assigned to. On "trial day," jurors were randomly assigned to one of nine courts, each presided over by an archon. Because it is unlikely that every player in this game would have been assigned to the same court, the Gamemaster restores the random element by choosing (and counting) only the first twelve marbles. In larger classes, she will count more marbles, and in smaller classes, fewer marbles. But she will never count them all. Neither will she disclose the color of the "uncounted" votes.

Setting a Punishment. If someone is adjudged guilty, then the prosecutor will initiate a second phase of the trial to determine the penalty. The procedures here will be similar to the initial trial, though shorter in duration. The prosecutor(s) will propose a penalty, the defenders will speak against it, and then there will be open discussion of the matter. Athenian lawcourts did not allow open discussion in the penalty phase, but it is allowed in the game to compensate for the brevity of the trial, compared to the daylong trials of ancient Athens.

Punishment for Frivolous Prosecutions. Athenian law included a provision to prevent what might be termed "frivolous" prosecutions. It stipulated that if a prosecutor failed to persuade at least 20 percent of the jurors to vote for "conviction," he would be subject to loss of political rights. Thus, for the purposes of the game, if a Prosecutor fails to persuade 20 percent of the jurors to vote for conviction, then she will automatically lose all of her votes in subsequent Assembly meetings and trials. Similarly, the archon in the case will be publicly censured for allowing an unworthy prosecution to go forward. (If the archon is censured by a majority vote of the Assembly, that student will lose 20 percent of his voting followers.)

Trial of Socrates: Special Procedures

If an archon agrees, any citizen can call for a trial of Socrates. In that event, the main evidence will consist of Socrates' own words as expressed in Plato's *Republic*. An abridgement of the *Republic* appears in Part Five of this game book. Students attacking or defending Socrates may wish to consult an unabridged version, available nearly anywhere, along with other materials: chapters from Xenophon's *Hellenica*, for example, or Thucydides' *History of the Peloponnesian War*. Socrates himself will not speak in his defense, but instead rely on others to do so.

In 399 BCE, Socrates was indicted as a "public offender" who failed to recognize the gods of the state, instead introducing his own "demoniacal beings," and who corrupted the youth of Athens. He was convicted and sentenced to death.

Historical Context. Socrates is an important figure to several of the factions of this game. Those most concerned are the followers of Thrasybulus and the followers of Socrates. The Thrasybulan democrats view Socrates as a dangerous enemy because he tutored Critias and other members of the Thirty Tyrants, and because his most scathing criticism is directed at the democracy; the Socratic faction draws its inspiration from both the beliefs of Socrates (generally antidemocratic, to be sure) and from the power of his mind. The Periclean democrats and the Solonian aristocrats are less concerned about the fate of Socrates.

Role of the Gamemaster

The Gamemaster's role is to do everything possible to make the game an intellectually broadening exploration of late-fifth-century BCE Athenian society and thought. The game, accordingly, is complex. As the myriad elements collide in innumerable permutations, chance will intervene in ways that no one can anticipate. If the game careens wildly from historical plausibility, the Gamemaster may intervene, perhaps by modifying the rules or roles.

Most roles are challenging, as are the accompanying texts. Students should not hesitate to discuss their confusion with the Gamemaster. If, by the third Game Session, you have not spoken privately with the Gamemaster or exchanged at least one e-mail, you are probably playing the game poorly. E-mail is a good way to initiate queries because the process of formulating a question in words often helps to clarify your thinking. The Gamemaster, in responding to such requests, will try to formulate a helpful response without betraying any secrets or objectives held by other characters in the game.

Advisory: How to Reclaim the Athenian Empire

Sparta's defeat of Athens and the recent civil war have deprived the city of most of its tribute revenue. The Athenian fleet has been all but demolished. Some democratic leaders want to restore the Athenian empire, and if they succeed nearly all Athenians will benefit (see the section on the Treasury of Athena, pp. 51–53 in Part II). But rebuilding even a small fleet of triremes is expensive, and there are risks in reconstituting the Athenian empire, as the calamitous Sicilian expedition and the debacle at Aegospotami have shown.

If the Athenian Assembly wishes to restore the empire, it must first vote to build a fleet of triremes. It can then vote to dispatch the fleet to any of the former tribute-paying districts: Ionia, the islands, Thrace and the northern regions, the Hellespont, and so on (see map on page 36 of the tribute districts). Each of these districts includes between twenty-seven and sixty-five city-states that are charged with paying tribute. The more city-states involved and the longer the mission, the greater the tribute revenue; but long missions are more likely to hit a storm or encounter an enemy fleet. The Assembly should elect one general or more to command any tribute-collection mission. Sparta will likely disapprove of Athenian remilitarization but may be more worried about the rise of Thebes. Expeditions to Ionia and the Hellespont may unsettle the Persians, although the Persian empire is in turmoil following the recent death of Darius II.

An official Assembly vote to build a fleet of triremes and embark on a mission to collect tribute can be accomplished in the final Assembly meeting (Session 6). The instructor will roll a die to determine whether any military expedition succeeded, and, if successful, the amount of tribute revenue collected. Factors influencing the odds of success include but are not limited to the duration and difficulty of the mission; the margin of the vote in favor of the mission (if the margin was great, enthusiasm for the project was strong and recruitment in the navy will be easy); the leadership abilities of the commanding general(s); and the favor of the gods, as influenced by the pig sacrifice and prayer of the day (and signified through a die roll).

BASIC OUTLINE OF THE GAME

This game has three distinct phases: Setup, when the instructor introduces the mechanics of the game, describes its historical context and major texts, and assigns students to roles and factions; Game Play, when student players seek to win by debating and voting on major issues and policies; and Postmortem, when the class discusses what happened, compares it to the historical outcome, and ponders the major issues and texts from another perspective.

Phase I: Setup

SESSION 1

INTRODUCTION TO ATHENS IN 403 BCE: THE HISTORICAL CONTEXT

The instructor will explain the mechanics of the game and lead a discussion on Athenian history. Alternatively, he or she may play a micro (one-session) Reacting game, "Athens Besieged: Debating Surrender," which outlines the situation in Athens during the winter of 405–404 BCE after the destruction of the Athenian fleet at Aegospotami. Deprived of food and cowering behind the city walls, Athenians debated whether to surrender, which would likely lead to the slaughter of Athens's men and the enslavement of its women and children, or to hold out and devise some means of saving its people—and perhaps even its democracy. The game may not follow history and no outcome is predetermined. Dice are likely to be involved.

Required Reading

- Game book: Introduction and Historical Background, pp. 2–53.

REMAINING SETUP SESSIONS

The remaining Setup sessions will include a lecture and discussion on Athenian democracy, with particular attention paid to Pericles' funeral oration and Plato's *Republic*. Players will receive their roles (as faction members or Indeterminates) and will be randomly assigned to jobs (President of the Assembly, archon, or Herald). They will meet with their factions or, if they are Indeterminates, meet privately with the Gamemaster.

Required Reading

- Core Text #1, Funeral Oration, pp. 89–94.
- Core Text #2, Plato's *Republic*, pp. 95–199.

Students must be prepared both to discuss what these two primary texts reveal about Athenian views of democracy and to place them within the historical, political, social, and economic context of Athens in 403 BCE, as described in the Historical Background section of the game book. A clear distillation of Socrates' critique of democracy appears in Part III of *Republic* (Book 4, section 434a; see Core Texts, p. 154). To prepare for this discussion, it is particularly helpful to read Plato's *Republic* from the perspective of your character in the game—considering, for example, how a Solonian aristocrat would react to Socrates' comments about oligarchies (see *Republic*, Part V, in Core Texts, pp. 194–99).

Phase II: Game Play

This phase of the game will consist of the six sessions, five of them at the Assembly and one in the lawcourts. The Game Sessions will unfold in a predictable sequence: when players arrive at the Assembly or the lawcourts, they will likely sit with their factions. Indeterminates will sit wherever they wish. Those with leadership roles (President, Herald, archons) will commence the sessions—with a pig sacrifice, for example—and a debate will follow. Players will propose laws or offer indictments. These debates will function chiefly to persuade Indeterminates to vote in a particular way, or to persuade one faction to ally with another. All of the debates will likely culminate in a vote.

Members within factions, meeting outside of class, will likely assign each member to speak (and write) on particular topics. For example, the Solonian aristocrats may assign Xenophon to speak in favor of the Reconciliation Agreement in Assembly Session 1, while Callias will be asked to call for restricting the vote to property owners in Session 2, and Aristarchus to oppose payment for jurors and Assembly members in Session 3. Every member of the faction is expected to participate in all sessions and debates, but particular players have special responsibilities and rhetorical duties; initial tasks will be worked out during the Setup phase.

Remember that, by the start of the Game Sessions, every factional player will have three sets of responsibilities: those of her faction (outlined in the factional role sheets); those of her individual player identity (outlined in her personal role sheet); and those of her position within the Athenian government (Assembly President, Herald, or archon). Every Indeterminate player will have two sets of responsibilities: those outlined in her personal role sheet, and those of her position within the Athenian government (Assembly President, Herald, or archon).

The following provides an outline for a class with six Game Sessions. Your instructor may schedule more or fewer than six classes.

GAME BEGINS

GAME SESSION 1

RECONCILIATION AGREEMENT

Leader: President 1

Main Agenda Topic

- Should Athenians forget the "past wrongs" of the supporters of the Thirty?
- Should they be prohibited from filing lawsuits against the supporters of the Thirty?

Other Agenda Topics

- No other agenda items may be discussed.

Required Reading

- Xenophon's *Hellenica* (Core Texts, pp. 226–35).

Supplemental Texts

All of the supplemental texts may be found on the Perseus website at www.perseus.tufts.edu.

- Thucydides on the horrors of the civil war (Thucydides, Book 3, chapters 69–85, usually cited as Thuc. 3.69–85).
- Thucydides on the horrors of ancient warfare (Thuc. 7.75–87).

GAME SESSION 2

ELECTORATE

Leader: President 2

Main Agenda Topic

- Should metics and worthy slaves be admitted to and allowed to vote in the Pnyx?
- Should they be allowed to serve as jurors in the lawcourts?

Other Agenda Topics

- The President may choose a second topic, but must announce that topic in time for players to prepare for it in advance.

Required Reading:

- Plato's *Protagoras* (Core Texts, pp. 200–02).

Supplemental Texts

- Aristophanes' *Ecclesiaszusae* (also known as *The Assemblywomen*).
- Review Plato's *Republic*, Part III (Core Texts, pp. 147–71) for Socrates' views on the roles of the family and women in an ideal state.

GAME SESSION 3

SOCIAL WELFARE

Leader: President 3

Main Agenda Topic

- Should Assemblymen and jurors be paid?

Other Agenda Topics

- The President may choose a second topic, but must announce that topic in time for players to prepare for it in advance.

Required Reading

- Xenophon's "The Estate Manager" from *The Economist* (Core Texts, pp. 213–226).

Supplemental Texts

- "The Constitution of the Athenians" by Pseudo-Xenophon (also known as the "Old Oligarch").

GAME SESSION 4

TRIAL DAY

Leader: the Archon (or Archons)

Main Agenda Topic

- This session is reserved for a trial. If no archon requests a trial in advance, then the GM will ask President 4 to hold an Assembly session and announce the topic in advance.

Required Reading for a trial of Socrates

- Plato's *Republic*, Part II (Core Texts, pp. 118–47).

Supplemental Text for a trial of Socrates

- Plato's *Apology*

GAME SESSION 5

GOVERNANCE

Leader: President 5

Main Agenda Topic

- Should laws and major decisions be made by the Assembly, or by a governing council?
- If the latter, how should the council members be chosen?

Other Agenda Topics

- The President may choose a second topic, but must announce that topic in time for players to prepare for it in advance.

Required Reading

- Plutarch's *Life of Lycurgus* (Core Texts, pp. 202–08).
- Review Plato's *Republic*, Part II (Core Texts, pp. 118–47), which summarizes Socrates' views on proper education for the so-called guardians of his ideal state.

GAME SESSION 6

REMILITARIZATION/RESTORATION OF THE ATHENIAN EMPIRE

Leader: President 6

Main Agenda Topic

- Should Athens rebuild its fleet, recommence tribute collection, and reconstitute its empire?

Other Agenda Topics

- The President may choose a second topic or more, and may do so without warning.

Required Reading

- Plutarch's *Life of Cimon* (Core Texts, pp. 209–13).

Supplemental Texts

- Thucydides' *Melian Dialogue* (Thuc. 5.84–116) on the excesses of the empire.
- Athenian tribute lists on the successes of the empire and its revenues.

Phase III: Postmortem Discussion

After the final Game Session, the Gamemaster will direct discussion during the final class (or classes) of the Postmortem phase, indicating the victors and uncovering any secrets. She will also relate the actual historical events of the period. If the game's outcomes differed from history, the class will discuss how and why. Finally, students will discuss their own "true" views on the central issues and texts, especially Plato's *Republic*.

Writing and Speaking Assignments

Although your instructor will outline the exact writing and speaking requirements for your class, she will likely adhere to several general principles as well. Players assigned to factions will likely write two essays, one during the first half of the game (Game Sessions 1–3), the other during the second half (Game Sessions 4–6). The suggested topics for each player within a faction are outlined in the factional role sheets. The writing assignments for Indeterminates vary by role.

Within factions, students who write a paper on a particular topic will likely make an oral presentation on that topic in the Assembly or lawcourts. But teams/factions should always function collectively: whenever one player makes a speech, the others should be prepared to help out. When a player is advocating for a particular law or making an indictment in a lawcourt, players on the other side of the issue should be thinking of hard questions and rebuttals. Everyone should speak frequently.

Historians You Should Draw Upon in Your Writings and Speeches

The period covered by this game witnessed the emergence of historical writing as a field of intellectual inquiry. For thousands of years, scribes and priests of earlier civilizations had chronicled the stories of kings and battles, such as appear in the Hebrew Bible of the ancient Israelites and the *Mahabharata* of the early Hindus. But all three of the founders of historical writing in the Western world—Herodotus,

Thucydides, and Xenophon—were major figures in fifth-century Greece. Herodotus wrote about the Persian Wars early in the century. Thucydides and Xenophon, who may be players in your game, wrote about the Peloponnesian War. They had witnessed some of the events about which they wrote, and sought written or oral confirmation from participants in events they did not observe. Perhaps the most important source on Athenian political development is the *Athenian Constitution*, in which Aristotle (or one of his students) charts the development of Athenian political institutions from about 630 to 403 BCE.

In writing papers or giving speeches, you can cite any of these sources—just as Athenians of the time might have done. (Though Aristotle was not alive in 403 BCE, he knew some of the people who lived at this time and may have had access to written sources that have since been lost. Therefore you may include quotations and facts from the people he cites.) These historical accounts may provide much of the evidence you need to bolster your arguments and write powerful papers.

TIP

Often passages from classical texts are identified by their book, chapter, and line. Therefore Thuc 1.1.1 would refer to Thucydides' *History of the Peloponnesian War*, Book 1, Chapter 1, Line 1.

Herodotus. Herodotus was born in Halicarnassus, a city in the southwest corner of modern-day Turkey. He wrote about interactions between Greeks and Persians in a work he called the *Histories*, meaning, merely, the "Inquiries." His account of the Persian War is rich and thorough, with a broad chronological and geographical sweep. It is flavored by stories, folktales, accounts recorded by other travelers, and detailed descriptions of places he himself visited in his quest to discover the source of the conflict between Greeks and Persians. In his text, you will find information about Peisistratus and the Tyrant Slayers (1.59), the battle at Marathon that Athenians considered their "finest moment" (6.105), the rise of the Athenian navy (7.140–145), and the sack of Athens by the Persian king Xerxes (8.40–60).

Thucydides. Thucydides (born ca. 460 BCE) belonged to an aristocratic Athenian family that owned property in Thrace and enjoyed access to revenues from the gold mines there. Like Herodotus, Thucydides chose to write about the war that defined his own age: in his case, the Peloponnesian War. As he himself writes, he "wrote the history of the war . . . beginning at the moment that it broke out, believing that it would be a great war and more worthy of telling than any that had preceded it . . . [since] there was nothing on so great a scale, either in war or in other matters [as this war]" (Thuc. 1.1.1). Among the most distinctive features of his history are the long and detailed speeches he puts in the mouths of the historical figures of the period. He describes his historical methodology for writing these speeches in some detail: "Some I heard myself, others I got from various quarters; it was in all cases difficult to carry them word for word in one's memory, so my habit has been to make the speakers say what was in my opinion demanded of them by the various occasions, of course adhering as closely as possible to the general sense of what they really said" (1.22.1). These speeches give readers a vivid sense of participating in a session of the Assembly and listening to the political figures of the day advocate for actions and policies.

Thucydides could offer an insider's perspective on many of the war's events. He had suffered, for instance, from the plague that killed many Athenians in the early years of the war (2.47–55). His perspective on the Athenian military was similarly profound; he had been elected general in 424 and, after failing to prevent Amphipolis from surrendering to Sparta that year, had been exiled from Athens (5.26). He spent the next twenty years travelling from Athenian to Peloponnesian allies and back, thus seeing the war from both the Spartan and the Athenian perspective. He eventually returned to Athens during the final siege of the city.

His *History* breaks off (literally in mid-sentence) near the end of the twenty-first year of the war (411 BCE). Not long afterward, another great Greek historian, Xenophon, picks up the account in his *Hellenica* exactly where Thucydides left off, describing the final seven years of the war and its aftermath. Reading both of these authors in succession gives us a very full depiction of the war, including the events leading up to it and its subsequent impact on Athens, Sparta, and the other Greek city-states. Thucydides envisioned his text as a "possession for all time" (Thuc. 1.22)—and so it has been.

If you want to know what ancient civil war was like and how it led to the breakdown of moral order, read Thucydides' description of the conflict at Corcyra (3.69–85). The finest description of the virtues of Athenian democracy appears in the funeral oration that Thucydides has Pericles deliver in 430 BCE (see Core Texts, p. 89). When the island of Melos attempts to withdraw from the empire and stop paying tribute to Athens, the Athenians give the Melians a choice: surrender and pay the tribute or be destroyed. Thucydides composes speeches for the Athenian envoys that contain a stark indictment of Athenian power and cruelty, saying, "For ourselves, we shall not trouble you with specious pretenses—either of how we have a right to our empire because we overthrew the Mede, or are now attacking you because of wrong that you have done us—and make a long speech which would not be believed; and in return we hope that you, instead of thinking to influence us by saying that you did not join the Spartans, although their colonists, or that you have done us no wrong, will aim at what is feasible, holding in view the real sentiments of us both; since you know as well as we do that right, as the world goes, is only in question between equals in power, while *the strong do what they can and the weak suffer what they must*" (5.89). True to their word, the Athenians follow this speech by killing all of the men and enslaving all of the women and children. For a vivid description of the horrors of military defeat, read Thucydides' description of the end of the Sicilian campaign (7.75–87); even more startling is his account of the panic in Athens when word of the defeat began to trickle into the city (8.1 and Plutarch's *Life of Nicias*, 29–30).

Xenophon. Xenophon, the son of Gryllus, an aristocrat, was born in Athens. Although he was actually born in 430 BCE, for the purposes of the game, he is assumed to be about 30 years old in 403. As a young man, he was a student of Socrates (see his *Symposium* and other Socratic dialogues written by him). In later life, he was a mercenary soldier and eventually an historian, first writing the *Hellenica*, which finishes the account of the Peloponnesian War where Thucydides left off, and then the *Anabasis*, which describes his return to Greece after serving as a mercenary in Persia. These historical works provide a glimpse into Xenophon's politics, especially the *Education of Cyrus* and the *Constitution of Sparta*. Another text, the *Constitution of Athens*, by someone known as the Old Oligarch, seems to reflect Xenophon's views about democracy so closely that earlier generations of scholars believed it to have been written by Xenophon. Although you should not quote directly from any of these sources, they will give you general ideas about Xenophon's political views.

A NOTE ON PRIMARY SOURCES

Some of this material by Herodotus, Thucydides, and Xenophon appears in the Core Texts section. Translations of every text can be found easily in your school's library (look for the collection of Greek texts published as the Loeb series or ask the librarian for assistance) or online. Some excellent online resources are the Perseus website (www.perseus.tufts.edu; the website includes almost all of the Loeb volumes) and the Internet Classics Archive (http://classics.mit.edu/index.html); both of these resources are searchable. Published translations that are now in the public domain can also be found on Google scholar.

PART 4: ROLES AND FACTIONS

OVERVIEW OF FACTIONS

Thrasybulans

Thrasybulans (also known as the Followers of Thrasybulus) believe that Athenian greatness over the past century has been a product of its increasingly vital democracy. A half-century ago, Pericles strengthened the democracy by expanding the power of the Assembly, ensuring that all officials (except generals) would be chosen by random lottery, and paying citizens to serve as jurors. Pericles also promoted Athenian imperialism, which helped finance the democracy. But he failed to appreciate the extent to which enemies of the democracy would seek to destroy it from within—a major factor in Athens's loss to Sparta. Thrasybulans maintain that Athens must protect its democracy by putting on trial those who assisted the Thirty Tyrants, including "teachers" like Socrates who persuaded wealthy young men to despise democracy and mock the idea of citizens governing themselves. Thrasybulans propose to broaden the electorate by granting citizenship to patriotic metics and even some slaves. They also seek to rebuild the Athenian navy and resume tribute-collection missions.

Periclean Democrats

Pericleans believe that the more moderate democratic system erected by Pericles forever changed human affairs. Under his guidance, democracy unleashed the collective talents and abilities of the Athenian people. In his famous funeral oration (see Core Texts, p. 89), Pericles declared that Athens was "the school of Greece," teaching the world that the best form of government was controlled by the people themselves. Periclean democrats call for the restoration of the Athenian Assembly, in which six thousand citizens gathered to debate policies and enact laws. Lest some people gain too much influence in this body, however, Pericleans insist that government officials be chosen by random lottery and serve only one-year terms. Citizens should receive modest payment to attend the Assembly and serve as jurors. Athens's defeat during the Peloponnesian War was due to the negligence and greed of a few generals, not to defects in its democracy. Athenians must forget their past differences and pull together to rebuild the glory of democratic Athens—and to restore the Athenian empire. However, the radical proposals of the Thrasybulans, such as granting more rights and power to metics and slaves, must be rejected.

Solonian Aristocrats

Solonian aristocrats define themselves most clearly in opposition to the democrats. In their view, power-hungry demagogues, over the past century, have pandered to the poor citizens of Athens. Time and again the Assembly roared its approval as leather-lunged orators, including scoundrels such as Alcibiades and Cleon, trumpeted the virtues of "democracy." These demagogues believed everyone should have a voice in the government, per Pericles' declaration that no Athenian citizen seeking a government position should be "hindered" by his own "obscurity" (see Core Texts, p. 91). Pericles' funeral oration insists that every male citizen, however ill-tempered, drunken, or stupid, must be accorded an equal chance to voice his opinion, vote for laws and dispense justice, and serve in executive positions in the government.

This view is wrong. By giving citizens an equal share of power over the state, Athenian democracy has ensured that it will be poorly governed. Athens should return to the constitution of the wise Solon, which gives a small governing council, elected from the property-owning citizens of Athens, the power to make all important decisions. These men were natural leaders experienced at managing people, running large farms, and planning for the future. They should again lead the state. Athens, too, should relinquish its empire and abandon its policy of extorting tribute payments from other Greek city-states. Rather than build warships, it should reduce overall expenditures while focusing on defending the city. It should extend its walls to protect more farms and the families that either own or work them.

Followers of Socrates

The followers of Socrates agree with much of the Solonians' critique of Athenian democracy: the notion that six thousand citizens can make wise decisions while screaming at each other in the Pnyx is absurd, as is the selection of government officials by random lottery. But the Solonian aristocrats err in believing that well-to-do farmers and property owners are best suited to rule. Like any other skill, ruling requires special talents and traits. Rulers must be chosen for their intelligence, character, and commitment to the pursuit of truth and justice. They must undergo rigorous education to hone their skills as philosophers. Athens should be ruled by a governing council, but not one randomly "elected" by the mob of Athenian citizens, or culled from among the city's richest oligarchs. Instead, the finest young minds—men and women of a pure philosophical disposition—should be recruited to serve on the council. They should receive further education from philosophers such as Socrates. As rulers, they should receive no payment beyond what is necessary for their subsistence. The council should be open to men and women, slaves and foreigners alike. This enlightened form of government can provide a model for wise rule everywhere.

Indeterminates

The Indeterminates are not members of any faction at the outset of game, nor do they function as a faction. On the contrary, they may well have divergent views and opinions. Although Indeterminates (excepting the metic Lysias) are expected to cast votes even in the first Assembly session, they are barred from publicly joining any faction until the final Game Session. At that point, they may sit with the faction of their choice and proclaim their affiliation with it.

PUBLIC BIOGRAPHIES OF ATHENIAN LEADERS, 403 BCE

The following descriptions report what is generally known about these prominent figures in Athens. Your game will likely include many, but not all, of these figures. It may also include some figures not listed below.

All of the listed figures are frequent and effective speakers in the Assembly and the lawcourts. Whenever any of these speakers addresses the Assembly, five hundred Assembly members vote as he recommends. (The number of followers may change during the game according to the efforts of the speaker and the whims of the gods.) An exception is the metic Lysias who, though wealthy and influential, is not an Athenian citizen. At the outset of the game, he cannot officially attend the Assembly or serve as a juror in the lawcourts.

Most of the leaders—the finest speakers in Athens—are well-to-do or wealthy. This is true of even the most ardent supporters of Thrasybulus, much of whose support comes from the poorer citizens (those of the thetes class—the oarsmen). Wealthy individuals are more likely to have spent years honing their speaking skills by studying with prominent rhetoricians such as Gorgias, Isocrates, Thrasymachus, and Socrates. And fame begets more fame. Prominent speakers become celebrities after being lampooned in the comedies of Aristophanes, Eupolis, and Cratalus.

But Athenians know that their predominantly wealthy leaders do not reflect the demographic patterns of the citizenry as a whole. When the game opens in 403 BCE, Athens has eighteen thousand adult male citizens. About half of these citizens own property. For the purposes of the game, the property owners are classified as hoplites (armored foot-soldiers); the others are classified as thetes, the rowers of the triremes.

> In 431, at the outset of the war, Athens had forty-three thousand adult male citizens. Of these, twenty-five thousand were property owners and eighteen thousand thetes. The Great War has decimated the ranks of adult male Athenians. Every Athenian family has suffered grievous losses. For further demographic and economic information on Athens, see the Historical Background section, pages 20–53.

Players may wish to undertake research about themselves and other figures in the game. This is not quite as easy as it may seem. A son's name is often indistinguishable from that of his father or grandfather; and often very little is known even about the prominent leaders of ancient Athens.

List of Possible Players: A Fact Sheet

NAME	PRONUNCIATION	AGE	DEME/DISTRICT	OCCUPATION & NOTES
THRASYBULANS				
Thrasybulus	thra-SIHB-yoo-lus	48	Stiria	General
Lycon	LYE-con	65	Thoricus	Wealthy; father of Autolycus
Meletus	MEH-lee-tus	30	Piraeus	Served with Thrasybulus
Kephisophon	che-PHIZ-oh-phon	31	Kerameikos	Potter and vase painter
Damnippus	dam-NIP-us	32	Decelea	Friend of Lysias
PERICLEAN DEMOCRATS				
Anytus	AH-noo-tus	48	Euonymon	Wealthy owner of a tannery
Archinus	ar-KINE-us	32	Coele	General
Theozotides	thee-oh-zoh-TIE-dez	46	Authmoneus	Farmer
Aristogeiton	ah-ris-toe-GUY-ton	37	Rhamnous	Served with Thrasybulus
Euclides	you-KLY-deez	31	Thoricus	Gem cutter
SOLONIAN ARISTOCRATS				
Callias	CAL-lee-ahs	47	Alopece	Wealthy owner of silver mines
Aristarchus	air-ihs-TAR-kuss	45	Athens	Landowner and farmer; now poor
Xenophon	ZEN-oh-fahn	30	Erchia	Knight, philosopher, writer
Miltiades	mill-TYE-ah-DEEZ	67	Laciadae	Wealthy; helped in surrender
Phormisius	for-MIS-ee-us	38	Eleusis	Served with Thrasybulus
FOLLOWERS OF SOCRATES				
Crito	CRY-toh	66	Alopece	Wealthy landowner
Simon	[as in English]	37	Kyda	Shoemaker
Aristocles	ah-RISS-toh-kleez	30	Collytus	Rich landowning family
Eryximachus	er-rux-E-mah-khos	50	Coele	Physician; defendant in trial
Antaeus	an-TEE-us	38	Aphidna	Wrestler
INDETERMINATES				
Gorgias, Younger	gore-GEE-us	31	Coele	Rhetorician, logician
Thucydides	thoo-SIH-de-DEEZ	60	Halimous	Exiled general, writer
Lithicles	LITH-ah-kleez	42	Scambonidae	Stonemason
Diognetus	dee-AHG-nee-tus	47	Scambonidae	Famous boxer

Epeius	eh-PEE-us	32	Cydantidae	Silver mines
Lysias	LI-see-as	41	Thurii (foreign)	Metic, owner of weapons factory
Thearion	thay-AR-e-on	32	Collytus	Baker
Rhinon	RYE-non	56	Paenia	Farmer
Herodion	her-OH-dee-un	69	Piraeus	Philosopher, shoemaker

Thrasybulans

Thrasybulus. Leader of the Thrasybulans, Thrasybulus, 48 years old, has been a prominent figure in promoting the democracy since 411 BCE, when he helped put down an attempt by oligarchs to overthrow the government. He also served as a general during the Great War, winning several major naval battles. His reputation was tarnished, however, when, after the victory at Arginousae, he failed along with the other commanders to rescue Athenian sailors whose ships had been sunk. Thousands perished. Despite that, Thrasybulus has had recent success as the leader of the democratic army that defeated the Thirty Tyrants and drove them from Athens. Though once very wealthy, he lost much of his property during the reign of the Thirty. He still owns slaves.

Lycon. An ardent supporter of Thrasybulus and defender of the democracy, Lycon, 65, is well known for his exuberant partying. Comic poets have often made fun of him and his licentious, foreign-born wife. But last year the Thirty Tyrants executed Lycon's son, Autolycus, a famous wrestler and ardent democrat. Lycon has entered public life to avenge his son's death, making no secret of his vow to punish the enemies of the democracy. Lycon owns several properties and farms and a few slaves.

Meletus. The son of a playwright, Meletus, 30, served in the Great War as an oarsman (thetes). A native of Piraeus, he joined Thrasybulus's men in the battle that defeated the Thirty Tyrants at Munychia, one of the ports there. He remains a follower of Thrasybulus. He is ranked as a hoplite, though gossipers hint that he is nearly broke. He still owns one or two slaves.

Kephisophon. A potter and vase painter, Kephisophon, 31, works in the pottery shop of Bakkhios in the Kerameikos (pottery district) of Athens, and married Bakkhios's daughter. Bakkhios was a financial supporter of Thrasybulus during the insurgency and Kephisophon is known to be a follower of Thrasybulus. He did not serve in the Great War. Although he lacks money of his own—his two slaves are the property of his wife—he will likely inherit the profitable Bakkhios pottery works someday.

Damnippus. An unusually well-spoken leader of the Assembly, Damnippus, 32, is from Decelea, in the foothills of Mount Parnes. Decelea was seized by Theban and Spartan soldiers, who used it as a raiding base during the final years of the war. Damnippus moved to Athens and is frequently seen in the company of the metic Lysias. Little else is known about him.

Periclean Democrats

Anytus. Having inherited his father's tannery, Anytus, 48, is very wealthy. He served during the Great War as a general. But his failure to relieve the Athenian garrison at Pylos in 425 BCE led to him being charged with treason. Though he was acquitted, rumors have persisted that he bribed the jurors—apparently in new and inventive ways. After Anytus publicly criticized the Thirty Tyrants, they seized his property and exiled him. Afterward, he joined Thrasybulus and commanded a force that helped defeat the Thirty in Piraeus. Although Anytus marched into Athens with the victorious army led by Thrasybulus, he now leads the Pericleans, or the moderate democrats. He owns many slaves and is one of the richest men in Athens.

Archinus. Archinus, 32, served in the Great War and was elected general. He was among those who helped negotiate Athens's surrender to the Spartans; but when the Thirty Tyrants began their reign of terror, he fled Athens, joined Thrasybulus, and became a commander of some of the democratic troops. He grew close to Anytus, another democratic commander, and is now a key figure among the Periclean Democrats. He owns only a few slaves.

Theozotides. A middling farmer from the western slopes of Mount Pentele, Theozotides, 46, served as a hoplite during the Great War. His farm was razed by Spartans and now is nearly worthless. He owns only two slaves. An effective speaker, he is a leader of the Periclean Democrats. He came to public attention by proposing that orphans of soldiers killed fighting the Thirty be granted assistance from the state.

Aristogeiton. Until the last few years Aristogeiton, 37, was rarely seen in Athens. Though his namesake is one of the legendary "Tyrant Slayers," this farmer is from the remote village of Rhamnous on the northeastern coast of Attica, looking out toward the island of Euboea. After the Spartans destroyed the Athenian navy two years ago, Aristogeiton took the lead in carting grain and livestock from Euboea to help feed the Athenians. Then he fought with Thrasybulus at the battle of Munychia, where Critias fell dead. For a time it was rumored that this descendent of the "Tyrant Slayers" had also killed Critias, but this was untrue. Aristogeiton has made a name for himself as a dynamic speaker in the Assembly.

Euclides. Euclides, 31, is a gem cutter from Thoricus on the eastern coast of Attica. His forceful speeches in the Assembly have caused Athenians to wonder about his background, though little is known about him.

Solonian Aristocrats

Callias. The scion of one of the oldest and wealthiest families in all Greece, Callias, 47, inherited the family silver mines in Laurium, in the southeastern corner of Attica. Just twenty years before the game starts he was the richest man in Greece, with a large annual income from the mines of about six talents and additional income from the agricultural activity on his land in other parts of Attica. He once owned three lavish houses and about a thousand slaves, though most of them ran away during the Great War. He served as a general during the war and officiated as a member of the priestly family that presided over the mysteries at Eleusis. Rich men have customarily been the targets of comedic wit, and Callias's reputation for adultery has recently underscored his visibility in public life. The collapse of the Athenian economy has reportedly left him exposed to creditors. He still owns hundreds of slaves, but the lavish parties at his house in Melite are now rare.

Aristarchus. Once a wealthy landowner with farms near Mount Hymettus, Aristarchus, 45, now lives in Athens in greatly reduced circumstances. He has a single slave, and his house in Athens is home to a large number of women left behind when citizens fled the city. Aristarchus remained in Athens during the reign of the Thirty; therefore rumors abound that he is "favorably disposed" toward them, though this has not been confirmed.

Xenophon. The son of a wealthy farmer from Erchia, east of Mount Hymettus, Xenophon, 30 (see the Counterfactuals section, p. 18, for information concerning his age), has already attracted considerable notice. An enthusiastic horseman and priest-in-training in Erchia, Xenophon has begun spending more time in Athens and frequenting Socrates' favorite spot in the Agora. Some say that Xenophon remained in Athens and even fought with his close friend Critias, though others dismiss such accusations as rumors. Xenophon points out that he has publicly criticized the Thirty and that for much of their reign, he was in Erchia, breaking in horses and learning to conduct sacrifices.

Miltiades. The son of Stesagoras, Miltiades, 67, claims to be related to the commander of the Greek armies that defeated the Persians earlier this century. When Pericles first proposed war against Sparta, Miltiades declared that this was unwise. During the Great War, rumors spread that he commanded a Spartan warship, though no proof of this was ever produced. Last year, when Athens was forced to capitulate to Sparta, Miltiades was among the team that was sent to negotiate terms of surrender. He played no role in the reign of the Thirty Tyrants but remained in Athens; he did not support either side during the civil war. Although his health is poor, he still commands an audience whenever he speaks, usually in support of the Solonian Aristocrats. Miltiades is wealthy enough to qualify for the "liturgical" class, which obliges him to spend vast sums in support of religious festivals and choral productions.

Phormisius. From the sacred city of Eleusis, Phormisius, 38, has proven to be a formidable speaker in both the Assembly and the lawcourts. Little is known about his background.

Followers of Socrates

Crito. Crito's family consisted of a respected band of farmers in the Alopece district, just beyond one of the city gates of Athens. While most farmers fared badly during the war, Crito's farms appear not to have been badly ravaged by Spartan invasions—perhaps because they were so close to the city. Indeed, he seems to have profited from the war and is now very wealthy, the owner of scores of slaves. As a result he frequently has to defend himself in the lawcourts against frivolous lawsuits. At 66, a mature statesman, Crito is perhaps the most influential of Socrates' many supporters. Crito owns many properties, warehouses, and slave quarters.

Simon. Known as Simon the Shoemaker, Simon, 37, is the owner of a shoemaker's shop in the southwest corner of the Agora. Socrates, who often can be seen shoeless, frequents the shop, which has consequently become a gathering place for his supporters. Adept at logic and rhetoric, Simon has become—against all expectations—a celebrated speaker in the Assembly and lawcourts. He owns one slave who works in his shop. Simon, too, is a devoted follower of Socrates, so much so that he often is moved to take down some leather from his storeroom and write down particularly interesting bits of conversations between Socrates and other patrons of the shop.

Aristocles. Too young to serve in the Great War, Aristocles, 30, did not fight in any major battles and only took up arms at the end of the struggle with Sparta. Like his older brothers, Adeimantus and Glaucon, Aristocles is a son of Ariston and a member of an ancient and wealthy family of landholders. Though Aristocles was a wrestler as a teenager, he became one of Socrates' most devoted disciples. He is wealthy and owns many estates and several slaves.

Eryximachus. The son of Acumenus, a figure of some sexual scandal, Eryximachus, 50, himself became entangled in public furor. In 415 BCE, on the eve of the departure of the great fleet for Sicily, public outrage erupted over the mutilation of the herms, the phallic statues placed at the entrances to homes and public buildings in Athens. Although Alcibiades was held to be chiefly responsible for that outrage, an "Eryximachus" was also identified as one of the malicious vandals. Eryximachus has recently won a lawsuit confirming his innocence of that crime. But rumors continue to plague him as he carries on his work in Athens as a physician. He is a man of some wealth and substance, which is surprising considering his lineage. He, along with Socrates, is one of the guests at the banquet described in Plato's *Symposium*.

Antaeus. A large man with a booming voice, Antaeus, 38, was a well-known wrestler who nearly competed in the Olympic Games. Little else is known about him.

Indeterminates

Gorgias the Younger. The son of Gorgias of Leontini, a famous Sophist, Gorgias the Younger, 31, has followed in his father's footsteps and established a Logic Shop near the Agora. He teaches incessantly, offering free lectures and demonstrations. It is rumored that he is courting a prominent young woman—or is it a young man?—and he needs to boost his income to prove his worth.

Thucydides. Younger Athenians know little of Thucydides, 60, a bookish old man with a slight Thracian accent. He is related to Cimon, the famous Athenian general who once fought for Sparta before the Great War. Thucydides is also related, through marriage, to Thracian royalty. His family ran several gold mines near Mount Pangaeus. Thucydides, educated in Athens, was named an Athenian general in 424 BCE and charged with defending Amphipolis, an Athenian fortress in Macedon. But Amphipolis fell to the Spartans, a defeat that caused many of the tribute states in the region to break free of Athens. During a hasty and illegal trial, Thucydides was convicted of treason and exiled for twenty years—a decision that was controversial among Athenians. He returned to Athens just last year. It is said that he spent his two decades in exile writing an account of the Great War.

Lithicles of Scambonidae. A master stonemason and an ox of a man, Lithicles, 42, led several construction teams that completed (and repaired) the Long Walls to Piraeus. But last year, the Spartan conquerors dismantled a two-mile section of the Long Walls to ensure Athens's vulnerability to Spartan phalanxes. Lithicles, who insists that the walls be rebuilt, has taken an increasingly vocal position in the Assembly.

Diognetus. The son of Niceratus, a self-made man who built a fortune operating silver mines, and the half-brother of Nicias, a powerful politician and general whom many blame for the debacle in Sicily (and who perished there), Diognetus, 47, was a victorious *choregos* (khore-E-gus)—producer and director of a series of tragedies for the Dionysian festival of 415. Although the entire family promoted religious festivals, liturgies, and other philanthropies, Diognetus cultivates his passion for theater, sculpture, and architecture. "Our bodies will die," he is fond of saying, "but we will live through our arts forever."

Epeius. A formidable and guileful boxer, Epeius, 32, from Scambonidae in Athens, excels in logic and debate. Whenever he speaks, enthusiasts of sports roar their approval.

Lysias. A metic, Lysias, 41, is the younger son of Cephalus, who established a profitable shield factory in Piraeus. Cephalus (who was originally from Syracuse in Sicily) became very wealthy, as did his sons. During the reign of the Thirty Tyrants, Polemarchus, Lysias's brother, tried to sneak shields and other weapons to Thrasybulus and his insurgents. But the plot was discovered and the Thirty executed Polemarchus by forcing him to drink hemlock. The Thirty confiscated the shield factory and other family properties. Lysias nevertheless managed to send Thrasybulus some weapons and enough money to hire two hundred mercenaries to fight for the democrats. Although, as a metic, he is not entitled to vote in the Assembly, he is quickly gaining a reputation as an excellent speaker and writer of speeches for others.

Thearion. "Only in Athens!" some Athenians say of Thearion, 32, the celebrity baker turned Assembly speaker. For a time, Thearion was the talk of the town. His loaves, baked in the shape of animals, were staples at all the best parties. He expanded his bakery, moved it to a choice spot in the Agora, and attracted the wealthiest clients. Important people confided in him, and soon he was giving instructive speeches in the Assembly and lawcourts. "Only in Athens!"

Rhinon. The son of a farming family from Paeania near Mount Hymettos, Rhinon, 56, became famous last year when people at the Assembly were debating whether to surrender. Many of Athens's inhabitants were starving; most speakers said that there was no choice but to give up. But Rhinon instantly became famous with his ringing declaration: "Better dead than ruled by Spartan dogs!" Rhinon later fought alongside Thrasybulus and the insurgents and helped defeat the Thirty at Piraeus.

Herodion. A shoemaker, Herodion has long been a respected "country" philosopher. His friends praise him as a simple man who speaks from his heart ("because he has no brains," the comic poet Eupolis once sniffed). Eupolis's jibe did not silence Herodion, but last year, before Athens's surrender to Sparta, Herodion, then 68, referred to "our hated enemy, Xerxes"—forgetting that Xerxes had been dead for half a century. This provided comedic poets with plenty of jokes, while many listeners shook their heads at the old man's supposed folly. Since then, however, Herodion's much younger wife, Praxagora, has been widely credited with giving him a new outlook on life.

PART 5: CORE TEXTS

PERICLES

Funeral Oration, 431 BCE

In his great history, Thucydides (ca. 460 BCE–ca. 395 BCE) reconstructs over one hundred speeches by the principal figures of the war. Perhaps no speech was more important than the oration by the Athenian statesman Pericles, delivered on the occasion of the first public funeral for the war's dead in 431 BCE. Pericles argues that the soldiers died for a worthy cause—preserving Athenian democracy—and he proceeds to list its merits. Using the funeral service to enshrine a political system might seem unusual, but it was the Athenian custom to group the dead bodies by tribe and bury them in a common grave rather than in private family tombs—a practice which epitomizes the Athenian democracy's insistence on viewing all citizens as equals. Pericles' speech has long been regarded as one of the finest defenses of democracy, although a close reading reveals that the democracy of Pericles was quite different from the democratic systems of the modern world.

Thucydides was not a wholly dispassionate observer of the events he chronicled. Early in the war he had been an Athenian general; after losing a key battle he was punished in court with a twenty-year exile. He proceeded to travel throughout Greece, interviewing participants in the war, gathering letters, and writing an account of the conflict. His resulting work is widely regarded as a masterpiece—the first scientific work of history. Thucydides is generally critical of democracy, though he acknowledges that it works well when led by a brilliant statesman like Pericles.

As you read, consider the following questions:

- *How much does Pericles say about the dead? What is the real subject of his speech?*
- *A funeral oration reveals what a society considers worth celebrating or remembering. What does this oration tell you about what the Athenians most valued?*
- *The praise of Athens is also an implicit criticism of Sparta, Athens's enemy. What can you gather about Sparta here, or what might make it less admirable in Pericles' eyes?*

SOURCE: *Thucydides,* History of the Peloponnesian War, *trans. Richard Crawley (New York: E. P. Dutton, 1910); edited and abridged by Lisa Cox for this game book.*

After the first deaths in the war with Sparta, Pericles, son of Xanthippus, was chosen to give the eulogy. When the proper time arrived, he advanced from the sepulcher to an elevated platform in order to be heard by as many of the crowd as possible, and spoke as follows:

"Most of my predecessors in this place have commended him who made this speech part of the law, telling us that it is well that it should be delivered at the burial of those who fall in battle. For myself, I should have thought that the worth which had displayed itself in deeds, would be sufficiently rewarded by honors also shown by deeds; such as you now see in this funeral prepared at the people's cost. And I could have wished that the reputations of many brave men were not to be imperiled in the mouth of a single individual, to stand or fall according as he spoke well or ill. For it is hard to speak properly upon a subject where it is even difficult to convince your hearers that you are speaking the truth. On the one hand, the friend who is familiar with every fact of the story, may think that some point has not been set forth with that fullness which he wishes and knows it to deserve; on the other, he who is a stranger to the matter may be led by envy to suspect exaggeration if he hears anything above his own nature. For men can endure to hear others praised only so long as they can severally persuade themselves of their own ability to equal the actions recounted: when this point is passed, envy comes in and with it incredulity. However since our ancestors have stamped this custom with their approval, it becomes my duty to obey the law and to try to satisfy your several wishes and opinions as best I may.

"I shall begin with our ancestors: it is both just and proper that they should have the honor of the first mention on an occasion like the present. They dwelt in the country without break in the succession from generation to generation, and handed it down free to the present time by their valor. And if our more remote ancestors deserve praise, much more do our own fathers, who added to their inheritance the empire which we now possess, and spared no pains to be able to leave their acquisitions to us of the present generation. Lastly, there are few parts of our dominions that have not been augmented by those of us here, who are still more or less in the vigor of life; while the mother country has been furnished by us with everything that can enable her to depend on her own resources whether for war or for peace. That part of our history which tells of the military achievements which gave us our several possessions, or of the ready valor with which either we or our fathers stemmed the tide of Hellenic or foreign aggression, is a theme too familiar to my hearers for me to spend much time on, and I shall therefore pass it by. But what was the road by which we reached our position, what the form of government under which our greatness grew, what the national habits out of which it sprang; these are questions which I may try to solve before I proceed to my panegyric [a public expression of praise] upon these men; since I think this to be a subject upon which on the present occasion a speaker may properly dwell, and to which the whole assemblage, whether citizens or foreigners, may listen with advantage.

"Our constitution does not copy the laws of neighboring states; we are rather a pattern to others than imitators ourselves. Its administration favors the many instead of the few; this is why it is called a democracy. If we look to the laws, they afford equal justice to all in their private differences; if to social standing, advancement in public life falls to reputation for capacity, class considerations not being allowed to interfere with merit; nor again does poverty bar the way, if a man is able to serve the state, he is not hindered by the obscurity of his condition. The freedom which we enjoy in our government extends also to our ordinary life. There, far from exercising a jealous surveillance over each other, we do not feel called upon to be angry with our neighbor for doing what he likes, or even to indulge in those injurious looks which cannot fail to be offensive, although they inflict no positive penalty. But all this ease in our private relations does not make us lawless as citizens. Against this fear is our chief safeguard, teaching us to obey the magistrates and the laws, particularly such as regard the protection of the injured, whether they are actually on the statute book, or belong to that code which, although unwritten, yet cannot be broken without acknowledged disgrace.

"Further, we provide plenty of means for the mind to refresh itself from business. We celebrate games and sacrifices all the year round, and the elegance of our private establishments forms a daily source of pleasure and helps to banish the spleen; while the magnitude of our city draws the produce of the world into our harbor, so that to the Athenian the fruits of other countries are as familiar a luxury as those of his own.

"If we turn to our military policy, there also we differ from our antagonists. We throw open our city to the world, and never by alien acts exclude foreigners from any opportunity of learning or observing, although the eyes of an enemy may occasionally profit by our liberality; trusting less in system and policy than to the native spirit of our citizens; while in education, where our rivals from their very cradles by a painful discipline seek after manliness, at Athens we live exactly as we please, and yet are just as ready to encounter every legitimate danger. In proof of this it may be noticed that the Lacedaemonians [another name for the Spartans] do not invade our country alone, but bring with them all their confederates; while we Athenians advance unsupported into the territory of a neighbor, and fighting upon a foreign soil usually vanquish with ease men who are defending their homes. Our united force was never yet encountered by any enemy, because we have at once to attend to our marine and to dispatch our citizens by land upon a hundred different services; so that, wherever they engage with some such fraction of our strength, a success against a detachment is magnified into a victory over the nation, and a defeat into a reverse suffered at the hands of our entire people. And yet if with habits not of labor but of ease, and courage not of art but of nature, we are still willing to encounter danger, we have the double advantage of escaping the experience of hardships in anticipation and of facing them in the hour of need as fearlessly as those who are never free from them.

"Nor are these the only points in which our city is worthy of admiration. We cultivate refinement without extravagance and knowledge without effeminacy; wealth we employ more for use than for show, and place the real disgrace of poverty not in owning to the fact but in declining the struggle against it. Our public men have, besides politics, their private affairs to attend to, and our ordinary citizens, though occupied with the pursuits of industry, are still fair judges of public matters; for, unlike any other nation, regarding him who takes no part in these duties not as unambitious but as useless, we Athenians are able to judge at all events if we cannot originate, and instead of looking on discussion as a stumbling-block in the way of action, we think it an indispensable preliminary to any wise action at all. Again, in our enterprises we present the singular spectacle of daring and deliberation, each carried to its highest point, and both united in the same persons; although usually decision is the fruit of ignorance, hesitation of reflection. But the palm of courage will surely be adjudged most justly to those, who best know the difference between hardship and pleasure and yet are never tempted to shrink from danger.

Pericles suggests that Athens deserves its empire through its virtue. How might Athenians see that their empire is a kind of "generosity"?

"In generosity we are equally singular, acquiring our friends by conferring not by receiving favors. Yet, of course, the doer of the favor is the firmer friend of the two, in order by continued kindness to keep the recipient in his debt; while the debtor feels less keenly from the very consciousness that the return he makes will be a payment, not a free gift. And it is only the Athenians who, fearless of consequences, confer their benefits not from calculations of expediency, but in the confidence of liberality.

"In short, I say that as a city we are the school of Hellas; while I doubt if the world can produce a man, who where he has only himself to depend upon, is equal to so many emergencies, and graced by so happy a versatility as the Athenian. And that is no mere boast thrown out for the occasion, but plain matter of fact, the power of the state acquired by these habits proves.

"For Athens alone of her contemporaries is found when tested to be greater than her reputation, and alone gives no occasion to her assailants to blush at the antagonist by whom they have been worsted, or to her subjects to question her title by merit to rule. Rather, the admiration of the present and succeeding ages will be ours, since we have not left our power without witness, but have shown it by mighty proofs; and far from needing a Homer for our panegyrist, or other of his craft whose verses might charm for the moment only for the impression which they gave to melt at the touch of fact, we have forced every sea and land to be the highway of our daring, and everywhere, whether for evil or for good, have left imperishable monuments behind us.

"Such is the Athens for which these men, in the assertion of their resolve not to lose her, nobly fought and died; and well may every one of their survivors be ready to suffer in her cause.

"Indeed if I have dwelt at some length upon the character of our country, it has been to show that our stake in the struggle is not the same as theirs who have no such blessings to lose, and also that the panegyric of the men over whom I am now speaking might be by definite proofs established. That panegyric is now in a great measure complete; for the Athens that I have celebrated is only what the heroism of these and their like have made her, men whose fame, unlike that of most Hellenes, will be found to be only commensurate with their deserts. And if a test of worth be wanted, it is to be found in their closing scene, and this not only in the cases in which it set the final seal upon their merit, but also in those in which it gave the first intimation of their having any. For there is justice in the claim that steadfastness in his country's battles should be as a cloak to cover a man's other imperfections; since the good action has blotted out the bad, and his merit as a citizen more than outweighed his demerits as an individual. But none of these allowed either wealth with its prospect of future enjoyment to unnerve his spirit, or poverty with its hope of a day of freedom and riches to tempt him to shrink from danger. No, holding that vengeance upon their enemies was more to be desired than any personal blessings, and reckoning this to be the most glorious of hazards, they joyfully determined to accept the risk, to make sure of their vengeance and to let their wishes wait; and while committing to hope the uncertainty of final success, in the business before them they thought fit to act boldly and trust in themselves. Thus choosing to die resisting, rather than to live submitting, they fled only from dishonor, but met danger face to face, and after one brief moment, while at the summit of their fortune, escaped, not from their fear, but from their glory.

"So died these men as became Athenians. You, their survivors, must determine, to have as unfaltering a resolution in the field, though you may pray that it may have a happier issue. And not contented with ideas derived only from words of the advantages which are bound up with the defense of your country, though these would furnish a valuable text to a speaker even before an audience so alive to them as the present, you must yourselves realize the power of Athens, and feed your eyes upon her from day to day, till love of her fills your hearts and then when all her greatness shall break upon you, you must reflect that it was by courage, sense of duty, and a keen feeling of honor in action that men were enabled to win all this, and that no personal failure in an enterprise could make them consent to deprive their country of their valor, but they laid it at her feet as the most glorious contribution they could offer. For this offering of their lives made in common by them all, they each of them individually received that renown which never grows old, and for a sepulcher, not so much that in which their bones have been deposited, but that noblest of shrines wherein their glory is laid up to be eternally remembered upon every occasion on which deed or story shall call for its commemoration. For heroes have the whole earth for their tomb; and in lands far from their own, where the column with its epitaph declares it, there is enshrined in every breast a record unwritten with no tablet to preserve it, except that of the heart.

"These take as your model, and judging happiness to be the fruit of freedom and freedom of valor, never decline the dangers of war.

* * *

"Comfort, therefore, not condolence, is what I have to offer to the parents of the dead who may be here. Numberless are the chances to which, as they know, the life of man is subject; but fortunate indeed are they who draw for their lot a death so glorious as that which has caused your mourning, and to whom life has been so exactly measured as to terminate in the happiness in which it has been passed. Still I know that this is a hard saying, especially when those are in question of whom you will constantly be reminded by seeing in the homes of others blessings of which once you also boasted: for grief is felt not so much for the want of what we have never known, as for the loss of that to which we have been long accustomed. Yet you who are still of an age to beget children must bear up in the hope of having others in their stead; not only will they help you to forget those whom you have lost, but will be to the state at once a reinforcement and a security; for never can a fair or just policy be expected of the citizen who does not, like his fellows, bring to the decision the interests and apprehensions of a father. While those of you who have passed your prime must congratulate yourselves with the thought that the best part of your life was fortunate, and that the brief span that remains will be cheered by the fame of the departed. For it is only the love of honor that never grows old; and honor it is, not gain, as some would have it, that rejoices the heart of age and helplessness.

"Turning to the sons or brothers of the dead, I see an arduous struggle before you. When a man is gone, all are wont to praise him, and should your merit be ever so transcendent, you will still find it difficult not merely to overtake, but even to approach their renown. The living have envy to contend with, while those who are no longer in our path are honored with a goodwill into which rivalry does not enter. On the other hand, if I must say anything on the subject of female excellence to those of you who will now be in widowhood, it will be all comprised in this brief exhortation. Great will be your glory in not falling short of your natural character; and greatest will be hers who is least talked of among the men whether for good or for bad.

"My task is now finished. I have performed it to the best of my ability, and in word, at least, the requirements of the law are now satisfied. If deeds be in question, those who are here interred have received part of their honors already, and for the rest, their children will be brought up till manhood at the public expense; the state thus offers a valuable prize, as the garland of victory in this race of valor, for the reward both of those who have fallen and their survivors. And where the rewards for merit are greatest, there are found the best citizens.

"And now that you have brought to a close your lamentations for your relatives, you may depart."

PLATO

The Republic, ca. 390–370 BCE

PART I

Aristocles (perhaps a player in this game) is now more commonly known as Plato (ca. 428 BCE–ca. 348 BCE), the most famous follower of Socrates. Plato often chose to express his philosophical ideas in the form of dialogues rather than as treatises. Scholars generally consider his earlier, shorter dialogues to be more representative of the true Socrates than the later, more didactic works. The Republic *is somewhat transitional in that the opening, like the earlier dialogues, comes to an impasse regarding the nature of justice. Once Glaucon and Adeimantus press Socrates further, however, the dialogue becomes a wide-ranging exploration of justice, both in the individual soul and in the city. This exploration may go far beyond what Socrates himself said or believed, but for purposes of the game you will act on the assumption that this text is an accurate representation of Socrates' beliefs. You are encouraged to read the entire* Republic, *which more fully develops many of the ideas contained in these excerpts.*

In this first part, the question of justice is introduced and several inadequate definitions of it are proposed, whereupon Glaucon and Adeimantus renew the question and Socrates begins to construct an ideal city-state.

As you read, consider the following questions:

- *How do you think the unsuccessful definitions of justice presented by Cephalus, Polemarchus, and Thrasymachus set the stage for a deeper exploration of the question?*
- *How might the events of the Peloponnesian War, including the rise of the Thirty Tyrants, call into question these preliminary definitions of justice?*

Note that you will find in the margins occasional references to the traditional pagination numbers (e.g., 328b); you can use these to find your place in other translations.

SOURCE: *Plato,* The Republic, *trans. Benjamin Jowett (Oxford: Clarendon Press, 1894), with minor revisions for this edition. http://classics.mit.edu/Plato/republic.html (accessed February 1, 2015).*

Book 1

I went down yesterday to the Piraeus with Glaucon the son of Ariston,[1] that I might offer up my prayers to the goddess; and also because I wanted to see in what manner they would celebrate the festival, which was a new thing. I was delighted with the procession of the inhabitants; but that of the Thracians was equally, if not more, beautiful. When we had finished our prayers and viewed the spectacle, we turned in the direction of the city; and at that instant Polemarchus the son of Cephalus[2] chanced to catch sight of us from a distance as we were starting on our way home, and told his servant to run and bid us wait for him. The servant took hold of me by the cloak behind, and said: Polemarchus desires you to wait.

I turned round, and asked him where his master was.

There he is, said the youth, coming after you, if you will only wait.

Certainly we will, said Glaucon; and in a few minutes Polemarchus appeared, and with him Adeimantus, Glaucon's brother, Niceratus the son of Nicias,[3] and several others who had been at the procession.

Polemarchus said to me: I perceive, Socrates, that you and our companion are already on your way to the city.

You are not far wrong, I said.

But do you see, he rejoined, how many we are?

Of course.

And are you stronger than all these? For if not, you will have to remain where you are.

May there not be the alternative, I said, that we may persuade you to let us go?

But can you persuade us, if we refuse to listen to you? he said.

Certainly not, replied Glaucon.

Then we are not going to listen; of that you may be assured.

Adeimantus added: Has no one told you of the torch-race on horseback in honour of the goddess which will take place in the evening?

With horses! I replied: That is a novelty. Will horsemen carry torches and pass them one to another during the race?

Yes, said Polemarchus, and not only so, but a festival will be celebrated at night, which you certainly ought to see. Let us rise soon after supper and see this festival; there will be a gathering of young men, and we will have a good talk. Stay then, and do not be perverse.

---

1. Glaucon and Adeimantus were Plato's older brothers.

2. Cephalus was a wealthy metic, owner of a business that manufactured shields. His sons inherited his business and were targeted by the Thirty Tyrants. Polemarchus was executed; Lysias (not a participant in this dialogue) escaped and became a famous speechwriter. Lysias may also be a figure in the game.

3. Diognetus, another son of Nicias, may also be a figure in the game.

Glaucon said: I suppose, since you insist, that we must.

Very good, I replied.

Accordingly we went with Polemarchus to his house; and there we found his brothers Lysias and Euthydemus, and with them Thrasymachus the Chalcedonian,[4] Charmantides the Paeanian, and Cleitophon the son of Aristonymus. There too was Cephalus the father of Polemarchus, whom I had not seen for a long time, and I thought him very much aged. He was seated on a cushioned chair, and had a garland on his head, for he had been sacrificing in the court; and there were some other chairs in the room arranged in a semicircle, upon which we sat down by him. He saluted me eagerly, and then he said:— 328b

You don't come to see me, Socrates, as often as you ought: If I were still able to go and see you I would not ask you to come to me. But at my age I can hardly get to the city, and therefore you should come oftener to the Piraeus. For let me tell you, that the more the pleasures of the body fade away, the greater to me is the pleasure and charm of conversation. Do not then deny my request, but make our house your resort and keep company with these young men; we are old friends, and you will be quite at home with us.

I replied: There is nothing which for my part I like better, Cephalus, than conversing with aged men; for I regard them as travellers who have gone a journey which I too may have to go, and of whom I ought to enquire, whether the way is smooth and easy, or rugged and difficult. And this is a question which I should like to ask of you who have arrived at that time which the poets call the "threshold of old age"—Is life harder towards the end, or what report do you give of it?

Socrates does here what he always does: ask another man to enlighten him on something about which he himself feels ignorant.

I will tell you, Socrates, he said, what my own feeling is. Men of my age flock together; we are birds of a feather, as the old proverb says; and at our meetings the tale of my acquaintance commonly is—I cannot eat, I cannot drink; the pleasures of youth and love are fled away: there was a good time once, but now that is gone, and life is no longer life. Some complain of the slights which are put upon them by relations, and they will tell you sadly of how many evils their old age is the cause. But to me, Socrates, these complainers seem to blame that which is not really in fault. For if old age were the cause, I too being old, and every other old man, would have felt as they do. But this is not my own experience, nor that of others whom I have known. How well I remember the aged poet Sophocles, when in answer to the question, How does love suit with age, Sophocles,—are you still the man you were? Peace, he replied; most gladly have I escaped the thing of which you speak; I feel as if I had escaped from a mad and furious master. His words have often occurred to my mind since, and they seem as good to me now as at the time when he uttered them. For certainly old age has a great sense of calm and freedom; when the passions relax their hold, then, as Sophocles says, we are freed from the grasp

---

4. Thrasymachus, a metic, taught rhetoric in Athens.

not of one mad master only, but of many. The truth is, Socrates, that these regrets, and also the complaints about relations, are to be attributed to the same cause, which is not old age, but men's characters and tempers; for he who is of a calm and happy nature will hardly feel the pressure of age, but to him who is of an opposite disposition youth and age are equally a burden.

I listened in admiration, and wanting to draw him out, that he might go on—Yes, Cephalus, I said: but I rather suspect that people in general are not convinced by you when you speak thus; they think that old age sits lightly upon you, not because of your happy disposition, but because you are rich, and wealth is well known to be a great comforter.

You are right, he replied; they are not convinced: and there is something in what they say; not, however, so much as they imagine. I might answer them as Themistocles answered the Seriphian who was abusing him and saying that he was famous, not for his own merits but because he was an Athenian: "If you had been a native of my country or I of yours, neither of us would have been famous." And to those who are not rich and are impatient of old age, the same reply may be made; for to the good poor man old age cannot be a light burden, nor can a bad rich man ever have peace with himself.

May I ask, Cephalus, whether your fortune was for the most part inherited or acquired by you?

Acquired! Socrates; do you want to know how much I acquired? In the art of making money I have been midway between my father and grandfather: for my grandfather, whose name I bear, doubled and trebled the value of his patrimony, that which he inherited being much what I possess now; but my father Lysanias reduced the property below what it is at present: and I shall be satisfied if I leave to these my sons not less but a little more than I received.

That was why I asked you the question, I replied, because I see that you are indifferent about money, which is a characteristic rather of those who have inherited their fortunes than of those who have acquired them; the makers of fortunes have a second love of money as a creation of their own, resembling the affection of authors for their own poems, or of parents for their children, besides that natural love of it for the sake of use and profit which is common to them and all men. And hence they are very bad company, for they can talk about nothing but the praises of wealth.

That is true, he said.

Yes, that is very true, but may I ask another question? What do you consider to be the greatest blessing which you have reaped from your wealth?

One, he said, of which I could not expect easily to convince others. For let me tell you, Socrates, that when a man thinks himself to be near death, fears and cares enter into his mind which he never had before; the tales of a world below and the punishment which is exacted there of deeds done here were once a laughing matter to him, but now he is tormented with the thought that they may be true: either from the weakness of age, or because he is now drawing nearer to that other place, he has a clearer view of these things; suspicions and alarms crowd thickly upon him, and he begins to reflect and consider what wrongs he has done to others. . . . And the great blessing of riches, I do not say to every man, but to a good man, is, that he has had no occasion to deceive or to defraud others, either intentionally or unintentionally; and when he departs to the world below he is not in any apprehension about offerings due to the gods or debts which he owes to men. Now to this peace of mind the possession of wealth greatly contributes; and therefore I say, that, setting one thing against another, of the many advantages which wealth has to give, to a man of sense this is in my opinion the greatest.

Socrates' response here introduces the question that will dominate the rest of the book.

Well said, Cephalus, I replied; but as concerning justice, what is it?—to speak the truth and to pay your debts—no more than this? And even to this are there not exceptions? Suppose that a friend when in his right mind has deposited arms with me and he asks for them when he is not in his right mind, ought I to give them back to him? No one would say that I ought or that I should be right in doing so, any more than they would say that I ought always to speak the truth to one who is in his condition.

You are quite right, he replied.

But then, I said, speaking the truth and paying your debts is not a correct definition of justice.

Quite correct, Socrates, if Simonides[5] is to be believed, said Polemarchus interposing.

I fear, said Cephalus, that I must go now, for I have to look after the sacrifices, and I hand over the argument to Polemarchus and the company.

Is not Polemarchus your heir? I said.

To be sure, he answered, and went away laughing to the sacrifices.

Tell me then, O thou heir of the argument, what did Simonides say, and 331e
according to you truly say, about justice?

He said that the repayment of a debt is just, and in saying so he appears to me to be right. I should be sorry to doubt the word of such a wise and inspired man, but his meaning, though probably clear to you, is the reverse of clear to me. For he certainly does not mean, as we were now saying that I ought to return a deposit of arms or of anything else to one who asks for it when he is not in his right senses; and yet a deposit cannot be denied to be a debt.

True.

Then when the person who asks me is not in his right mind I am by no means to make the return?

Certainly not.

---

5. A respected poet of a previous generation.

When Simonides said that the repayment of a debt was justice, he did not mean to include that case?

Certainly not; for he thinks that a friend ought always to do good to a friend and never evil.

You mean that the return of a deposit of gold which is to the injury of the receiver, if the two parties are friends, is not the repayment of a debt—that is what you would imagine him to say?

Yes.

And are enemies also to receive what we owe to them?

To be sure, he said, they are to receive what we owe them, and an enemy, as I take it, owes to an enemy that which is due or proper to him—that is to say, evil.

Simonides, then, after the manner of poets, would seem to have spoken darkly of the nature of justice; for he really meant to say that justice is the giving to each

this he termed a debt.

eaning, he said.

f we asked him what due or proper thing is given

at answer do you think that he would make to us?

medicine gives drugs and meat and drink to human

ing is given by cookery, and to what?

tice gives, and to whom?

ided at all by the analogy of the preceding instances,

es good to friends and evil to enemies.

good to his friends and evil to his enemies in time

Or when they are on a voyage, amid the perils of the sea?

The pilot.

And in what sort of actions or with a view to what result is the just man most able to do harm to his enemy and good to his friends?

In going to war against the one and in making alliances with the other.

But when a man is well, my dear Polemarchus, there is no need of a physician?

No.

And he who is not on a voyage has no need of a pilot?

No.

Then in time of peace justice will be of no use?

I am very far from thinking so.

You think that justice may be of use in peace as well as in war?

Yes.

Like husbandry for the acquisition of grain?

Yes.

Or like shoemaking for the acquisition of shoes—that is what you mean?

Yes.

And what similar use or power of acquisition has justice in time of peace?

In contracts, Socrates, justice is of use.

And by contracts you mean partnerships?

Exactly.

But is the just man or the skilful player a more useful and better partner at a game of draughts?

The skilful player.

And in the laying of bricks and stones is the just man a more useful or better partner than the builder?

Quite the reverse.

Then in what sort of partnership is the just man a better partner than the harp-player, as in playing the harp the harp-player is certainly a better partner than the just man?

In a money partnership.

Yes, Polemarchus, but surely not in the use of money; for you do not want a just man to be your counsellor in the purchase or sale of a horse; a man who is knowing about horses would be better for that, would he not?

Certainly.

And when you want to buy a ship, the shipwright or the pilot would be better?

True.

Then what is that joint use of silver or gold in which the just man is to be preferred?

When you want a deposit to be kept safely.

You mean when money is not wanted, but allowed to lie?

Precisely.

That is to say, justice is useful when money is useless?

That is the inference.

And when you want to keep a pruning-hook safe, then justice is useful to the individual and to the state; but when you want to use it, then the art of the vine-dresser?

Clearly.

And when you want to keep a shield or a lyre, and not to use them, you would say that justice is useful; but when you want to use them, then the art of the soldier or of the musician?

Certainly.

And so of all the other things—justice is useful when they are useless, and useless when they are useful?

That is the inference.

Then justice is not good for much. But let us consider this further point: Is not he who can best strike a blow in a boxing match or in any kind of fighting best able to ward off a blow?

Certainly.

And he who is most skilful in preventing or escaping from a disease is best able to create one?

True.

And he is the best guard of a camp who is best able to steal a march upon the enemy?

Certainly.

Then he who is a good keeper of anything is also a good thief?

That, I suppose, is to be inferred.

Then if the just man is good at keeping money, he is good at stealing it.

That is implied in the argument.

Then after all the just man has turned out to be a thief. And this is a lesson which I suspect you must have learnt out of Homer; for he, speaking of Autolycus, the maternal grandfather of Odysseus, who is a favorite of his, affirms that

He was excellent above all men in theft and perjury.

And so, you and Homer and Simonides are agreed that justice is an art of theft; to be practised however "for the good of friends and for the harm of enemies"—that was what you were saying?

No, certainly not that, though I do not now know what I did say; but I still stand by the latter words.

Well, there is another question: By friends and enemies do we mean those who are so really, or only in seeming?

Surely, he said, a man may be expected to love those whom he thinks good, and to hate those whom he thinks evil.

Yes, but do not persons often err about good and evil: many who are not good seem to be so, and conversely?

That is true.

Then to them the good will be enemies and the evil will be their friends?

True.

And in that case they will be right in doing good to the evil and evil to the good?

Clearly.

But the good are just and would not do an injustice?

True.

Then according to your argument it is just to injure those who do no wrong?

Nay, Socrates; the doctrine is immoral.

Then I suppose that we ought to do good to the just and harm to the unjust?

I like that better.

But see the consequence: many a man who is ignorant of human nature has friends who are bad friends, and in that case he ought to do harm to them; and he has good enemies whom he ought to benefit; but, if so, we shall be saying the very opposite of that which we affirmed to be the meaning of Simonides.

Very true, he said: and I think that we had better correct an error into which we seem to have fallen in the use of the words "friend" and "enemy."

What was the error, Polemarchus? I asked.

We assumed that he is a friend who seems to be or who is thought good.

And how is the error to be corrected?

We should rather say that he is a friend who is, as well as seems, good; and that he who seems only, and is not good, only seems to be and is not a friend; and of an enemy the same may be said.

You would argue that the good are our friends and the bad our enemies?

Yes.

And instead of saying simply as we did at first, that it is just to do good to our friends and harm to our enemies, we should further say: It is just to do good to our friends when they are good and harm to our enemies when they are evil?

Yes, that appears to me to be the truth.

But ought the just to injure any one at all?

Undoubtedly he ought to injure those who are both wicked and his enemies.

When horses are injured, are they improved or deteriorated?

The latter.

Deteriorated, that is to say, in the good qualities of horses, not of dogs?

Yes, of horses.

And dogs are deteriorated in the good qualities of dogs, and not of horses?

Of course.

And will not men who are injured be deteriorated in that which is the proper virtue of man?

Certainly.

And that human virtue is justice?

To be sure.

Then men who are injured are of necessity made unjust? That is the result. But can the musician by his art make men unmusical?

Certainly not.

Or the horseman by his art make them bad horsemen?

Impossible.

And can the just by justice make men unjust, or speaking generally can the good by virtue make them bad?

Assuredly not.

Any more than heat can produce cold?

It cannot.

Or drought moisture?

Clearly not.

Nor can the good harm any one?

Impossible.

And the just is the good?

Certainly.

Then to injure a friend or any one else is not the act of a just man, but of the opposite, who is the unjust?

I think that what you say is quite true, Socrates.

Then if a man says that justice consists in the repayment of debts, and that good is the debt which a man owes to his friends, and evil the debt which he owes to his enemies—to say this is not wise; for it is not true, if, as has been clearly shown, the injuring of another can be in no case just.

I agree with you, said Polemarchus.

Then you and I are prepared to take up arms against any one who attributes such a saying to Simonides or Bias or Pittacus, or any other wise man or seer?

I am quite ready to do battle at your side, he said.

* * *

Yes, I said; but if this definition of justice also breaks down, what other can be offered?

Several times in the course of the discussion Thrasymachus had made an attempt to get the argument into his own hands, and had been put down by the rest of the company, who wanted to hear the end. But when Polemarchus and I had done speaking and there was a pause, he could no longer hold his peace; and, gathering himself up, he came at us like a wild beast, seeking to devour us. We were quite panic-stricken at the sight of him.

He roared out to the whole company: What folly, Socrates, has taken possession of you all? And why, silly billies, do you knock under to one another? I say that if you want really to know what justice is, you should not only ask but answer, and you should not seek honour to yourself from the refutation of an opponent, but have your own answer; for there is many a one who can ask and cannot answer. And now I will not have you say that justice is duty or advantage or profit or gain or interest, for this sort of nonsense will not do for me; I must have clearness and accuracy.

I was panic-stricken at his words, and could not look at him without trembling. Indeed I believe that if I had not fixed my eye upon him, I should have been struck dumb: but when I saw his fury rising, I looked at him first, and was therefore able to reply to him.

Thrasymachus, I said, with a quiver, don't be hard upon us. Polemarchus and I may have been guilty of a little mistake in the argument, but I can assure you that the error was not intentional. If we were seeking for a piece of gold, you would not imagine that we were "knocking under to one another," and so losing our chance of finding it. And why, when we are seeking for justice, a thing more precious than many pieces of gold, do you say that we are weakly yielding to one another and not doing our utmost to get at the truth? Nay, my good friend, we are most willing and anxious to do so, but the fact is that we cannot. And if so, you people who know all things should pity us and not be angry with us.

How characteristic of Socrates! he replied, with a bitter laugh—that's your ironical style! Did I not foresee—have I not already told you, that whatever he was asked he would refuse to answer, and try irony or any other shuffle, in order that he might avoid answering?

You are a philosopher, Thrasymachus, I replied, and well know that if you ask a person what numbers make up twelve, taking care to prohibit him whom you ask from answering twice six, or three times four, or six times two, or four times three, "for this sort of nonsense will not do for me"—then obviously, that is your way of putting the question, no one can answer you. But suppose that he were to retort, "Thrasymachus, what do you mean? If one of these numbers which you forbid be the true answer to the question, am I falsely to say some other number which is not the right one?—Is that your meaning?"—How would you answer him?

Just as if the two cases were at all alike! he said.

Why should they not be? I replied; and even if they are not, but only appear to be so to the person who is asked, ought he not to say what he thinks, whether you and I forbid him or not?

I presume then that you are going to make one of the forbidden answers?

I dare say that I may, notwithstanding the danger, if upon reflection I approve of any of them.

But what if I give you an answer about justice other and better, he said, than any of these? What do you deserve to have done to you?

Done to me!—as becomes the ignorant, I must learn from the wise—that is what I deserve to have done to me.

What, and no payment! A pleasant notion!

I will pay when I have the money, I replied.

But you have, Socrates, said Glaucon: and you, Thrasymachus, need be under no anxiety about money, for we will all make a contribution for Socrates.

Yes, he replied, and then Socrates will do as he always does—refuse to answer himself, but take and pull to pieces the answer of some one else.

Why, my good friend, I said, how can any one answer who knows, and says that he knows, just nothing; and who, even if he has some faint notions of his own, is told by a man of authority not to utter them? The natural thing is, that the speaker should be some one like yourself who professes to know and can tell what he knows. Will you then kindly answer, for the edification of the company and of myself?

Glaucon and the rest of the company joined in my request and Thrasymachus, as any one might see, was in reality eager to speak; for he thought that he had an excellent answer, and would distinguish himself. But at first he insisted on my answering; at length he consented to begin. Behold, he said, the wisdom of Socrates; he refuses to teach himself, and goes about learning of others, to whom he never even says thank you.

That I learn of others, I replied, is quite true; but that I am ungrateful I wholly deny. Money I have none, and therefore I pay in praise, which is all I have: and how ready I am to praise any one who appears to me to speak well you will very soon find out when you answer; for I expect that you will answer well.

Listen, then, he said; I proclaim that justice is nothing else than the interest of the stronger. And now why do you not applaud me? But of course you won't.

Let me first understand you, I replied. Justice, as you say, is the interest of the stronger. What, Thrasymachus, is the meaning of this? You cannot mean to say that because Polydamas, the pancratiast, is stronger than we are, and finds the eating of beef conducive to his bodily strength, that to eat beef is therefore equally for our good who are weaker than he is, and right and just for us?

That's abominable of you, Socrates; you take the words in the sense which is most damaging to the argument.

Not at all, my good sir, I said; I am trying to understand them; and I wish that you would be a little clearer.

Well, he said, have you never heard that forms of government differ; there are tyrannies, and there are democracies, and there are aristocracies?

Yes, I know.

And the government is the ruling power in each state?

Certainly.

And the different forms of government make laws democratical, aristocratical, tyrannical, with a view to their several interests; and these laws, which are made by them for their own interests, are the justice which they deliver to their subjects, and him who transgresses them they punish as a breaker of the law, and unjust. And that is what I mean when I say that in all states there is the same principle of justice, which is the interest of the government; and as the government must be supposed to have power, the only reasonable conclusion is, that everywhere there is one principle of justice, which is the interest of the stronger.

Now I understand you, I said; and whether you are right or not I will try to discover.[6]

* * *

6. Omitted is Socrates' refutation of Thrasymachus's argument. Book I (in the traditional divisions) ends as many of the shorter Socratic dialogues do, with a refutation of the position that another holds, but with no solution to the problem.

With these words I was thinking that I had made an end of the discussion; but the end, in truth, proved to be only a beginning. For Glaucon, who is always the most pugnacious of men, was dissatisfied at Thrasymachus' retirement; he wanted to have the battle out. So he said to me: Socrates, do you wish really to persuade us, or only to seem to have persuaded us, that to be just is always better than to be unjust?

Book II

357a

Glaucon and Adeimantus express their frustration with the argument and push Socrates to help them formulate a more satisfying account of what constitutes justice.

I should wish really to persuade you, I replied, if I could.

Then you certainly have not succeeded. Let me ask you now:—How would you arrange goods—are there not some which we welcome for their own sakes, and independently of their consequences, as, for example, harmless pleasures and enjoyments, which delight us at the time, although nothing follows from them?

I agree in thinking that there is such a class, I replied.

Is there not also a second class of goods, such as knowledge, sight, health, which are desirable not only in themselves, but also for their results?

Certainly, I said.

And would you not recognize a third class, such as gymnastic, and the care of the sick, and the physician's art; also the various ways of money-making—these do us good but we regard them as disagreeable; and no one would choose them for their own sakes, but only for the sake of some reward or result which flows from them?

There is, I said, this third class also. But why do you ask?

Because I want to know in which of the three classes you would place justice?

In the highest class, I replied,—among those goods which he who would be happy desires both for their own sake and for the sake of their results.

Then the many are of another mind; they think that justice is to be reckoned in the troublesome class, among goods which are to be pursued for the sake of rewards and of reputation, but in themselves are disagreeable and rather to be avoided.

I know, I said, that this is their manner of thinking, and that this was the thesis which Thrasymachus was maintaining just now, when he censured justice and praised injustice. But I am too stupid to be convinced by him.

I wish, he said, that you would hear me as well as him, and then I shall see whether you and I agree. For Thrasymachus seems to me, like a snake, to have been charmed by your voice sooner than he ought to have been; but to my mind the nature of justice and injustice have not yet been made clear. Setting aside their rewards and results, I want to know what they are in themselves, and how they inwardly work in the soul. If you please, then, I will revive the argument of Thrasymachus. And first I will speak of the nature and origin of justice according to the common view of them. Secondly, I will show that all men who practice justice do so against their will, of necessity, but not as a good. And thirdly, I will argue that there is reason in this view, for the life of the unjust is after all better far than the life of the just—if what they say is true, Socrates, since I myself am not of their opinion. But still I acknowledge that I am perplexed when I hear the voices of

Thrasymachus and myriads of others dinning in my ears; and, on the other hand, I have never yet heard the superiority of justice to injustice maintained by any one in a satisfactory way. I want to hear justice praised in respect of itself; then I shall be satisfied, and you are the person from whom I think that I am most likely to hear this; and therefore I will praise the unjust life to the utmost of my power, and my manner of speaking will indicate the manner in which I desire to hear you too praising justice and censuring injustice. Will you say whether you approve of my proposal?

Indeed I do; nor can I imagine any theme about which a man of sense would oftener wish to converse.

I am delighted, he replied, to hear you say so, and shall begin by speaking, as I proposed, of the nature and origin of justice.

They say that to do injustice is, by nature, good; to suffer injustice, evil; but that the evil is greater than the good. And so when men have both done and suffered injustice and have had experience of both, not being able to avoid the one and obtain the other, they think that they had better agree among themselves to have neither; hence there arise laws and mutual covenants; and that which is ordained by law is termed by them lawful and just. This they affirm to be the origin and nature of justice;—it is a mean or compromise, between the best of all, which is to do injustice and not be punished, and the worst of all, which is to suffer injustice without the power of retaliation; and justice, being at a middle point between the two, is tolerated not as a good, but as the lesser evil, and honored by reason of the inability of men to do injustice. For no man who is worthy to be called a man would ever submit to such an agreement if he were able to resist; he would be mad if he did. Such is the received account, Socrates, of the nature and origin of justice.

Now that those who practice justice do so involuntarily and because they have not the power to be unjust will best appear if we imagine something of this kind: having given both to the just and the unjust power to do what they will, let us watch and see whither desire will lead them; then we shall discover in the very act the just and unjust man to be proceeding along the same road, following their interest, which all natures deem to be their good, and are only diverted into the path of justice by the force of law. The liberty which we are supposing may be most completely given to them in the form of such a power as is said to have been possessed by Gyges the ancestor of Croesus the Lydian.

According to the tradition, Gyges was a shepherd in the service of the king of Lydia; there was a great storm, and an earthquake made an opening in the earth at the place where he was feeding his flock. Amazed at the sight, he descended into the opening, where, among other marvels, he beheld a hollow brazen horse, having doors, at which he stooping and looking in saw a dead body of stature, as appeared to him, more than human, and having nothing on but a gold ring; this he took from the finger of the dead and reascended. Now the shepherds met together, according to custom, that they might send their monthly report about the flocks to the king; into their assembly he came having the ring on his finger, and as he was sitting among them he chanced to turn the facet of the ring inside his hand, when instantly he became invisible to the rest of the company and they began to speak of him as if he were no longer present. He was astonished at this, and again touching the ring he turned the facet outwards and reappeared; he made several trials of the ring, and always with the same result—when he turned the facet inwards he became invisible, when outwards he reappeared. Whereupon he contrived to be chosen one of the messengers who were sent to the court; where as soon as he arrived he seduced the queen, and with her help conspired against the king and slew him, and took the kingdom. Suppose now that there were two such magic rings, and the just put on one of them and the unjust the other; no man can be imagined to be of such an iron nature that he would stand fast in justice. No man would keep his hands off what was not his own when he could safely take what he liked out of the market, or go into houses and lie with any one at his pleasure, or kill or release from prison whom he would, and in all respects be like a God among men. Then the actions of the just would be as the actions of the unjust; they would both come at last to the same point. And this we may truly affirm to be a great proof that a man is just, not willingly or because he thinks that justice is any good to him individually, but of necessity, for wherever any one thinks that he can safely be unjust, there he is unjust. For all men believe in their hearts that injustice is far more profitable to the individual than justice, and he who argues as I have been supposing, will say that they are right. If you could imagine any one obtaining this power of becoming invisible, and never doing any wrong or touching what was another's, he would be thought by the lookers-on to be a most wretched idiot, although they would praise him to one another's faces, and keep up appearances with one another from a fear that they too might suffer injustice.[7]

* * *

I had always admired the genius of Glaucon and Adeimantus, but on hearing these words I was quite delighted. . . . [I said:] There is something truly divine in being able to argue as you have done for the superiority of injustice, and remaining unconvinced by your own arguments. And I do believe that you are not convinced—this I infer from your general character, for had I judged only from your speeches I should have mistrusted you. But now, the greater my confidence in you, the greater is my difficulty in knowing what to say. For I am in a strait between two; on the one hand I feel that I am unequal to the task; and my inability is brought home to me by the fact that you were not satisfied with the answer 368a

7. Omitted are additional arguments made by Glaucon and his brother Adeimantus in support of the position that it is better to be unjust than just.

which I made to Thrasymachus, proving, as I thought, the superiority which justice has over injustice. And yet I cannot refuse to help, while breath and speech remain to me; I am afraid that there would be an impiety in being present when justice is evil spoken of and not lifting up a hand in her defense. And therefore I had best give such help as I can.

Glaucon and the rest entreated me by all means not to let the question drop, but to proceed in the investigation. They wanted to arrive at the truth, first, about the nature of justice and injustice, and secondly, about their relative advantages. I told them, what I really thought, that the enquiry would be of a serious nature, and would require very good eyes. Seeing then, I said, that we are no great wits, I think that we had better adopt a method which I may illustrate thus; suppose that a short-sighted person had been asked by some one to read small letters from a distance; and it occurred to some one else that they might be found in another place which was larger and in which the letters were larger—if they were the same and he could read the larger letters first, and then proceed to the lesser—this would have been thought a rare piece of good fortune.

Very true, said Adeimantus; but how does the illustration apply to our enquiry?

I will tell you, I replied; justice, which is the subject of our enquiry, is, as you know, sometimes spoken of as the virtue of an individual, and sometimes as the virtue of a State.

True, he replied.

And is not a State larger than an individual?

It is.

Note how Socrates shifts the discussion here from the question of justice in the individual to justice in the state.

Then in the larger the quantity of justice is likely to be larger and more easily discernible. I propose therefore that we enquire into the nature of justice and injustice, first as they appear in the State, and secondly in the individual, proceeding from the greater to the lesser and comparing them.

That, he said, is an excellent proposal.

And if we imagine the State in process of creation, we shall see the justice and injustice of the State in process of creation also.

I dare say.

When the State is completed there may be a hope that the object of our search will be more easily discovered.

Yes, far more easily.

But ought we to attempt to construct one? I said; for to do so, as I am inclined to think, will be a very serious task. Reflect therefore.

I have reflected, said Adeimantus, and am anxious that you should proceed.

A State, I said, arises, as I conceive, out of the needs of mankind; no one is self-sufficing, but all of us have many wants. Can any other origin of a State be imagined?

There can be no other.

Then, as we have many wants, and many persons are needed to supply them, one takes a helper for one purpose and another for another; and when these partners and helpers are gathered together in one habitation the body of inhabitants is termed a State.

True, he said.

And they exchange with one another, and one g
under the idea that the exchange will be for their gooc

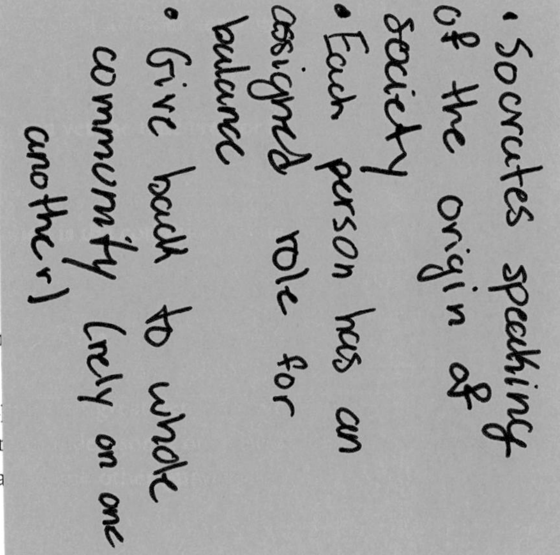

Very true.

Then, I said, let us begin and create in idea a State
necessity, who is the mother of our invention.

Of course, he replied.

Now the first and greatest of necessities is food, w
and existence.

Certainly.

The second is a dwelling, and the third clothing a

True.

And now let us see how our city will be able to su
may suppose that one man is a husbandman, another
weaver—shall we add to them a shoemaker, or perha
our bodily wants?

Quite right.

The barest notion of a State must include four or five men.

Clearly.

And how will they proceed? Will each bring the result of his labors into a common stock?—the individual husbandman, for example, producing for four, and laboring four times as long and as much as he need in the provision of food with which he supplies others as well as himself; or will he have nothing to do with others and not be at the trouble of producing for them, but provide for himself alone a fourth of the food in a fourth of the time, and in the remaining three-fourths of his time be employed in making a house or a coat or a pair of shoes, having no partnership with others, but supplying himself all his own wants?

Adeimantus thought that he should aim at producing food only and not at producing everything.

Probably, I replied, that would be the better way; and when I hear you say this, I am myself reminded that we are not all alike; there are diversities of natures among us which are adapted to different occupations.

Very true. 370b

And will you have a work better done when the workman has many occupations, or when he has only one?

When he has only one.

Further, there can be no doubt that a work is spoilt when not done at the right time?

No doubt.

For business is not disposed to wait until the doer of the business is at leisure; but the doer must follow up what he is doing, and make the business his first object.

He must.

This point—that specialization in the state is beneficial and in accordance with men's natures—becomes a critical one as the argument proceeds.

And if so, we must infer that all things are produced more plentifully and easily and of a better quality when one man does one thing which is natural to him and does it at the right time, and leaves other things.

Undoubtedly.

Then more than four citizens will be required; for the husbandman will not make his own plough or mattock, or other implements of agriculture, if they are to be good for anything. Neither will the builder make his tools—and he too needs many; and in like manner the weaver and shoemaker.

True.

Then carpenters, and smiths, and many other artisans, will be sharers in our little State, which is already beginning to grow?

True.

Yet even if we add cowherds, shepherds, and other herdsmen, in order that our husbandmen may have oxen to plough with, and builders as well as husbandmen may have draught cattle, and curriers and weavers fleeces and hides,—still our State will not be very large.

That is true; yet neither will it be a very small State which contains all these.

Then, again, there is the situation of the city—to find a place where nothing need be imported is well-nigh impossible.

Impossible.

Then there must be another class of citizens who will bring the required supply from another city?

There must.

But if the trader goes empty-handed, having nothing which they require who would supply his need, he will come back empty-handed.

That is certain.

And therefore what they produce at home must be not only enough for themselves, but such both in quantity and quality as to accommodate those from whom their wants are supplied.

Very true.

Then more husbandmen and more artisans will be required?

They will.

Not to mention the importers and exporters, who are called merchants?

Yes.

Then we shall want merchants?

We shall.

And if merchandise is to be carried over the sea, skilful sailors will also be needed, and in considerable numbers?

Yes, in considerable numbers.

Then, again, within the city, how will they exchange their productions? To secure such an exchange was, as you will remember, one of our principal objects when we formed them into a society and constituted a State.

Clearly they will buy and sell.

Then they will need a market-place, and a money-token for purposes of exchange.

Certainly.

Suppose now that a husbandman, or an artisan, brings some production to market, and he comes at a time when there is no one to exchange with him,—is he to leave his calling and sit idle in the market-place?

Not at all; he will find people there who, seeing the want, undertake the office of salesmen. In well-ordered States they are commonly those who are the weakest in bodily strength, and therefore of little use for any other purpose; their duty is to be in the market, and to give money in exchange for goods to those who desire to sell and to take money from those who desire to buy.

This want, then, creates a class of retail-traders in our State. Is not "retailer" the term which is applied to those who sit in the market-place engaged in buying and selling, while those who wander from one city to another are called merchants?

Yes, he said.

And there is another class of servants, who are intellectually hardly on the level of companionship; still they have plenty of bodily strength for labor, which accordingly they sell, and are called, if I do not mistake, hirelings, hire being the name which is given to the price of their labor.

True.

Then hirelings will help to make up our population?

Yes.

And now, Adeimantus, is our State matured and perfected?

I think so.

Where, then, is justice, and where is injustice, and in what part of the State did they spring up?

Probably in the dealings of these citizens with one another. I cannot imagine that they are more likely to be found anywhere else.

I dare say that you are right in your suggestion, I said; we had better think the matter out, and not shrink from the enquiry. Let us then consider, first of all, what will be their way of life, now that we have thus established them. Will they not produce grain, and wine, and clothes, and shoes, and build houses for themselves? And when they are housed, they will work, in summer, commonly, stripped and barefoot, but in winter substantially clothed and shod. They will feed on barley-meal and flour of wheat, baking and kneading them, making noble cakes and loaves; these they will serve up on a mat of reeds or on clean leaves, themselves reclining the while upon beds strewn with yew or myrtle. And they and their children will feast, drinking of the wine which they have made, wearing garlands on their heads, and hymning the praises of the gods, in happy converse with one another. And they will take care that their families do not exceed their means; having an eye to poverty or war.

Is Socrates being serious or ironical when he maintains that this simple society is healthiest and best? His next creation—a more complex, luxurious society—better describes contemporary Athens.

But, said Glaucon, interposing, you have not given them a relish to their meal.

True, I replied, I had forgotten; of course they must have a relish—salt, and olives, and cheese, and they will boil roots and herbs such as country people prepare; for a dessert we shall give them figs, and peas, and beans; and they will roast myrtle-berries and acorns at the fire, drinking in moderation. And with such a diet they may be expected to live in peace and health to a good old age, and bequeath a similar life to their children after them.

Yes, Socrates, he said, and if you were providing for a city of pigs, how else would you feed the beasts?

372d But what would you have, Glaucon? I replied.

Why, he said, you should give them the ordinary conveniences of life. People who are to be comfortable are accustomed to lie on sofas, and dine off tables, and they should have sauces and sweets in the modern style.

Yes, I said, now I understand: the question which you would have me consider is, not only how a State, but how a luxurious State is created; and possibly there is no harm in this, for in such a State we shall be more likely to see how justice and injustice originate. In my opinion the true and healthy constitution of the State is the one which I have described.

But if you wish also to see a State at fever heat, I have no objection. For I suspect that many will not be satisfied with the simpler way of life. They will be for adding sofas, and tables, and other furniture; also dainties, and perfumes, and incense, and courtesans, and cakes, all these not of one sort only, but in every variety; we must go beyond the necessaries of which I was at first speaking, such as houses, and clothes, and shoes: the arts of the painter and the embroiderer will have to be set in motion, and gold and ivory and all sorts of materials must be procured.

True, he said.

Then we must enlarge our borders; for the original healthy State is no longer sufficient. Now will the city have to fill and swell with a multitude of callings which are not required by any natural want; such as the whole tribe of hunters and actors, of whom one large class have to do with forms and colors; another will be the votaries of music—poets and their attendant train of rhapsodists, players, dancers, contractors; also makers of divers kinds of articles, including women's dresses. And we shall want more servants. Will not tutors be also in request, and nurses wet and dry, beauticians and barbers, as well as confectioners and cooks; and swineherds, too, who were not needed and therefore had no place in the former edition of our State, but are needed now? They must not be forgotten: and there will be animals of many other kinds, if people eat them.

Certainly.

And living in this way we shall have much greater need of physicians than before?

Much greater.

And the country which was enough to support the original inhabitants will be too small now, and not enough?

Quite true.

Then a slice of our neighbors' land will be wanted by us for pasture and tillage, and they will want a slice of ours, if, like ourselves, they exceed the limit of necessity, and give themselves up to the unlimited accumulation of wealth?

That, Socrates, will be inevitable.

And so we shall go to war, Glaucon. Shall we not?

Most certainly, he replied.

Then without determining as yet whether war does good or harm, thus much we may affirm, that now we have discovered war to be derived from causes which are also the causes of almost all the evils in States, private as well as public.

Undoubtedly.

And our State must once more enlarge; and this time there will be nothing short of a whole army, which will have to go out and fight with the invaders for all that we have, as well as for the things and persons whom we were describing above.

Why? he said; are they not capable of defending themselves?[8]

No, I said; not if we were right in the principle which was acknowledged by 374a
all of us when we were framing the State: the principle, as you will remember, was that one man cannot practice many arts with success.

Very true, he said.

But is not war an art?

Certainly.

And an art requiring as much attention as shoemaking?

Quite true.

And the shoemaker was not allowed by us to be husbandman, or a weaver, a builder—in order that we might have our shoes well made; but to him and to every other worker was assigned one work for which he was by nature fitted, and at that he was to continue working all his life long and at no other; he was not to let opportunities slip, and then he would become a good workman. Now nothing can be more important than that the work of a soldier should be well done. But is war an art so easily acquired that a man may be a warrior who is also a husbandman, or shoemaker, or other artisan; although no one in the world would be a good dice

---

8. Glaucon's question is a natural one. The practice of all Greek states, other than Sparta, was to employ citizen armies rather than professionally trained troops to fight wars and defend the state.

or draught player who merely took up the game as a recreation, and had not from his earliest years devoted himself to this and nothing else? No tools will make a man a skilled workman, or master of defense, nor be of any use to him who has not learned how to handle them, and has never bestowed any attention upon them. How then will he who takes up a shield or other implement of war become a good fighter all in a day, whether with heavy-armed or any other kind of troops?

Here Socrates introduces the important word "guardian" to describe those who will protect the state. The discussion now focuses on the character and training of these guardians.

Yes, he said, the tools which would teach men their own use would be beyond price.

And the higher the duties of the guardian, I said, the more time, and skill, and art, and application will be needed by him?

374e No doubt, he replied.

Will he not also require natural aptitude for his calling?

Certainly.

Then it will be our duty to select, if we can, natures which are fitted for the task of guarding the city?

It will.

And the selection will be no easy matter, I said; but we must be brave and do our best.

We must.

Is not the noble youth very like a well-bred dog in respect of guarding and watching?

What do you mean?

I mean that both of them ought to be quick to see, and swift to overtake the enemy when they see him; and strong too if, when they have caught him, they have to fight with him.

All these qualities, he replied, will certainly be required by them.

Well, and your guardian must be brave if he is to fight well?

Certainly.

And is he likely to be brave who has no spirit, whether horse or dog or any other animal? Have you never observed how invincible and unconquerable is spirit and how the presence of it makes the soul of any creature to be absolutely fearless and indomitable?

I have.

Then now we have a clear notion of the bodily qualities which are required in the guardian.

True.

And also of the mental ones; his soul is to be full of spirit?

Yes.

But are not these spirited natures apt to be savage with one another, and with everybody else?

A difficulty by no means easy to overcome, he replied.

Whereas, I said, they ought to be dangerous to their enemies, and gentle to their friends; if not, they will destroy themselves without waiting for their enemies to destroy them.

True, he said.

What is to be done then? I said; how shall we find a gentle nature which has also a great spirit, for the one is the contradiction of the other?

True.

He will not be a good guardian who is wanting in either of these two qualities; and yet the combination of them appears to be impossible; and hence we must infer that to be a good guardian is impossible.

I am afraid that what you say is true, he replied.

Here feeling perplexed I began to think over what had preceded. My friend, I said, no wonder that we are in a perplexity; for we have lost sight of the image which we had before us.

What do you mean? he said.

I mean to say that there do exist natures gifted with those opposite qualities.

And where do you find them?

Many animals, I replied, furnish examples of them; our friend the dog is a very good one: you know that well-bred dogs are perfectly gentle to their familiars and acquaintances, and the reverse to strangers.

Yes, I know.

Then there is nothing impossible or out of the order of nature in our finding a guardian who has a similar combination of qualities?

Certainly not.

Would not he who is fitted to be a guardian, besides the spirited nature, need to have the qualities of a philosopher?

I do not apprehend your meaning.

The trait of which I am speaking, I replied, may be also seen in the dog, and is remarkable in the animal.

What trait?

Why, a dog, whenever he sees a stranger, is angry; when an acquaintance, he welcomes him, although the one has never done him any harm, nor the other any good. Did this never strike you as curious?

The matter never struck me before; but I quite recognize the truth of your remark.

And surely this instinct of the dog is very charming;—your dog is a true philosopher.

Why?

Why, because he distinguishes the face of a friend and of an enemy only by the criterion of knowing and not knowing. And must not an animal be a lover of learning who determines what he likes and dislikes by the test of knowledge and ignorance?

Most assuredly.

And is not the love of learning the love of wisdom, which is philosophy?

They are the same, he replied.

And may we not say confidently of man also, that he who is likely to be gentle to his friends and acquaintances, must by nature be a lover of wisdom and knowledge?

That we may safely affirm.

Then he who is to be a really good and noble guardian of the State will require to unite in himself philosophy and spirit and swiftness and strength?

Undoubtedly.

PLATO

The Republic, ca. 390–370 BCE

PART II

In this section, Socrates explores how the guardians of the ideal state should be educated. Athenian education at the time was for the most part a private concern, so this undertaking would seem unusual to an Athenian audience—more in keeping with Spartan practice. Socrates concerns himself here with three kinds of education: 1) basic reading and writing; 2) physical education or gymnastics; and 3) study of the poets, who were seen as keepers of traditional Greek morality. Note that this education is only for the guardians, and that Socrates will distinguish between guardians proper—rulers—and auxiliaries, who will perform military, police, and executive functions. A third class of people would consist of everyone else and be ruled by the first two groups.

SOURCE: *Plato,* The Republic, *trans. Benjamin Jowett (Oxford: Clarendon Press, 1894), with minor revisions for this edition. http://classics.mit.edu/Plato/republic.html (accessed February 1, 2015).*

376c Then we have found the desired natures; and now that we have found them, how are they to be reared and educated? Will not this enquiry throw light on the greater enquiry which is our final end—How do justice and injustice grow up in States? For we do not want either to omit what is to the point or to draw out the argument to an inconvenient length.

Adeimantus thought that the enquiry would be of great service to us. Then, I said, my dear friend, the task must not be given up, even if somewhat long.

Certainly not.

Come then, and let us pass a leisure hour in story-telling, and our story shall be the education of our heroes.

By all means.

And what shall be their education? Can we find a better than the traditional sort?—and this has two divisions, gymnastic for the body, and music for the soul.[1]

True.

Shall we begin education with music, and go on to gymnastic afterwards?

By all means.

And when you speak of music, do you include literature or not?

I do.

And literature may be either true or false?

Yes.

And the young should be trained in both kinds, and we begin with the false?

I do not understand your meaning, he said.

You know, I said, that we begin by telling children stories which, though not wholly destitute of truth, are in the main fictitious; and these stories are told them when they are not of an age to learn gymnastics.

Very true.

That was my meaning when I said that we must teach music before gymnastics.

Quite right, he said.

You know also that the beginning is the most important part of any work, especially in the case of a young and tender thing; for that is the time at which the character is being formed and the desired impression is more readily taken.

Quite true.

And shall we just carelessly allow children to hear any casual tales which may be devised by casual persons, and to receive into their minds ideas for the most part the very opposite of those which we should wish them to have when they are grown up?

We cannot.

Then the first thing will be to establish a censorship of the writers of fiction, and let the censors receive any tale of fiction which is good, and reject the bad; and we will desire mothers and nurses to tell their children the authorized ones only. Let them fashion the mind with such tales, even more fondly than they mould the body with their hands; but most of those which are now in use must be discarded.

Of what tales are you speaking? he said.

You may find a model of the lesser in the greater, I said; for they are necessarily of the same type, and there is the same spirit in both of them.

Very likely, he replied; but I do not as yet know what you would term the greater.

---

1. The Greek word *mousike* can mean not only music but also literature. It encompasses the traditional works of Homer and other poets, which were sung to the accompaniment of a lyre.

Those, I said, which are narrated by Homer and Hesiod, and the rest of the poets, who have ever been the great story-tellers of mankind.[2]

377d But which stories do you mean, he said; and what fault do you find with them?

A fault which is most serious, I said; the fault of telling a lie, and, what is more, a bad lie. But when is this fault committed?

Whenever an erroneous representation is made of the nature of gods and heroes,—as when a painter paints a portrait not having the shadow of a likeness to the original.

Yes, he said, that sort of thing is certainly very blamable; but what are the stories which you mean?

First of all, I said, there was that greatest of all lies, in high places, which the poet told about Uranus, and which was a bad lie too,—I mean what Hesiod says that Uranus did, and how Cronus retaliated on him.[3] The doings of Cronus, and the sufferings which in turn his son inflicted upon him, even if they were true, ought certainly not to be lightly told to young and thoughtless persons; if possible, they had better be buried in silence. But if there is an absolute necessity for their mention, a chosen few might hear them in a mystery, and they should sacrifice not a common pig, but some huge and unprocurable victim; and then the number of the hearers will be very few indeed.

Why, yes, said he, those stories are extremely objectionable.

Yes, Adeimantus, they are stories not to be repeated in our State; the young man should not be told that in committing the worst of crimes he is far from doing anything outrageous; and that even if he chastises his father when he does wrong, in whatever manner, he will only be following the example of the first and greatest among the gods.

I entirely agree with you, he said; in my opinion those stories are quite unfit to be repeated.

Neither, if we mean our future guardians to regard the habit of quarrelling among themselves as of all things the basest, should any word be said to them of the wars in heaven, and of the plots and fightings of the gods against one another, for they are not true. No, we shall never mention the battles of the giants, or let them be embroidered on garments; and we shall be silent about the innumerable other quarrels of gods and heroes with their friends and relatives. If they would only believe us we would tell them that quarrelling is unholy, and that never up to this time has there been any quarrel between citizens; this is what old men and

---

2. The Greeks had no sacred scriptures, but you will better comprehend Plato's critique of the poets if you understand that Homer and, to a lesser degree, other older poets were seen as fundamental authorities on correct behavior.

3. Uranus, the original supreme god, was castrated by his son Cronus, who was, in turn, overthrown by his son Zeus.

old women should begin by telling children; and when they grow up, the poets also should be told to compose for them in a similar spirit. But the narrative of Hephaestus binding Hera his mother, or how on another occasion Zeus sent him flying for taking her part when she was being beaten, and all the battles of the gods in Homer—these tales must not be admitted into our State, whether they are supposed to have an allegorical meaning or not. For a young person cannot judge what is allegorical and what is literal; anything that he receives into his mind at that age is likely to become indelible and unalterable; and therefore it is most important that the tales which the young first hear should be models of virtuous thoughts.

There you are right, he replied; but if any one asks where are such models to be found and of what tales are you speaking—how shall we answer him?

I said to him, You and I, Adeimantus, at this moment are not poets, but founders of a State: now the founders of a State ought to know the general forms in which poets should cast their tales, and the limits which must be observed by them, but to make the tales is not their business.

Very true, he said; but what are these forms of theology which you mean?

Something of this kind, I replied:—God is always to be represented as he truly is, whatever be the sort of poetry, epic, lyric or tragic, in which the representation is given.

The Greeks believed in many gods, but the supreme god, Zeus, is sometimes referred to simply as "god" or "the god." What sort of understanding of divinity does Socrates present here, and how might it challenge conventional beliefs?

Right.

And is he not truly good? And must he not be represented as such?

Certainly.

And no good thing is hurtful?

No, indeed.

And that which is not hurtful hurts not?

Certainly not.

And that which hurts not does no evil?

No.

And can that which does no evil be a cause of evil?

Impossible.

And the good is advantageous?

Yes.

And therefore the cause of well-being?

Yes.

It follows therefore that the good is not the cause of all things, but of the good only?

Assuredly.

Then God, if he be good, is not the author of all things, as the many assert, but he is the cause of a few things only, and not of most things that occur to men. For few are the goods of human life, and many are the evils, and the good is to be attributed to God alone; of the evils the causes are to be sought elsewhere, and not in him.

That appears to me to be most true, he said.

Then we must not listen to Homer or to any other poet who is guilty of the folly of saying that two casks *Lie at the threshold of Zeus, full of lots, one of good, the other of evil lots,* and that he to whom Zeus gives a mixture of the two *Sometimes meets with evil fortune, at other times with good.*

* * *

And if any one asserts that the violation of oaths and treaties, which was really the work of Pandarus, was brought about by Athena and Zeus, or that the strife and contention of the gods was instigated by Themis and Zeus, he shall not have our approval; neither will we allow our young men to hear the words of Aeschylus, that *God plants guilt among men when he desires utterly to destroy a house.*

And if a poet writes of the sufferings of Niobe—the subject of the tragedy in which these iambic verses occur—or of the house of Pelops, or of the Trojan war or on any similar theme, either we must not permit him to say that these are the works of God, or if they are of God, he must devise some explanation of them such as we are seeking; he must say that God did what was just and right, and they were the better for being punished; but that those who are punished are miserable, and that God is the author of their misery—the poet is not to be permitted to say; though he may say that the wicked are miserable because they require to be punished, and are benefited by receiving punishment from God; but that God being good is the author of evil to any one is to be strenuously denied, and not to be said or sung or heard in verse or prose by any one whether old or young in any well-ordered commonwealth. Such a fiction is suicidal, ruinous, impious.

I agree with you, he replied, and am ready to give my assent to the law.

Let this then be one of our rules and principles concerning the gods, to which our poets and reciters will be expected to conform—that God is not the author of all things, but of good only.

That will do, he said.

And what do you think of a second principle? Shall I ask you whether God is a magician, and of a nature to appear insidiously now in one shape, and now in another—sometimes himself changing and passing into many forms, sometimes deceiving us with the semblance of such transformations; or is he one and the same immutably fixed in his own proper image?

I cannot answer you, he said, without more thought.

Well, I said; but if we suppose a change in anything, that change must be effected either by the thing itself, or by some other thing?

Most certainly.

And things which are at their best are also least liable to be altered or discomposed; for example, when healthiest and strongest, the human frame is least liable to be affected by meats and drinks, and the plant which is in the fullest vigor also suffers least from winds or the heat of the sun or any similar causes.

Of course.

And will not the bravest and wisest soul be least confused or deranged by any external influence?

True.

And the same principle, as I should suppose, applies to all composite things—furniture, houses, garments; when good and well made, they are least altered by time and circumstances.

Very true.

Then everything which is good, whether made by art or nature, or both, is least liable to suffer change from without?

True.

But surely God and the things of God are in every way perfect?

Of course they are.

Then he can hardly be compelled by external influence to take many shapes?

He cannot.

But may he not change and transform himself?

Clearly, he said, that must be the case if he is changed at all.

And will he then change himself for the better and fairer, or for the worse and more unsightly?

If he change at all he can only change for the worse, for we cannot suppose him to be deficient either in virtue or beauty.

Very true, Adeimantus; but then, would any one, whether God or man, desire to make himself worse?

Impossible.

Then it is impossible that God should ever be willing to change; being, as is supposed, the fairest and best that is conceivable, every god remains absolutely and for ever in his own form.

That necessarily follows, he said, in my judgment.

Then, I said, my dear friend, let none of the poets tell us that *The gods, taking the disguise of strangers from other lands, walk up and down cities in all sorts of forms,* and let no one slander Proteus and Thetis, neither let any one, either in tragedy or in any other kind of poetry, introduce Hera disguised in the likeness of a priestess asking an alms *For the life-giving daughters of Inachus the river of Argos;*—let us have no more lies of that sort. Neither must we have mothers under the influence of the poets scaring their children with a bad version of these myths—telling how certain gods, as they say, "Go about by night in the likeness of so many strangers and in divers forms"; but let them take heed lest they make cowards of their children, and at the same time speak blasphemy against the gods.

Heaven forbid, he said.

But although the gods are themselves unchangeable, still by witchcraft and deception they may make us think that they appear in various forms?

Perhaps, he replied.

Well, but can you imagine that God will be willing to lie, whether in word or deed, or to put forth a phantom of himself?

I cannot say, he replied.

Do you not know, I said, that the true lie, if such an expression may be allowed, is hated of gods and men?

What do you mean? he said.

I mean that no one is willingly deceived in that which is the truest and highest part of himself, or about the truest and highest matters; there, above all, he is most afraid of a lie having possession of him.

Still, he said, I do not comprehend you.

The reason is, I replied, that you attribute some profound meaning to my words; but I am only saying that deception, or being deceived or uninformed about the highest realities in the highest part of themselves, which is the soul, and in that part of them to have and to hold the lie, is what mankind least like;—that, I say, is what they utterly detest.

There is nothing more hateful to them.

And, as I was just now remarking, this ignorance in the soul of him who is deceived may be called the true lie; for the lie in words is only a kind of imitation and shadowy image of a previous affection of the soul, not pure unadulterated falsehood. Am I not right?

Perfectly right.

The true lie is hated not only by the gods, but also by men?

Yes.

Whereas the lie in words is in certain cases useful and not hateful; in dealing with enemies—that would be an instance; or again, when those whom we call our friends in a fit of madness or illusion are going to do some harm, then it is useful and is a sort of medicine or preventive; also in the tales of mythology, of which we were just now speaking—because we do not know the truth about ancient times, we make falsehood as much like truth as we can, and so turn it to account.

Very true, he said.

But can any of these reasons apply to God? Can we suppose that he is ignorant of antiquity, and therefore has recourse to invention?

That would be ridiculous, he said.

Then the lying poet has no place in our idea of God?

I should say not.

Or perhaps he may tell a lie because he is afraid of enemies? That is inconceivable.

But he may have friends who are senseless or mad?

But no mad or senseless person can be a friend of God.

Then no motive can be imagined why God should lie?

None whatever.

Then the superhuman and divine is absolutely incapable of falsehood?

Yes.

Then is God perfectly simple and true both in word and deed; he changes not; he deceives not, either by sign or word, by dream or waking vision.

Your thoughts, he said, are the reflection of my own.

You agree with me then, I said, that this is the second type or form in which we should write and speak about divine things. The gods are not magicians who transform themselves, neither do they deceive mankind in any way.

I grant that.

Then, although we are admirers of Homer, we do not admire the lying dream which Zeus sends to Agamemnon; neither will we praise the verses of Aeschylus in which Thetis says that Apollo at her nuptials

> *Was celebrating in song her fair progeny whose days were to be long, and to know no sickness. And when he had spoken of my lot as in all things blessed of heaven he raised a note of triumph and cheered my soul. And I thought that the word of Phoebus being divine and full of prophecy, would not fail. And now he himself who uttered the strain, he who was present at the banquet, and who said this—he it is who has slain my son.*

These are the kind of sentiments about the gods which will arouse our anger; and he who utters them shall be refused a chorus; neither shall we allow teachers to make use of them in the instruction of the young, meaning, as we do, that our guardians, as far as men can be, should be true worshippers of the gods and like them.

Existing poetry is also morally unsound because it presents gods and heroes exhibiting moral failings, thus presenting the young with bad examples to emulate.

I entirely agree, he said, in these principles, and promise to make them my laws.

Book III 386a

Such then, I said, are our principles of theology—some tales are to be told, and others are not to be told to our disciples from their youth upwards, if we mean them to honor the gods and their parents, and to value friendship with one another.

Yes; and I think that our principles are right, he said.

But if they are to be courageous, must they not learn other lessons besides these, and lessons of such a kind as will take away the fear of death? Can any man be courageous who has the fear of death in him?

Certainly not, he said.

And can he be fearless of death, or will he choose death in battle rather than defeat and slavery, who believes the world below to be real and terrible?

Impossible.

Then we must assume a control over the narrators of this class of tales as well as over the others, and beg them not simply to refrain from presenting a gloomy picture of the underworld but rather to commend the world below, intimating to them that their descriptions are untrue, and will do harm to our future warriors.

That will be our duty, he said.

Then, I said, we shall have to obliterate many obnoxious passages, beginning with the verses, *I would rather be a serf on the land of a poor and portionless man than rule over all the dead who have come to naught [Achilles in the underworld, Odyssey 11]*. We must also expunge the verse, which tells us how Pluto feared *Lest the mansions grim and squalid which the gods abhor should be seen both of mortals and immortals [Iliad 20]*.[4]

* * *

And we must beg Homer and the other poets not to be angry if we strike out these and similar passages, not because they are unpoetical, or unattractive to the popular ear, but because the greater the poetical charm of them, the less are they meet for the ears of boys and men who are meant to be free, and who should fear slavery more than death.

Undoubtedly.

Also we shall have to reject all the terrible and appalling names that describe the world below—Cocytus and Styx, ghosts under the earth, and sapless shades, and any similar words of which the very mention causes a shudder to pass through the inmost soul of him who hears them. I do not say that these horrible stories may not have a use of some kind; but there is a danger that the nerves of our guardians may be rendered too excitable and effeminate by them.

There is a real danger, he said.

Then we must have no more of them.

True.

Another and a nobler strain must be composed and sung by us.

Clearly.

And shall we proceed to get rid of the weepings and wailings of famous men?

They will go with the rest.

But shall we be right in getting rid of them? Reflect: our principle is that the good man will not consider death terrible to any other good man who is his comrade.

Yes; that is our principle.

And therefore he will not sorrow for his departed friend as though he had suffered anything terrible?

He will not.

Such a one, as we further maintain, is sufficient for himself and his own happiness, and therefore is least in need of other men.

True, he said.

And for this reason the loss of a son or brother, or the deprivation of fortune, is to him of all men least terrible.

Assuredly.

And therefore he will be least likely to lament, and will bear with the greatest equanimity any misfortune of this sort which may befall him.

---

4. Omitted are additional examples from Homer. Note how ancient Greeks use quotations from Greek literature to strengthen their argument.

Yes, he will feel such a misfortune far less than another.

Then we shall be right in getting rid of the lamentations of famous men, and making them over to women (and not even to women who are good for anything), or to men of a baser sort, that those who are being educated by us to be the defenders of their country may scorn to do the like.

That will be very right.

Then we will once more entreat Homer and the other poets not to depict Achilles, who is the son of a goddess, first lying on his side, then on his back, and then on his face; then starting up and sailing in a frenzy along the shores of the barren sea; now taking the sooty ashes in both his hands and pouring them over his head, or weeping and wailing in the various modes which Homer has delineated. Nor should he describe Priam the kinsman of the gods as praying and beseeching, *Rolling in the dirt, calling each man loudly by his name [Iliad 22].* Still more earnestly will we beg of him at all events not to introduce the gods lamenting and saying, *Alas! my misery! Alas! that I bore the harvest to my sorrow [Thetis in Iliad 18].*

* * *

For if, my sweet Adeimantus, our youth seriously listen to such unworthy representations of the gods, instead of laughing at them as they ought, hardly will any of them deem that he himself, being but a man, can be dishonored by similar actions; neither will he rebuke any inclination which may arise in his mind to say and do the like. And instead of having any shame or self-control, he will be always whining and lamenting on slight occasions.

Yes, he said, that is most true.

Yes, I replied; but that surely is what ought not to be, as the argument has just proved to us; and by that proof we must abide until it is disproved by a better.

It ought not to be.[5]

* * *

Again, truth should be highly valued; if, as we were saying, a lie is useless to the gods, and useful only as a medicine to men, then the use of such medicines should be restricted to physicians; private individuals have no business with them.

Clearly not, he said.

Then if any one at all is to have the privilege of lying, the rulers of the State should be the persons; and they, in their dealings either with enemies or with their own citizens, may be allowed to lie for the public good. But nobody else should meddle with anything of the kind; and although the rulers have this privilege, for a private man to lie to them in return is to be deemed a more heinous fault than for the

The idea that lies may be justified under certain circumstances will prove to be important as the argument progresses.

5. Omitted is a brief discussion of the evils of uncontrolled laughter.

patient or the pupil of a gymnasium not to speak the truth about his own bodily illnesses to the physician or to the trainer, or for a sailor not to tell the captain what is happening about the ship and the rest of the crew, and how things are going with himself or his fellow sailors.

Most true, he said.

If, then, the ruler catches anybody beside himself lying in the State . . . he will punish him for introducing a practice which is equally subversive and destructive of ship or State.

Most certainly, he said, if our idea of the State is ever carried out.

In the next place our youth must be temperate?

Certainly.

Are not the chief elements of temperance, speaking generally, obedience to commanders and self-control in sensual pleasures?

True.

Then we shall approve such language as that of Diomede in Homer, *Friend, sit still and obey my word [Iliad 4]* and the verses which follow, *The Greeks marched breathing prowess, . . . in silent awe of their leaders [Odyssey 3–4]* and other sentiments of the same kind.

We shall.

What of this line, *O heavy with wine, who hast the eyes of a dog and the heart of a stag [Odyssey 1]*—and of the words which follow? Would you say that these, or any similar impertinences which private individuals are supposed to address to their rulers, whether in verse or prose, are well or ill spoken?

They are ill spoken.

They may very possibly afford some amusement, but they do not conduce to temperance. And therefore they are likely to do harm to our young men—you would agree with me there?

Yes.

And then, again, to make the wisest of men say that nothing in his opinion is more glorious than *When the tables are full of bread and meat, and the cup-bearer carries round wine which he draws from the bowl and pours into the cups [Odyssey 9]*. Is it fit or conducive to temperance for a young man to hear such words? Or the verse *The saddest of fates is to die and meet destiny from hunger [Odyssey 12]*? What would you say again to the tale of Zeus, who, while other gods and men were asleep and he the only person awake, lay devising plans, but forgot them all in a moment through his lust, and was so completely overcome at the sight of Hera that he would not even go into the hut, but wanted to lie with her on the ground, declaring that he had never been in such a state of rapture before, even when they first met one another . . . or that other tale of how Hephaestus, because of similar goings on, cast a chain around Ares and Aphrodite *[Odyssey 8]*?

Indeed, he said, I am strongly of opinion that they ought not to hear that sort of thing.

But any deeds of endurance which are done or told by famous men, these they ought to see and hear; as, for example, what is said in the verses, *He smote his breast, and thus reproached his heart, Endure, my heart; far worse hast thou endured [Odyssey 20]!*

Certainly, he said.

In the next place, we must not let them be receivers of gifts or lovers of money.

Certainly not.

Neither must we sing to them of *Gifts persuading gods, and persuading reverend kings.* Neither is Phoenix, the tutor of Achilles, to be approved or deemed to have given his pupil good counsel when he told him that he should take the gifts of the Greeks and assist them; but that without a gift he should not lay aside his anger. Neither will we believe or acknowledge Achilles himself to have been such a lover of money that he took Agamemnon's or that when he had received payment he restored the dead body of Hector, but that without payment he was unwilling to do so.

Undoubtedly, he said, these are not sentiments which can be approved.

Loving Homer as I do, I hardly like to say that in attributing these feelings to Achilles, or in believing that they are truly to him, he is guilty of downright impiety. As little can I believe the narrative of his insolence to Apollo . . . or his insubordination to the river-god, on whose divinity he is ready to lay hands; or his offering to the dead Patroclus of his own hair, which had been previously dedicated to the other river-god Spercheius, and that he actually performed this vow; or that he dragged Hector round the tomb of Patroclus, and slaughtered the captives at the pyre; of all this I cannot believe that he was guilty, any more than I can allow our citizens to believe that he, the wise Cheiron's pupil, the son of a goddess and of Peleus who was the gentlest of men and third in descent from Zeus, was so disordered in his wits as to be at one time the slave of two seemingly inconsistent passions, meanness, not untainted by avarice, combined with overweening contempt of gods and men.

You are quite right, he replied.

And let us equally refuse to believe, or allow to be repeated, the tale of Theseus son of Poseidon, or of Peirithous son of Zeus, going forth as they did to perpetrate a horrid rape; or of any other hero or son of a god daring to do such impious and dreadful things as they falsely ascribe to them in our day: and let us further compel the poets to declare either that these acts were not done by them, or that they were not the sons of gods;—both in the same breath they shall not be permitted to affirm. We will not have them trying to persuade our youth that the gods are the authors of evil, and that heroes are no better than men—sentiments which, as we were saying, are neither pious nor true, for we have already proved that evil cannot come from the gods.

Assuredly not.

And further they are likely to have a bad effect on those who hear them; for everybody will begin to excuse his own vices when he is convinced that similar wickednesses are always being perpetrated by *the kindred of the gods*. . . . And therefore let us put an end to such tales, lest they engender laxity of morals among the young.

By all means, he replied.

But now that we are determining what classes of subjects are or are not to be spoken of, let us see whether any have been omitted by us. The manner in which gods and demigods and heroes and the world below should be treated has been already laid down.

Very true.

And what shall we say about men? That is clearly the remaining portion of our subject.

Clearly so.

But we are not in a condition to answer this question at present, my friend.

Why not?

Because, if I am not mistaken, we shall have to say that poets and story-tellers are guilty of making the gravest misstatements when they tell us that wicked men are often happy, and the good miserable; and that injustice is profitable when undetected, but that justice is a man's own loss and another's gain—these things we shall forbid them to utter, and command them to sing and say the opposite.

To be sure we shall, he replied.

But if you admit that I am right in this, then I shall maintain that you have implied the principle for which we have been all along contending.

I grant the truth of your inference.

That such things are or are not to be said about men is a question which we cannot determine until we have discovered what justice is, and how naturally advantageous to the possessor, whether he seems to be just or not.

Most true, he said.

393c Enough of the subjects of poetry: let us now speak of the style; and when this has been considered, both matter and manner will have been completely treated.

* * *

The form of poetry is also a concern. Socrates distinguishes here between narration—as when Homer describes someone doing or saying something—and imitation—as when Homer, or particularly the tragic poets, presents direct speech.

In saying this, I intended to imply that we must come to an understanding about the mimetic[6] art—whether the poets, in narrating their stories, are to be allowed by us to imitate, and if so, whether in whole or in part, and if the latter, in what parts; or should all imitation be prohibited?

You mean, I suspect, to ask whether tragedy and comedy shall be admitted into our State?

---

6. Mimetic, from the Greek *mimesis*, means imitative.

Yes, I said; but there may be more than this in question: I really do not know as yet, but whither the argument may blow, thither we go.

And go we will, he said.

Then, Adeimantus, let me ask you whether our guardians ought to be imitators; or rather, has not this question been decided by the rule already laid down that one man can only do one thing well, and not many; and that if he attempt many, he will altogether fail of gaining much reputation in any?

Certainly.

And this is equally true of imitation; no one man can imitate many things as well as he would imitate a single one?

He cannot.

Then the same person will hardly be able to play a serious part in life, and at the same time to be an imitator and imitate many other parts as well; for even when two species of imitation are nearly allied, the same persons cannot succeed in both, as, for example, the writers of tragedy and comedy—did you not just now call them imitations?

Yes, I did; and you are right in thinking that the same persons cannot succeed in both.

Any more than they can be rhapsodists and actors at once?

True.

Neither are comic and tragic actors the same; yet all these things are but imitations.

They are so.

And human nature, Adeimantus, appears to have been coined into yet smaller pieces, and to be as incapable of imitating many things well, as of performing well the actions of which the imitations are copies.

Quite true, he replied.

If then we adhere to our original notion and bear in mind that our guardians, setting aside every other business, are to dedicate themselves wholly to the maintenance of freedom in the State, making this their craft, and engaging in no work which does not bear on this end, they ought not to practice or imitate anything else; if they imitate at all, they should imitate from youth upward only those characters which are suitable to their profession—the courageous, temperate, holy, free, and the like; but they should not depict or be skilful at imitating any kind of illiberality or baseness, lest from imitation they should come to be what they imitate. Did you never observe how imitations, beginning in early youth and continuing far into life, at length grow into habits and become a second nature, affecting body, voice, and mind?

Yes, certainly, he said.

Then, I said, we will not allow those for whom we profess a care and of whom we say that they ought to be good men, to imitate a woman, whether young or old, quarrelling with her husband, or striving and vaunting against the gods in conceit of her happiness, or when she is in affliction, or sorrow, or weeping; and certainly not one who is in sickness, love, or labor.

Very right, he said.

Neither must they represent slaves, male or female, performing the offices of slaves?

They must not.

And surely not bad men, whether cowards or any others, who do the reverse of what we have just been prescribing, who scold or mock or revile one another in drink or out of in drink, or who in any other manner sin against themselves and their neighbors in word or deed, as the manner of such is. Neither should they be trained to imitate the action or speech of men or women who are mad or bad; for madness, like vice, is to be known but not to be practiced or imitated.

Very true, he replied.

Neither may they imitate smiths or other artificers, or oarsmen, or boatswains, or the like?

How can they, he said, when they are not allowed to apply their minds to the callings of any of these?

Nor may they imitate the neighing of horses, the bellowing of bulls, the murmur of rivers and roll of the ocean, thunder, and all that sort of thing?

Nay, he said, if madness be forbidden, neither may they copy the behavior of madmen.

You mean, I said, if I understand you aright, that there is one sort of narrative style which may be employed by a truly good man when he has anything to say, and that another sort will be used by a man of an opposite character and education.

And which are these two sorts? he asked.

Suppose, I answered, that a just and good man in the course of a narration comes on some saying or action of another good man,—I should imagine that he will like to impersonate him, and will not be ashamed of this sort of imitation: he will be most ready to play the part of the good man when he is acting firmly and wisely; in a less degree when he is overtaken by illness or love or drink, or has met with any other disaster. But when he comes to a character which is unworthy of him, he will not make a study of that; he will disdain such a person, and will assume his likeness, if at all, for a moment only when he is performing some good action; at other times he will be ashamed to play a part which he has never practiced, nor will he like to fashion and frame himself after the baser models; he feels the employment of such an art, unless in jest, to be beneath him, and his mind revolts at it.

So I should expect, he replied.

Then he will adopt a mode of narration such as we have illustrated out of Homer, that is to say, his style will be both imitative and narrative; but there will be very little of the former, and a great deal of the latter. Do you agree?

Certainly, he said; that is the model which such a speaker must necessarily take.

But there is another sort of character who will narrate anything, and, the worse lie is, the more unscrupulous he will be; nothing will be too bad for him: and he will be ready to imitate anything, not as a joke, but in right good earnest, and before a large company. As I was just now saying, he will attempt to represent the roll of thunder, the noise of wind and hall, or the creaking of wheels, and pulleys, and the various sounds of flutes; pipes, trumpets, and all sorts of instruments: he will bark like a dog, bleat like a sheep, or crow like a cock; his entire art will consist in imitation of voice and gesture, and there will be very little narration.

That, he said, will be his mode of speaking.

These, then, are the two kinds of style?

Yes.

And you would agree with me in saying that one of them is simple and has but slight changes; and if the harmony and rhythm are also chosen for their simplicity, the result is that the speaker, if he speaks correctly, is always pretty much the same in style, and he will keep within the limits of a single harmony (for the changes are not great), and in like manner he will make use of nearly the same rhythm?

That is quite true, he said.

Whereas the other requires all sorts of harmonies and all sorts of rhythms, if the music and the style are to correspond, because the style has all sorts of changes.

That is also perfectly true, he replied.

And do not the two styles, or the mixture of the two, comprehend all poetry, and every form of expression in words? No one can say anything except in one or other of them or in both together.

They include all, he said.

And shall we receive into our State all the three styles, or one only of the two unmixed styles? Or would you include the mixed?

I should prefer only to admit the pure imitator of virtue.

Yes, I said, Adeimantus, but the mixed style is also very charming: and indeed the pantomimic, which is the opposite of the one chosen by you, is the most popular style with children and their attendants, and with the world in general.

I do not deny it.

But I suppose you would argue that such a style is unsuitable to our State, in which human nature is not twofold or manifold, for one man plays one part only?

Yes; quite unsuitable.

And this is the reason why in our State, and in our State only, we shall find a shoemaker to be a shoemaker and not a pilot also, and a husbandman to be a husbandman and not a juror also, and a soldier a soldier and not a trader also, and the same throughout?

True, he said.

And therefore when any one of these pantomimic gentlemen, who are so clever that they can imitate anything, comes to us, and makes a proposal to exhibit himself and his poetry, we will fall down and worship him as a sweet and holy and wonderful being; but we must also inform him that in our State such as he are not permitted to exist; the law will not allow them. And so when we have anointed him with myrrh, and set a garland of wool upon his head, we shall send him away to another city. For we mean to employ for our souls' health the rougher and severer poet or story-teller, who will imitate the style of the virtuous only, and will follow those models which we prescribed at first when we began the education of our soldiers.

We certainly will, he said, if we have the power.

Then now, my friend, I said, that part of music or literary education which relates to the story or myth may be considered to be finished; for the matter and manner have both been discussed.

I think so too, he said.[7]

* * *

401b But shall our superintendence go no further, and are the poets only to be required by us to express the image of the good in their works, on pain, if they do anything else, of expulsion from our State? Or is the same control to be extended to other artists, and are they also to be prohibited from exhibiting the opposite forms of vice and intemperance and meanness and indecency in sculpture and building and the other creative arts; and is he who cannot conform to this rule of ours to be prevented from practicing his art in our State, lest the taste of our citizens be corrupted by him? We would not have our guardians grow up amid images of moral deformity, as in some noxious pasture, and there browse and feed upon many a baneful herb and flower day by day, little by little, until they silently gather a festering mass of corruption in their own soul. Let our artists rather be those who are gifted to discern the true nature of the beautiful and graceful; then will our youth dwell in a land of health, amid fair sights and sounds, and receive the good in everything; and beauty, the effluence of fair works, shall flow into the eye and ear, like a health-giving breeze from a purer region, and insensibly draw the soul from earliest years into likeness and sympathy with the beauty of reason.

Socrates sums up the goals of music—or arts—education.

There can be no nobler training than that, he replied.

And therefore, I said, Glaucon, musical training is a more potent instrument than any other, because rhythm and harmony find their way into the inward places of the soul, on which they mightily fasten, imparting grace, and making the soul of him who is rightly educated graceful, or of him who is ill-educated ungraceful; and also because he who has received this true education of the inner being will most shrewdly perceive omissions or faults in art and nature, and with a true taste, while he praises and rejoices over and receives into his soul the good, and becomes noble and good, he will justly blame and hate the bad, now in the days of his youth,

7. Omitted is a section on the types of melody conducive to courage and self-control.

even before he is able to know the reason why; and when reason comes he will recognize and salute the friend with whom his education has made him long familiar.

Yes, he said, I quite agree with you in thinking that our youth should be trained in music and on the grounds which you mention.

Just as in learning to read, I said, we were satisfied when we knew the letters of the alphabet, which are very few, in all their recurring sizes and combinations; not slighting them as unimportant whether they occupy a space large or small, but everywhere eager to make them out; and not thinking ourselves perfect in the art of reading until we recognize them wherever they are found:

True—

Or, as we recognize the reflection of letters in the water, or in a mirror, only when we know the letters themselves; the same art and study giving us the knowledge of both:

Exactly—

Even so, as I maintain, neither we nor our guardians, whom we have to educate, can ever become musical until we and they know the essential forms, in all their combinations, and can recognize them and their images wherever they are found, not slighting them either in small things or great, but believing them all to be within the sphere of one art and study.

Most assuredly.

And when a beautiful soul harmonizes with a beautiful form, and the two are cast in one mould, that will be the fairest of sights to him who has an eye to see it?

The fairest indeed.

And the fairest is also the loveliest?

That may be assumed.

And the man who has the spirit of harmony will be most in love with the loveliest; but he will not love him who is of an inharmonious soul?

That is true, he replied, if the deficiency be in his soul; but if there be any merely bodily defect in another he will be patient of it, and will love all the same.

I perceive, I said, that you have or have had experiences of this sort, and I agree. But let me ask you another question: Has excess of pleasure any affinity to temperance?

How can that be? he replied; pleasure deprives a man of the use of his faculties quite as much as pain.

Or any affinity to virtue in general?

None whatever.

Any affinity to wantonness and intemperance?

Yes, the greatest.

And is there any greater or keener pleasure than that of sensual love?

No, nor a madder.

Whereas true love is a love of beauty and order—temperate and harmonious?

Quite true, he said.

Then no intemperance or madness should be allowed to approach true love?

Certainly not.

Then mad or intemperate pleasure must never be allowed to come near the lover and his beloved; neither of them can have any part in it if their love is of the right sort?

No, indeed, Socrates, it must never come near them.

Then I suppose that in the city which we are founding you would make a law to the effect that a friend should use no other familiarity to his love than a father would use to his son, and then only for a noble purpose, and he must first have the other's consent; and this rule is to limit him in all his intercourse, and he is never to be seen going further, or, if he exceeds, he is to be deemed guilty of coarseness and bad taste.

I quite agree, he said.

Thus much of music, which makes a fair ending; for what should be the end of music if not the love of beauty?

I agree, he said.

403c After music comes gymnastic, in which our youth are next to be trained.[8]

* * *

410c Neither are the two arts of music and gymnastic really designed, as is often supposed, the one for the training of the soul, the other for the training of the body.

What then is the real object of them?

I believe, I said, that the teachers of both have in view chiefly the improvement of the soul.

How can that be? he asked.

Did you never observe, I said, the effect on the mind itself of exclusive devotion to gymnastic, or the opposite effect of an exclusive devotion to music?

In what way shown? he said.

The one producing a temper of hardness and ferocity, the other of softness and effeminacy, I replied.

Yes, he said, I am quite aware that the mere athlete becomes too much of a savage, and that the mere musician is melted and softened beyond what is good for him.

---

8. The argument for the correct form of physical education is omitted here, but you are encouraged to read it at the traditional pagination 403c–410b. Much of Socrates' discussion focuses on military preparation—an important part of the training of all Greek men—but he emphasizes that physical education is also aimed at building good character. This means it would include simplicity in diet and the use of physicians only for healing wounds or illnesses in otherwise healthy people. Excessive care of the body when one is no longer able to perform one's job is incompatible with virtue.

Yet surely, I said, this ferocity only comes from spirit, which, if rightly educated, would give courage, but, if too much intensified, is liable to become hard and brutal.

That I quite think.

On the other hand the philosopher will have the quality of gentleness. And this also, when too much indulged, will turn to softness, but, if educated rightly, will be gentle and moderate.

True.

And in our opinion the guardians ought to have both these qualities?

Assuredly.

And both should be in harmony?

Beyond question.

And the harmonious soul is both temperate and courageous?

Yes.

And the inharmonious is cowardly and boorish?

Very true.

And, when a man allows music to play upon him and to pour into his soul through the funnel of his ears those sweet and soft and melancholy airs of which we were just now speaking, and his whole life is passed in warbling and the delights of song; in the first stage of the process the passion or spirit which is in him is tempered like iron, and made useful, instead of brittle and useless. But, if he carries on the softening and soothing process, in the next stage he begins to melt and waste, until he has wasted away his spirit and cut out the sinews of his soul; and he becomes a feeble warrior.

Very true.

If the element of spirit is naturally weak in him the change is speedily accomplished, but if he have a good deal, then the power of music weakening the spirit renders him excitable;—on the least provocation he flames up at once, and is speedily extinguished; instead of having spirit he grows irritable and passionate and is quite impracticable.

Exactly.

And so in gymnastics, if a man takes violent exercise and is a great feeder, and the reverse of a great student of music and philosophy, at first the high condition of his body fills him with pride and spirit, and he becomes twice the man that he was.

Certainly.

And what happens? If he do nothing else, and holds no converse with the Muses, does not even that intelligence which there may be in him, having no taste of any sort of learning or enquiry or thought or culture, grow feeble and dull and blind, his mind never waking up or receiving nourishment, and his senses not being purged of their mists?

True, he said.

And he ends by becoming a hater of philosophy, uncivilized, never using the weapon of persuasion,—he is like a wild beast, all violence and fierceness, and knows no other way of dealing; and he lives in all ignorance and evil conditions, and has no sense of propriety and grace.

That is quite true, he said.

And as there are two principles of human nature, one the spirited and the other the philosophical, some God, as I should say, has given mankind two arts answering to them (and only indirectly to the soul and body), in order that these two principles (like the strings of an instrument) may be relaxed or drawn tighter until they are duly harmonized.

That appears to be the intention.

And he who mingles music with gymnastic in the fairest proportions, and best attempers them to the soul, may be rightly called the true musician and harmonist in a far higher sense than the tuner of the strings.

You are quite right, Socrates.

And such a presiding genius will be always required in our State if the government is to last.

Yes, he will be absolutely necessary.

Such, then, are our principles of nurture and education: Where would be the use of going into further details about the dances of our citizens, or about their hunting and coursing, their gymnastic and equestrian contests? For these all follow the general principle, and having found that, we shall have no difficulty in discovering them.

I dare say that there will be no difficulty.

412b Very good, I said; then what is the next question? Must we not ask who are to be rulers and who subjects?

Certainly.

There can be no doubt that the elder must rule the younger.

Clearly.

And that the best of these must rule.

That is also clear.

Now, are not the best husbandmen those who are most devoted to husbandry?

Yes.

An exploration of who will make the best guardians, and a distinction between guardians proper and auxiliaries.

And as we are to have the best of guardians for our city, must they not be those who have most the character of guardians?

Yes.

And to this end they ought to be wise and efficient, and to have a special care of the State?

True.

And a man will be most likely to care about that which he loves?

To be sure.

And he will be most likely to love that which he regards as having the same interests with himself, and that of which the good or evil fortune is supposed by him at any time most to affect his own?

Very true, he replied.

Then there must be a selection. Let us note among the guardians those who in their whole life show the greatest eagerness to do what is for the good of their country, and the greatest repugnance to do what is against her interests.

Those are the right men.

And they will have to be watched at every age, in order that we may see whether they preserve their resolution, and never, under the influence either of force or enchantment, forget or cast off their sense of duty to the State.

* * *

Therefore we must enquire who are the best guardians of their own conviction that what they think the interest of the State is to be the rule of their lives. We must watch them from their youth upwards, and make them perform actions in which they are most likely to forget or to be deceived, and he who remembers and is not deceived is to be selected, and he who falls in the trial is to be rejected. That will be the way?

Yes.

And there should also be toils and pains and conflicts prescribed for them, in which they will be made to give further proof of the same qualities.

Very right, he replied.

And then, I said, we must try them with enchantments that is the third sort of test—and see what will be their behavior: like those who take colts amid noise and tumult to see if they are of a timid nature, so must we take our youth amid terrors of some kind, and again pass them into pleasures, and prove them more thoroughly than gold is proved in the furnace, that we may discover whether they are armed against all enchantments, and of a noble bearing always, good guardians of themselves and of the music which they have learned, and retaining under all circumstances a rhythmical and harmonious nature, such as will be most serviceable to the individual and to the State. And he who at every age, as boy and youth and in mature life, has come out of the trial victorious and pure, shall be appointed a ruler and guardian of the State; he shall be honored in life and death, and shall receive memorials of honor, the greatest that we have to give. But him who fails, we must reject. I am inclined to think that this is the sort of way in which our rulers and guardians should be chosen and appointed. I speak generally, and not with any pretension to exactness.

And, speaking generally, I agree with you, he said.

And perhaps the word "guardian" in the fullest sense ought to be applied to this higher class only who preserve us against foreign enemies and maintain peace among our citizens at home, that the one may not have the will, or the others the power, to harm us. The young men whom we before called guardians may be more properly designated auxiliaries and supporters of the principles of the rulers.

I agree with you, he said.

How then may we devise one of those needful falsehoods of which we lately spoke—just one royal lie[9] which may deceive the rulers, if that be possible, and at any rate the rest of the city?

414b What sort of lie? he said.

Nothing new, I replied; only an old Phoenician tale of what has often occurred before now in other places (as the poets say, and have made the world believe), though not in our time, and I do not know whether such an event could ever happen again, or could now even be made probable, if it did.

How your words seem to hesitate on your lips!

You will not wonder, I replied, at my hesitation when you have heard.

Speak, he said, and fear not.

Well then, I will speak, although I really know not how to look you in the face, or in what words to utter the audacious fiction, which I propose to communicate gradually, first to the rulers, then to the soldiers, and lastly to the people. They are to be told that their youth was a dream, and the education and training which they received from us, an appearance only; in reality during all that time they were being formed and fed in the womb of the earth, where they themselves and their arms and equipment were manufactured; when they were completed, the earth, their mother, sent them up; and so, their country being their mother and also their nurse, they are bound to advise for her good, and to defend her against attacks, and her citizens they are to regard as children of the earth and their own brothers.

You had good reason, he said, to be ashamed of the lie which you were going to tell.

True, I replied, but there is more coming; I have only told you half. Citizens, we shall say to them in our tale, you are brothers, yet God has framed you differently. Some of you have the power of command, and in the composition of these he has mingled gold, wherefore also they have the greatest honor; others he has made of silver, to be auxiliaries; others again who are to be husbandmen and craftsmen he has composed of brass and iron; and the species will generally be preserved in the children. But as all are of the same original stock, a golden parent will sometimes have a silver son, or a silver parent a golden son. And God proclaims as a first principle to the rulers, and above all else, that there is nothing which they should so anxiously guard, or of which they are to be such good guardians, as of the purity of the race. They should observe what elements mingle in their offspring; for if the

---

9. The Greek phrase *gennaion pseudos*, often called the "noble lie," is challenging to translate. *Pseudos*, the word Socrates has been using, both here and in his critique of the poets, can mean either "lie" or "fiction." Desmond Lee translates the *gennaion pseudos* as a "magnificent myth," arguing that the word "lie" is misleading; rather, it is a story accepted by all members of the community as a way to embody their ideals and unite them in the way that national traditions do.

son of a golden or silver parent has an admixture of brass and iron, then nature orders a transposition of ranks, and the eye of the ruler must not be pitiful towards the child because he has to descend in the scale and become a husbandman or artisan, just as there may be sons of artisans who having an admixture of gold or silver in them are raised to honor, and become guardians or auxiliaries. For an oracle says that when a man of brass or iron guards the State, it will be destroyed. Such is the tale; is there any possibility of making our citizens believe in it?

Not in the present generation, he replied; there is no way of accomplishing this; but their sons may be made to believe in the tale, and their sons' sons, and posterity after them.

I see the difficulty, I replied; yet the fostering of such a belief will make them care more for the city and for one another. Enough, however, of the fiction, which may now fly abroad upon the wings of rumor, while we arm our earth-born heroes, and lead them forth under the command of their rulers. Let them look round and select a spot where they can best suppress insurrection from within, and also defend themselves against enemies, who like wolves may come down on the fold from without; there let them encamp, and when they have encamped, let them sacrifice to the proper Gods and prepare their dwellings.

Just so, he said.

And their dwellings must be such as will shield them against the cold of winter 415e
and the heat of summer.

I suppose that you mean houses, he replied.

Yes, I said; but they must be the houses of soldiers, and not of shop-keepers.

What is the difference? he said.

That I will try to explain, I replied. To keep watchdogs, who, from want of discipline or hunger, or some evil habit, or evil habit or other, would turn upon the sheep and worry them, and behave not like dogs but wolves, would be a foul and monstrous thing in a shepherd?

Truly monstrous, he said.

And therefore every care must be taken that our auxiliaries, being stronger than our citizens, may not grow to be too much for them and become savage tyrants instead of friends and allies?

Yes, great care should be taken.

And would not a really good education furnish the best safeguard?

But they are well-educated already, he replied.

I cannot be so confident, my dear Glaucon, I said; I am much certain that they ought to be, and that true education, whatever that may be, will have the greatest tendency to civilize and humanize them in their relations to one another, and to those who are under their protection.

Very true, he replied.

And not only their education, but their habitations, and all that belongs to them, should be such as will neither impair their virtue as guardians, nor tempt them to prey upon the other citizens. Any man of sense must acknowledge that.

He must.

This austere way of life is for guardians and auxiliaries only.

Then let us consider what will be their way of life, if they are to realize our idea of them. In the first place, none of them should have any property of his own beyond what is absolutely necessary; neither should they have a private house or store closed against any one who has a mind to enter; their provisions should be only such as are required by trained warriors, who are men of temperance and courage; they should agree to receive from the citizens a fixed rate of pay, enough to meet the expenses of the year and no more; and they will go and live together like soldiers in a camp. Gold and silver we will tell them that they have from God; the diviner metal is within them, and they have therefore no need of the dross which is current among men, and ought not to pollute the divine by any such earthly admixture; for that commoner metal has been the source of many unholy deeds, but their own is undefiled. And they alone of all the citizens may not touch or handle silver or gold, or be under the same roof with them, or wear them, or drink from them. And this will be their salvation, and they will be the saviors of the State. But should they ever acquire homes or lands or moneys of their own, they will become housekeepers and husbandmen instead of guardians, enemies and tyrants instead of allies of the other citizens; hating and being hated, plotting and being plotted against, they will pass their whole life in much greater terror of internal than of external enemies, and the hour of ruin, both to themselves and to the rest of the State, will be at hand. For all which reasons may we not say that thus shall our State be ordered, and that these shall be the regulations appointed by us for guardians concerning their houses and all other matters?

Yes, said Glaucon.

Book IV

Here Adeimantus interposed a question: How would you answer, Socrates, said he, if a person were to say that you are making these people miserable, and that they are the cause of their own unhappiness? The city in fact belongs to them, but they are none the better for it. Other men acquire lands, and build large and handsome houses, and have everything handsome about them, offering sacrifices to the gods on their own account, and practicing hospitality; moreover, as you were saying just now, they have gold and silver, and all that is usual among the favorites of fortune. But your guardians seem no better than mercenaries who are quartered in the city and are always mounting guard.

Yes, I said; and you may add that they are only fed, and not paid in addition to their food, like other men; and therefore they cannot, if they would, take a journey of pleasure; they have no money to spend on a mistress or any other luxurious fancy, which, as the world goes, is thought to be happiness; and many other accusations of the same nature might be added.

But, said he, let us suppose all this to be included in the charge.

You mean to ask, I said, what will be our answer?

Yes.

If we proceed along the old path, my belief, I said, is that we shall find the answer. And our answer will be that, even as they are, our guardians may very likely be the happiest of men; but that our aim in founding the State was not the disproportionate happiness of any one class, but the greatest happiness of the whole; we thought that in a State which is ordered with a view to the good of the whole we should be most likely to find Justice, and in the ill-ordered State injustice: and, having found them, we might then decide which of the two is the happier. At present, I take it, we are fashioning the happy State, not piecemeal, or with a view of making a few happy citizens, but as a whole; and by-and-by we will proceed to view the opposite kind of State. Suppose that we were painting a statue, and some one came up to us and said, Why do you not put the most beautiful colors on the most beautiful parts of the body—the eyes ought to be purple, but you have made them black—to him we might fairly answer, Sir, you would not surely have us beautify the eyes to such a degree that they are no longer eyes; consider rather whether, by giving this and the other features their due proportion, we make the whole beautiful. And so I say to you, do not compel us to assign to the guardians a sort of happiness which will make them anything but guardians; for we too can clothe our husbandmen in royal apparel, and set crowns of gold on their heads, and bid them till the ground as much as they like, and no more. Our potters also might be allowed to repose on couches, and feast by the fireside, passing round the winecup, while their wheel is conveniently at hand, and working at pottery only as much as they like; in this way we might make every class happy—and then, as you imagine, the whole State would be happy. But do not put this idea into our heads; for, if we listen to you, the husbandman will be no longer a husbandman, the potter will cease to be a potter, and no one will have the character of any distinct class in the State. Now this is not of much consequence where the corruption of society, and pretension to be what you are not, is confined to cobblers; but when the guardians of the laws and of the government are only seemingly and not real guardians, then see how they turn the State upside down; and on the other hand they alone have the power of giving order and happiness to the State. We mean our guardians to be true saviors and not the destroyers of the State, whereas our opponent is thinking of peasants at a festival, who are enjoying a life of revelry, not of citizens who are doing their duty to the State. But, if so, we mean different things, and he is speaking of something which is not a State. And therefore we must consider whether in appointing our guardians we would look to their greatest happiness individually, or whether this principle of happiness does not rather reside in the State as a whole. But if the latter be the truth, then the guardians and auxiliaries, and all others equally with them, must be compelled or induced to do their own work in the best way. And thus the whole State will grow up in a noble order, and the several classes will receive the proportion of happiness which nature assigns to them.

I think that you are quite right.

I wonder whether you will agree with another remark which occurs to me.

What may that be?

There seem to be two causes of the deterioration of the arts.

What are they?

Wealth, I said, and poverty.

How do they act?

The process is as follows: When a potter becomes rich, will he take the same pains with his art?

Certainly not.

He will grow more and more indolent and careless?

Very true.

And the result will be that he becomes a worse potter?

Yes; he greatly deteriorates.

But, on the other hand, if he has no money, and cannot provide himself tools or instruments, he will not work well , nor will he teach his sons or apprentices to work well.

Certainly not.

Then, under the influence either of poverty or of wealth, workmen and their work are equally liable to degenerate?

That is evident.

Here, then, is a discovery of new evils, I said, against which the guardians will have to watch, or they will creep into the city unobserved.

What evils?

Wealth, I said, and poverty; the one is the parent of luxury and indolence, and the other of meanness and viciousness, and both of discontent.

That is very true, he replied; but still I should like to know, Socrates, how our city will be able to go to war, especially against an enemy who is rich and powerful, if deprived of the sinews of war.

There would certainly be a difficulty, I replied, in going to war with one such enemy; but there is no difficulty where there are two of them.

How so? he asked.

In the first place, I said, if we have to fight, our side will be trained warriors fighting against an army of rich men.

That is true, he said.

And do you not suppose, Adeimantus, that a single boxer who was perfect in his art would easily be a match for two stout and well-to-do gentlemen who were not boxers?

Hardly, if they came upon him at once.

What, not, I said, if he were able to run away and then turn and strike at the one who first came up? And supposing he were to do this several times under the heat of a scorching sun, might he not, being an expert, overturn more than one stout personage?

Certainly, he said, there would be nothing wonderful in that.

And yet rich men probably have a greater superiority in the science and practice of boxing than they have in military qualities.

Likely enough.

Then we may assume that our athletes will be able to fight with two or three times their own number?

I agree with you, for I think you are right.

And suppose that, before engaging, our citizens send an embassy to one of the two cities, telling them what is the truth: Silver and gold we neither have nor are permitted to have, but you may; do you therefore come and help us in war, and take the spoils of the other city: Who, on hearing these words, would choose to fight against lean wiry dogs, rather than, with the dogs on their side, against fat and tender sheep?

That is not likely; and yet there might be a danger to the poor State if the wealth of many States were to be gathered into one.

But how simple of you to use the term State at all of any but our own!

Why so?

You ought to speak of other States in the plural number; not one of them is a city, but many cities, as they say in the game. For indeed any city, however small, is in fact divided into two, one the city of the poor, the other of the rich; these are at war with one another; and in either there are many smaller divisions, and you would be wrong if you treated them all as a single State. But if you deal with them as many, and give the wealth or power or persons of the one to the others, you will always have a great many friends and not many enemies. And your State, while the wise order which has now been prescribed continues to prevail in her, will be the greatest of States, I do not mean in reputation, but in truth, though she number not more than a thousand defenders. A single State which is her equal you will hardly find, either among Greeks or barbarians, though many that appear to be as great or much greater.

That is most true, he said.

And what, I said, will be the best limit for our rulers to fix when they are considering the size of the State and the amount of territory which they are to include, and beyond which they will not go?

What limit would you propose?

I would allow the State to increase so far as is consistent with unity; that, I think, is the proper limit.

Very good, he said.

Here then, I said, is another order which will have to be conveyed to our guardians: Let our city be accounted neither large nor small, but one and self-sufficing.

And surely, said he, this is not a very severe order which we impose upon them.

And the other, said I, of which we were speaking before is lighter still,—I mean the duty of degrading the offspring of the guardians when inferior, and of elevating into the rank of guardians the offspring of the lower classes, when naturally superior. The intention was, that, in the case of the citizens generally, each individual should be put to the use for which nature intended him, one to one work, and then every man would do his own business, and be one and not many; and so the whole city would be one and not many.

Yes, he said; that is not so difficult.

The regulations which we are prescribing, my good Adeimantus, are not, as might be supposed, a number of great principles, but trifles all, if care be taken, as the saying is, of the one great thing,—a thing, however, which I would rather call, not great, but sufficient for our purpose.

What may that be? he asked.

Education, I said, and nurture: If our citizens are well educated, and grow into sensible men, they will easily see their way through all these, as well as other matters which I omit; such, for example, as marriage, the possession of women and the procreation of children, which will all follow the general principle that friends have all things in common, as the proverb says.[10]

That will be the best way of settling them.

Also, I said, the State, if once started well, moves with accumulating force like a wheel. For good nurture and education implant good constitutions, and these good constitutions taking root in a good education improve more and more, and this improvement affects the breed in man as in other animals.

Very possibly, he said.

Then to sum up: This is the point to which, above all, the attention of our rulers should be directed,—that music and gymnastic be preserved in their original form, and no innovation made. They must do their utmost to maintain them intact. And when any one says that mankind most regard "the newest song which the singers have" they will be afraid that he may be praising, not new songs, but a new *kind* of song; and this ought not to be praised, or conceived to be the meaning of the poet; for any musical innovation is full of danger to the whole State, and ought to be prohibited. So Damon tells me, and I can quite believe him;—he says that when modes of music change, the ways of the State always change with them.

Yes, said Adeimantus; and you may add my vote to Damon's and your own.

Then, I said, our guardians must lay the foundations of their fortress in music?

Yes, he said; the lawlessness of which you speak too easily steals in.

Yes, I replied, in the form of amusement; and at first sight it appears harmless.

Why, yes, he said, and there would be no harm except that little by little this disorder finds a home and quietly penetrates into manners and customs; from there, it issues with greater force and invades business dealings between men, and from there goes on to laws and constitutions, in utter recklessness, until at last, Socrates, it overthrows all private and public life.

Is that true? I said.

---

10. Socrates' interlocutors will press him further on this point in Part III.

That is my belief, he replied.

Then, as I was saying, our youth should be trained from the first in a stricter system, for if amusements become lawless, and the youths themselves become lawless, they can never grow up into well-conducted and virtuous citizens.

Very true, he said.

And when they have made a good beginning in play, and by the help of music have gained the habit of good order, then this habit of order, unlike the lawless play of the others, will accompany them in all their actions and be a principle of growth to them, and will correct any previous flaws in the State.

Very true, he said.

* * *

PLATO

The Republic, ca. 390–370 BCE

PART III

This section of The Republic *marks a return to the original question about the nature of justice. Now that the state has been formed, what in it makes it just, or where is justice to be found? Socrates assumes that the four cardinal virtues—wisdom, courage, temperance, and justice—must all be present in this ideal state, so he searches for each in turn.*

As you read this section, consider the following questions:

- *Which virtues are found in only a part of the state, and which in the whole?*
- *How is justice in the state defined?*

The answer to Glaucon's question of whether it pays for the individual to act justly, however, is interrupted by questions about the place of women and the family in the ideal state.

SOURCE: *Plato,* The Republic, *trans. Benjamin Jowett (Oxford: Clarendon Press, 1894), with minor revisions for this edition. http://classics.mit.edu/Plato/republic.html (accessed February 1, 2015).*

But where, amid all this, is justice? Son of Ariston, tell me where. Now that our city has been made habitable, light a candle and search, and get your brother and Polemarchus and the rest of our friends to help, and 427d
let us see where in it we can discover justice and where injustice, and in what they

differ from one another, and which of them the man who would be happy should have for his portion, whether seen or unseen by gods and men.

Nonsense, said Glaucon: did you not promise to search yourself, saying that for you not to help justice in her need would be an impiety?

I do not deny that I said so, and as you remind me, I will be as good as my word; but you must join.

We will, he replied.

Well, then, I hope to make the discovery in this way: I mean to begin with the assumption that our State, if rightly ordered, is perfect.

That is most certain.

And being perfect, is therefore wise and valiant and temperate and just.

That is likewise clear.

And whichever of these qualities we find in the State, will the one not found be the residue?

Very good.

If there were four things, and we were searching for one of them, wherever it might be, the one sought for might be known to us from the first, and there would be no further trouble; or we might know the other three first, and then the fourth would clearly be the one left.

Very true, he said.

And is not a similar method to be pursued about the virtues, which are also four in number?

Clearly.

First among the virtues found in the State, wisdom comes into view, and in this I detect a certain peculiarity.

What is that?

The State which we have been describing is said to be wise as being good in counsel?

Very true.

And good counsel is clearly a kind of knowledge, for not by ignorance, but by knowledge, do men counsel well?

Clearly.

And the kinds of knowledge in a State are many and diverse?

Of course.

There is the knowledge of the carpenter; but is that the sort of knowledge which gives a city the title of wise and good in counsel?

Certainly not; that would only give a city the reputation of skill in carpentering.

Then a city is not to be called wise because possessing a knowledge which counsels for the best about wooden implements?

Certainly not.

Nor by reason of a knowledge which advises about brazen pots, I said, nor as possessing any other similar knowledge?

Not by reason of any of them, he said.

Nor yet by reason of a knowledge which cultivates the earth; that would give the city the name of agricultural?

Yes.

Well, I said, and is there any knowledge in our recently founded State among any of the citizens which advises, not about any particular thing in the State, but about the whole, and considers how a State can best deal with itself and with other States?

There certainly is.

And what is knowledge, and among whom is it found? I asked.

It is the knowledge of the guardians, he replied, and found among those whom we were just now describing as perfect guardians.

And what is the name which the city derives from the possession of this sort of knowledge?

The name of good in counsel and truly wise.

And will there be in our city more of these true guardians or more smiths?

The smiths, he replied, will be far more numerous.

Will not the guardians be the smallest of all the classes who receive a name from the profession of some kind of knowledge?

Much the smallest.

And so by reason of the smallest part or class, and of the knowledge which resides in this presiding and ruling part of itself, the whole State, being thus constituted according to nature, will be wise; and this, which has the only knowledge worthy to be called wisdom, has been ordained by nature to be of all classes the least.

Most true.

Thus, then, I said, the nature and place in the State of one of the four virtues has somehow or other been discovered.

And, in my humble opinion, very satisfactorily discovered, he replied.

Again, I said, there is no difficulty in seeing the nature of courage; and in what part that quality resides which gives the name of courageous to the State.

How do you mean?

Why, I said, every one who calls any State courageous or cowardly, will be thinking of the part which fights and goes out to war on the State's behalf.

No one, he replied, would ever think of any other.

The rest of the citizens may be courageous or may be cowardly but their courage or cowardice will not, as I conceive, have the effect of making the city either the one or the other.

Certainly not.

The city will be courageous in virtue of a portion of herself which preserves under all circumstances that opinion about the nature of things to be feared and not to be feared in which our legislator educated them; and this is what you term courage.

I should like to hear what you are saying once more, for I do not think that I perfectly understand you.

I mean that courage is a kind of salvation.

Salvation of what?

Of the opinion respecting things to be feared, what they are and of what nature, which the law implants through education; and I mean by the words "under all circumstances" to intimate that in pleasure or in pain, or under the influence of desire or fear, a man preserves, and does not lose this opinion. Shall I give you an illustration?

If you please.

You know, I said, that dyers, when they want to dye wool for making the true sea-purple, begin by selecting their white color first; this they prepare and dress with much care and pains, in order that the white ground may take the purple hue in full perfection. The dyeing then proceeds; and whatever is dyed in this manner becomes a fast color, and no washing either with lyes or without them can take away the bloom. But, when the ground has not been duly prepared, you will have noticed how poor is the look either of purple or of any other color.

Yes, he said; I know that they have a washed-out and ridiculous appearance.

Then now, I said, you will understand what our object was in selecting our soldiers, and educating them in music and gymnastic; we were contriving influences which would prepare them to take the dye of the laws in perfection, and the color of their opinion about dangers and of every other opinion was to be indelibly fixed by their nurture and training, not to be washed away by such potent lyes as pleasure—mightier agent far in washing the soul than any soda or lye; or by sorrow, fear, and desire, the mightiest of all other solvents. And this sort of universal saving power of true opinion in conformity with law about real and false dangers I call and maintain to be courage, unless you disagree.

But I agree, he replied; for I suppose that you mean to exclude mere uninstructed courage, such as that of a wild beast or of a slave—this, in your opinion, is not the courage which the law ordains, and ought to have another name.

Most certainly.

Then I may infer courage to be such as you describe?

Why, yes, said I, you may, and if you add the words "of a citizen," you will not be far wrong;—hereafter, if you like, we will carry the examination further, but at present we are seeking not for courage but justice; and for the purpose of our enquiry we have said enough.

You are right, he replied.

Two virtues remain to be discovered in the State—first temperance, and then justice, which is the end of our search.

Very true.

Now, can we find justice without troubling ourselves about temperance?

I do not know how that can be accomplished, he said, nor do I desire that justice should be brought to light and temperance lost sight of; and therefore I wish that you would do me the favor of considering temperance first.

Certainly, I replied, I should not be justified in refusing your request.

Then consider, he said.

Yes, I replied; I will; and as far as I can at present see, the virtue of temperance has more of the nature of harmony and symphony than the preceding.

How so? he asked.

Temperance, I replied, is the ordering or controlling of certain pleasures and desires; this is curiously enough implied in the saying of "a man being his own master" and other traces of the same notion may be found in language.

No doubt, he said.

There is something ridiculous in the expression "master of himself"; for the master is also the servant and the servant the master; and in all these modes of speaking the same person is denoted.

Certainly.

The meaning is, I believe, that in the human soul there is a better and also a worse principle; and when the better has the worse under control, then a man is said to be master of himself; and this is a term of praise: but when, owing to evil education or association, the better principle, which is also the smaller, is overwhelmed by the greater mass of the worse—in this case he is blamed and is called the slave of self and unprincipled.

Yes, there is reason in that.

And now, I said, look at our newly created State, and there you will find one of these two conditions realized; for the State, as you will acknowledge, may be justly called master of itself, if the words "temperance" and "self-mastery" truly express the rule of the better part over the worse.

Yes, he said, I see that what you say is true.

Let me further note that the manifold and complex pleasures and desires and pains are generally found in children and women and servants, and in the freemen so called who are of the lowest and more numerous class.

Certainly, he said.

Whereas the simple and moderate desires which follow reason, and are under the guidance of mind and true opinion, are to be found only in a few, and those the best born and best educated.

Very true.

These two, as you may perceive, have a place in our State; and the meaner desires of these are held down by the virtuous desires and wisdom of the few.

That I perceive, he said.

Then if there be any city which may be described as master of its own pleasures and desires, and master of itself, ours may claim such a designation?

Certainly, he replied.

It may also be called temperate, and for the same reasons?

Yes.

And if there be any State in which rulers and subjects will be agreed as to the question who are to rule, that again will be our State?

Undoubtedly.

And the citizens being thus agreed among themselves, in which class will temperance be found—in the rulers or in the subjects?

In both, as I should imagine, he replied.

Do you observe that we were not far wrong in our guess that temperance was a sort of harmony?

Why so?

Why, because temperance is unlike courage and wisdom, each of which resides in a part only, the one making the State wise and the other valiant; not so temperance, which extends to the whole, and runs through all the notes of the scale, and produces a harmony of the weaker and the stronger and the middle class, whether you suppose them to be stronger or weaker in wisdom or power or numbers or wealth, or anything else. Most truly then may we deem temperance to be the agreement of the naturally superior and inferior, as to the right to rule of either, both in states and individuals.

I entirely agree with you.

And so, I said, we may consider three out of the four virtues to have been discovered in our State. The last of those qualities which make a state virtuous must be justice, if we only knew what that was.

The inference is obvious.

The time then has arrived, Glaucon, when, like huntsmen, we should surround the thicket, and look sharp that justice does not steal away, and pass out of sight and escape us; for beyond a doubt she is somewhere in this country: watch therefore and strive to catch a sight of her, and if you see her first, let me know.

Would that I could! But you should regard me rather as a follower who has just eyes enough to see what you show him—that is about as much as I am good for.

Offer up a prayer with me and follow.

I will, but you must show me the way.

Here is no path, I said, and the wood is dark and perplexing; still we must push on.

Let us push on.

Here I saw something: Halloo! I said, I begin to perceive a track, and I believe that the quarry will not escape.

Good news, he said.

Truly, I said, we are stupid fellows.

Why so?

Why, my good sir, at the beginning of our enquiry, ages ago, there was justice tumbling out at our feet, and we never saw her; nothing could be more ridiculous. Like people who go about looking for what they have in their hands—that was the way with us—we looked not at what we were seeking, but at what was far off in the distance; and therefore, I suppose, we missed her.

What do you mean?

I mean to say that in reality for a long time past we have been talking of justice, and have failed to recognize her.

I grow impatient at the length of your preface.

Well then, tell me, I said, whether I am right or not: You remember the original principle which we were always laying down at the foundation of the State, that one man should practice one thing only, the thing to which his nature was best adapted;—now justice is this principle or a part of it.

Yes, we often said that one man should do one thing only.

Further, we affirmed that justice was doing one's own business, and not being a busybody; we said so again and again, and many others have said the same to us.

Yes, we said so.

Then to do one's own business in a certain way may be assumed to be justice. Can you tell me whence I derive this inference?

I cannot, but I should like to be told.

Because I think that this is the only virtue which remains in the State when the other virtues of temperance and courage and wisdom are abstracted; and, that this is the ultimate cause and condition of the existence of all of them, and while remaining in them is also their preservative; and we were saying that if the three were discovered by us, justice would be the fourth or remaining one.

That follows of necessity.

If we are asked to determine which of these four qualities by its presence contributes most to the excellence of the State, whether the agreement of rulers and subjects, or the preservation in the soldiers of the opinion which the law ordains about the true nature of dangers, or wisdom and watchfulness in the rulers, or whether this other which I am mentioning, and which is found in children and women, slave and freeman, artisan, ruler, subject,—the quality, I mean, of every one doing his own work, and not being a busybody, would claim the palm—the question is not so easily answered.

Certainly, he replied, there would be a difficulty in saying which.

Then the power of each individual in the State to do his own work appears to compete with the other political virtues, wisdom, temperance, courage.

Yes, he said.

And the virtue which enters into this competition is justice?

Exactly.

Let us look at the question from another point of view: Are not the rulers in a State those to whom you would entrust the office of determining suits at law?

Certainly.

And are suits decided on any other ground but that a man may neither take what is another's, nor be deprived of what is his own?

Yes; that is their principle.

Which is a just principle?

Yes.

Then on this view also justice will be admitted to be the having and doing what is a man's own, and belongs to him?

Very true.

Think, now, and say whether you agree with me or not. Suppose a carpenter to be doing the business of a cobbler, or a cobbler of a carpenter; and suppose them to exchange their implements or their duties, or the same person to be doing the work of both, or whatever be the change; do you think that any great harm would result to the State?

Not much.

434a But when the cobbler or any other man whom nature designed to be a trader, having his heart lifted up by wealth or strength or the number of his followers, or any like advantage, attempts to force his way into the class of warriors, or a warrior into that of legislators and guardians, for which he is unfitted, and either to take the implements or the duties of the other; or when one man is trader, legislator, and warrior all in one, then I think you will agree with me in saying that this interchange and this meddling of one with another is the ruin of the State.

Strategy alert! Socrates' point marks a significant attack on the practice of Athenian democracy.

Most true.

Seeing then, I said, that there are three distinct classes, any meddling of one with another, or the change of one into another, is the greatest harm to the State, and may be most justly termed evil-doing?

Precisely.

And the greatest degree of evil-doing to one's own city would be termed by you injustice?

Certainly.

This then is injustice; and on the other hand when the trader, the auxiliary, and the guardian each do their own business, that is justice, and will make the city just.

I agree with you.

We will not, I said, be over-positive as yet; but if, on trial, this conception of justice be verified in the individual as well as in the State, there will be no longer any room for doubt; if it be not verified, we must have a fresh enquiry.[1]

* * *

1. Omitted is the argument that establishes a tripartite soul. In brief, Socrates argues that the internal conflict we sometimes feel is best explained by positing three parts of the soul, corresponding to the three parts of the state. The reasoning part of the soul corresponds to the guardians proper, the desiring part corresponds to the great mass of workers, and the spirited part—that which feels anger or indignation—corresponds to the auxiliaries in the just state. A just person, like a just state, is one whose soul maintains each of these parts in proper relation. The passage omitted is important for a larger understanding of the *Republic*, but less so for purposes of the Reacting game.

Polemarchus, who was sitting a little way off, just beyond Adeimantus, began to whisper to him: stretching forth his hand, he took hold of the upper part of his coat by the shoulder, and drew him towards him, leaning forward himself so as to be quite close and saying something in his ear, of which I only caught the words, "Shall we let him off, or what shall we do?"

Book V

449b

Certainly not, said Adeimantus, raising his voice.

Who is it, I said, whom you are refusing to let off?

You, he said.

I repeated, Why am I especially not to be let off?

Why, he said, we think that you are lazy, and mean to cheat us out of a whole chapter which is a very important part of the story; and you fancy that we shall not notice your airy way of proceeding; as if it were self-evident to everybody, that in the matter of women and children "friends have all things in common."

Socrates' interlocutors wish to understand more fully what Socrates means when he speaks of a community of women and children.

And was I not right, Adeimantus?

Yes, he said; but what is right in this particular case, like everything else, requires to be explained; for community may be of many kinds. Please, therefore, say what sort of community you mean. We have been expecting that you would tell us something about the family life of your citizens—how they will bring children into the world, and rear them when they have arrived, and, in general, what is the nature of this community of women and children—for we are of opinion that the right or wrong management of such matters will have a great and paramount influence on the State for good or for evil. And now, since the question is still undetermined, and you are taking in hand another State, we have resolved, as you heard, not to let you go until you give an account of all this.

To that resolution, said Glaucon, you may regard me as saying Agreed.

And without more ado, said Thrasymachus, you may consider us all to be equally agreed.

I said, You know not what you are doing in thus assailing me: What an argument are you raising about the State! Just as I thought that I had finished, and was only too glad that I had laid this question to sleep, and was reflecting how fortunate I was in your acceptance of what I then said, you ask me to begin again at the very foundation, ignorant of what a hornet's nest of words you are stirring. Now I foresaw this gathering trouble, and avoided it.

For what purpose do you conceive that we have come here, said Thrasymachus,—to look for gold, or to hear discourse?

Yes, but discourse should have a limit.

Yes, Socrates, said Glaucon, and the whole of life is the only limit which wise men assign to the hearing of such discourses. But never mind about us; take heart yourself and answer the question in your own way: What sort of community of women and children is this which is to prevail among our guardians? And how shall we manage the period between birth and education, which seems to require the greatest care? Tell us how these things will be.

Yes, my simple friend, but the answer is the reverse of easy; many more doubts arise about this than about our previous conclusions. For the practicability of what is said may be doubted; and even if practicable, whether it is for the best may also be doubtful. Hence I feel a reluctance to approach the subject, lest our aspiration, my dear friend, turn out to be a dream only.

Fear not, he replied, for your audience will not be hard on you; they are not skeptical or hostile.

I said: My good friend, I suppose that you mean to encourage me by these words.

Yes, he said.

Then let me tell you that you are doing just the reverse; the encouragement which you offer would have been all very well had I myself believed that I knew what I was talking about: to declare the truth about matters of high interest which a man honors and loves among wise men who love him need occasion no fear or faltering in his mind; but to carry on an argument when you are yourself only a hesitating enquirer, which is my condition, is a dangerous and slippery thing; and the danger is not that I shall be laughed at (that is a childish fear), but that I shall miss the truth where I have most need to be sure of my footing, and drag my friends after me in my fall. And I pray Nemesis not to visit upon me the words which I am going to utter. For I do indeed believe that to be an involuntary homicide is less a crime than to be a deceiver about beauty or goodness or justice in the matter of laws. And that is a risk I would rather run among enemies than among friends, and therefore you do well to encourage me.

Glaucon laughed and said: Well then, Socrates, in case you and your argument do us any serious injury you shall be acquitted beforehand of the crime and shall not be held to be a deceiver; take courage then and speak.

Well, I said, the law says that when a man is acquitted he is free from guilt, and what holds at law may hold in argument.

Then why should you mind?

Well, I replied, I suppose that I must retrace my steps and say what I perhaps ought to have said before in the proper place. The part of the men has been played out, and now properly enough comes the turn of the women. Of them I will proceed to speak, and the more readily since I am invited by you. For men born and educated like our citizens, the only way, in my opinion, of arriving at a right conclusion about the possession and use of women and children is to follow the path on which we originally started, when we said that the men were to be the guardians and watchdogs of the herd.

True.

Let us further suppose the birth and education of our women to be subject to similar or nearly similar regulations; then we shall see whether the result accords with our design.

What do you mean?

What I mean may be put into the form of a question, I said: Are dogs divided into hes and shes, or do they share equally in hunting and in keeping watch and in the other duties of dogs? Or do we entrust to the males the entire and exclusive care of the flocks, while we leave the females at home, under the idea that the bearing and suckling their puppies is labor enough for them?

No, he said, they share alike; the only difference between them is that the males are stronger and the females weaker.

But can you use different animals for the same purpose, unless they are trained in the same way?

You cannot.

Then, if women are to have the same duties as men, they must have the same nurture and education?

Yes.

The education which was assigned to the men was music and gymnastic.

Yes.

Then women must be taught music and gymnastic and also the art of war, which they must practice like the men?

That is the inference, I suppose.

I should rather expect, I said, that several of our proposals, if they are carried out, being unusual, may appear ridiculous.

No doubt of it.

Yes, and the most ridiculous thing of all will be the sight of women naked in the palaestra, exercising with the men, especially when they are no longer young. They certainly will not be a vision of beauty, any more than the enthusiastic old men who in spite of wrinkles and ugliness continue to frequent the gymnasia.

Yes, indeed, he said: according to present notions the proposal would be thought ridiculous.

But then, I said, as we have determined to speak our minds, we must not fear the jests which will be directed against this sort of innovation; how they will talk of women's attainments both in music and gymnastic, and above all about their wearing armor and riding upon horseback!

Very true, he replied.

Yet having begun we must go forward to the rough places of the law; at the same time begging of these gentlemen for once in their life to be serious. Not long ago, as we shall remind them, the Greeks were of the opinion, which is still generally received among the barbarians, that the sight of a naked man was ridiculous and improper; and when first the Cretans and then the Spartans introduced the custom, the wits of that day might equally have ridiculed the innovation.

No doubt.

But when experience showed that to let all things be uncovered was far better than to cover them up, and the ludicrous effect to the outward eye vanished before the better principle which reason asserted, then the man was perceived to be a fool who directs the shafts of his ridicule at any other sight but that of folly and vice, or seriously inclines to weigh the beautiful by any other standard but that of the good.

Very true, he replied.

First, then, whether the question is to be put in jest or in earnest, let us come to an understanding about the nature of woman: Is she capable of sharing either wholly or partially in the actions of men, or not at all? And is the art of war one of those arts in which she can or cannot share? That will be the best way of commencing the enquiry, and will probably lead to the fairest conclusion.

That will be much the best way.

Shall we take the other side first and begin by arguing against ourselves; in this manner the adversary's position will not be undefended.

Why not? he said.

Then let us put a speech into the mouths of our opponents. They will say: "Socrates and Glaucon, no adversary need convict you, for you yourselves, at the first foundation of the State, admitted the principle that everybody was to do the one work suited to his own nature." And certainly, if I am not mistaken, such an admission was made by us. "And do not the natures of men and women differ very much indeed?" And we shall reply: Of course they do. Then we shall be asked, "Should not the tasks assigned to men and to women be different, and such as are agreeable to their different natures?" Certainly they should. "But if so, have you not fallen into a serious inconsistency in saying that men and women, whose natures are so entirely different, ought to perform the same actions?"—What defense will you make for us, my good Sir, against any one who offers these objections?

That is not an easy question to answer when asked suddenly; and I shall and I do beg of you to draw out the case on our side.

These are the objections, Glaucon, and there are many others of a like kind, which I foresaw long ago; they made me afraid and reluctant to take in hand any law about the possession and nurture of women and children.

By Zeus, he said, the problem to be solved is anything but easy.

Why yes, I said, but the fact is that when a man is out of his depth, whether he has fallen into a little swimming bath or into mid-ocean, he has to swim all the same.

Very true.

And must not we swim and try to reach the shore: we will hope that Arion's dolphin or some other miraculous help may save us?

I suppose so, he said.

Well then, let us see if any way of escape can be found. We acknowledged—did we not?—that different natures ought to have different pursuits, and that men's and women's natures are different. And now what are we saying?—that different natures ought to have the same pursuits—this is the inconsistency which is charged upon us.

Precisely.

Verily, Glaucon, I said, glorious is the power of the art of contradiction!

Why do you say so?

Because I think that many a man falls into the practice against his will. When he thinks that he is reasoning he is really disputing, just because he cannot define and divide, and so know that of which he is speaking; and he will pursue a merely verbal opposition in the spirit of contention and not of fair discussion.

Yes, he replied, such is very often the case; but what has that to do with us and our argument?

A great deal; for there is certainly a danger of our getting unintentionally into a verbal opposition.

In what way?

Why, we valiantly and pugnaciously insist upon the verbal truth, that different natures ought to have different pursuits, but we never considered at all what was the meaning of sameness or difference of nature, or why we distinguished them when we assigned different pursuits to different natures and the same to the same natures.

Why, no, he said, that was never considered by us.

I said: Suppose that by way of illustration we were to ask the question whether there is not an opposition in nature between bald men and hairy men; and if this is admitted by us, then, if bald men are cobblers, we should forbid the hairy men to be cobblers, and conversely?

That would be a jest, he said.

Yes, I said, a jest; and why? Because we never meant when we constructed the State, that the opposition of natures should extend to every difference, but only to those differences which affected the pursuit in which the individual is engaged; we should have argued, for example, that a physician and one who is in mind a physician may be said to have the same nature.

True.

Whereas the physician and the carpenter have different natures?

Certainly.

And if, I said, the male and female sex appear to differ in their fitness for any art or pursuit, we should say that such pursuit or art ought to be assigned to one or the other of them; but if the difference consists only in women bearing and men begetting children, this does not amount to a proof that a woman differs from a man in respect of the sort of education she should receive; and we shall therefore continue to maintain that our guardians and their wives ought to have the same pursuits.

Very true, he said.

Next, we shall ask our opponent how, in reference to any of the pursuits or arts of civic life, the nature of a woman differs from that of a man?

That will be quite fair.

And perhaps he, like yourself, will reply that to give a sufficient answer on the instant is not easy; but after a little reflection there is no difficulty.

Yes, perhaps.

Suppose then that we invite him to accompany us in the argument, and then we may hope to show him that there is nothing peculiar in the constitution of women which would affect them in the administration of the State.

By all means.

Let us say to him: Come now, and we will ask you a question:—when you spoke of a nature gifted or not gifted in any respect, did you mean to say that one man will acquire a thing easily, another with difficulty; a little learning will lead the one to discover a great deal; whereas the other, after much study and application, no sooner learns than he forgets; or again, did you mean, that the one has a body which is a good servant to his mind, while the body of the other is a hindrance to him?—would not these be the sort of differences which distinguish the man gifted by nature from the one who is ungifted?

No one will deny that.

And can you mention any pursuit of mankind in which the male sex has not all these gifts and qualities in a higher degree than the female? Need I waste time in speaking of the art of weaving, and the management of pancakes and preserves, in which womankind does really appear to be great, and in which for her to be beaten by a man is of all things the most absurd?

You are quite right, he replied, in maintaining the general inferiority of the female sex: although many women are in many things superior to many men, yet on the whole what you say is true.

And if so, my friend, I said, there is no special faculty of administration in a state which a woman has because she is a woman, or which a man has by virtue of his sex, but the gifts of nature are alike diffused in both; all the pursuits of men are the pursuits of women also, but in all of them a woman is inferior to a man.

Very true.

Then are we to impose all our enactments on men and none of them on women?

That will never do.

One woman has a gift of healing, another not; one is a musician, and another has no music in her nature?

Very true.

And one woman has a turn for gymnastic and military exercises, and another is unwarlike and hates gymnastics?

Certainly.

And one woman is a philosopher, and another is an enemy of philosophy; one has spirit, and another is without spirit?

That is also true.

Then one woman will have the temper of a guardian, and another not. Was not the selection of the male guardians determined by differences of this sort?

Yes.

Men and women alike possess the qualities which make a guardian; they differ only in their comparative strength or weakness.

Obviously.

And those women who have such qualities are to be selected as the companions and colleagues of men who have similar qualities and whom they resemble in capacity and in character?

Very true.

And ought not the same natures to have the same pursuits?

They ought.

Then, as we were saying before, there is nothing unnatural in assigning music and gymnastic to the wives of the guardians—to that point we come round again.

Certainly not.

The law which we then enacted was agreeable to nature, and therefore not an impossibility or mere aspiration; and the contrary practice, which prevails at present, is in reality a violation of nature.

That appears to be true.

We had to consider, first, whether our proposals were possible, and secondly whether they were the most beneficial?

Yes.

And the possibility has been acknowledged?

Yes.

The very great benefit has next to be established?

Quite so.

You will admit that the same education which makes a man a good guardian will make a woman a good guardian; for their original nature is the same?

Yes.

I should like to ask you a question.

What is it?

Would you say that all men are equal in excellence, or is one man better than another?

The latter.

And in the commonwealth which we were founding do you conceive the guardians who have been brought up on our model system to be more perfect men, or the cobblers whose education has been cobbling?

What a ridiculous question!

You have answered me, I replied: Well, and may we not further say that our guardians are the best of our citizens?

By far the best.

And will not their wives be the best women?

Yes, by far the best.

And can there be anything better for the interests of the State than that the men and women of a State should be as good as possible?

There can be nothing better.

And this is what the arts of music and gymnastic, when present in such manner as we have described, will accomplish?

Certainly.

Then we have made an enactment not only possible but in the highest degree beneficial to the State?

True.

Then let the wives of our guardians strip, for their virtue will be their robe, and let them share in the toils of war and the defense of their country; only in the distribution of labors the lighter are to be assigned to the women, who are the weaker natures, but in other respects their duties are to be the same. And as for the man who laughs at naked women exercising their bodies from the best of motives, in his laughter he is plucking "a fruit of unripe wisdom," and he himself is ignorant of what he is laughing at, or what he is about;—for that is, and ever will be, the best of sayings, "That the useful is the noble and the hurtful is the base."

Very true.

457c Here, then, is one difficulty in our law about women, which we may say that we have now escaped; the wave has not swallowed us up alive for enacting that the guardians of either sex should have all their pursuits in common; to the utility and also to the possibility of this arrangement the consistency of the argument with itself bears witness.

The equality of women has been laid out as a first "wave" of difficulty. Socrates introduces a second wave to overcome: abolition of the family and creation of a community of women and children.

Yes, that was a mighty wave which you have escaped.

Yes, I said, but a greater is coming; you will realize this when you see the next.

Go on; let me see.

The law, I said, which is the sequel of this and of all that has preceded, is to the following effect,—"that the wives of our guardians are to be common, and their children are to be common, and no parent is to know his own child, nor any child his parent."

Yes, he said, that is a much greater wave than the other; and the possibility as well as the utility of such a law are far more questionable.

I do not think, I said, that there can be any dispute about the very great utility of having wives and children in common; the possibility is quite another matter, and will be very much disputed.

I think that a good many doubts may be raised about both.

You imply that the two questions must be combined, I replied. Now I meant that you should admit the utility; and in this way, as I thought; I should escape from one of them, and then there would remain only the possibility.

But that little attempt is detected, and therefore you will please give a defense of both.

Well, I said, I submit to my fate. Yet grant me a little favor: let me feast my mind with the dream as day dreamers are in the habit of feasting themselves when they are walking alone; for before they have discovered any means of effecting their wishes—that is a matter which never troubles them—they would rather not tire themselves by thinking about possibilities; but assuming that what they desire is already granted to them, they proceed with their plan, and delight in detailing what they mean to do when their wish has come true—that is a way which they have of not doing much good to a capacity which was never good for much. Now I myself am beginning to lose heart, and I should like, with your permission, to pass over the question of possibility at present. Assuming therefore the possibility of the proposal, I shall now proceed to enquire how the rulers will carry out these arrangements, and I shall demonstrate that our plan, if executed, will be of the greatest benefit to the State and to the guardians. First of all, then, if you have no objection, I will endeavor with your help to consider the advantages of the measure; and hereafter the question of possibility.

I have no objection; proceed.

First, I think that if our rulers and their auxiliaries are to be worthy of the name which they bear, there must be willingness to obey in the one and the power of command in the other; the guardians must themselves obey the laws, and they must also imitate the spirit of them in any details which are entrusted to their care.

That is right, he said.

You, I said, who are their legislator, having selected the men, will now select the women and give them to them;—they must be as far as possible of like natures with them; and they must live in common houses and meet at common meals, None of them will have anything specially his or her own; they will be together, and will be brought up together, and will associate at gymnastic exercises. And so they will be drawn by a necessity of their natures to have intercourse with each other—necessity is not too strong a word, I think?

Yes, he said;—necessity, not geometrical, but another sort of necessity which lovers know, and which is far more convincing and constraining to the mass of mankind.

True, I said; and this, Glaucon, like all the rest, must proceed after an orderly fashion; in a city of the blessed, licentiousness is an unholy thing which the rulers will forbid.

Yes, he said, and it ought not to be permitted.

Then clearly the next thing will be to make marriage sacred in the highest degree, and what is most beneficial will be deemed sacred?

Exactly.

And how can marriages be made most beneficial?—that is a question which I put to you, because I see in your house dogs for hunting, and of the nobler sort of birds not a few. Now, I ask you, have you ever attended to their pairing and breeding?

In what particulars?

Why, in the first place, although they are all of a good sort, are not some better than others?

True.

And do you breed from them all indifferently, or do you take care to breed from the best only?

From the best.

And do you take the oldest or the youngest, or only those of ripe age?

I choose only those of ripe age.

And if care was not taken in the breeding, your dogs and birds would greatly deteriorate?

Certainly.

And the same of horses and animals in general?

Undoubtedly.

Good heavens! My dear friend, I said, what consummate skill will our rulers need if the same principle holds of the human species!

Certainly, the same principle holds; but why does this involve any particular skill?

Because, I said, our rulers will often have to use medicines. You know that when patients do not need medicines, but have only to be put under a regimen, an inferior doctor is considered good enough; but when medicine has to be given, then the doctor should be more skilled.

That is quite true, he said; but to what are you alluding?

I mean, I replied, that our rulers will find a considerable dose of falsehood and deceit necessary for the good of their subjects: we were saying that the use of all these things regarded as medicines might be of advantage.

And we were very right.

And this lawful use of them seems likely to be needed in the regulations of marriages and births.

How so?

Why, I said, the principle has been already laid down that the best of either sex should be united with the best as often, and the inferior with the inferior, as seldom as possible; and that they should rear the offspring of the one sort of union, but not of the other, if the flock is to be maintained in first-rate condition. Now these goings on must be a secret which the rulers only know, or there will be a further danger of our guardian herd breaking out into rebellion.

Very true.

Should we not appoint certain festivals at which we will bring together the brides and bridegrooms, and sacrifices will be offered and suitable marriage songs composed by our poets: the number of weddings is a matter which must be left to the discretion of the rulers, whose aim will be to preserve the average of population? There are many other things which they will have to consider, such as the effects of wars and diseases and any similar agencies, in order as far as this is possible to prevent the State from becoming either too large or too small.

Certainly, he replied.

We shall have to invent some ingenious kind of lots which the less worthy may draw on each occasion of our bringing them together, and then they will accuse their own ill-luck and not the rulers.

To be sure, he said.

And I think that our braver and better youth, besides their other honors and rewards, might have greater facilities of intercourse with women given them; their bravery will be a reason, and such fathers ought to have as many sons as possible.

True.

And the proper officers, whether male or female or both, for offices are to be held by women as well as by men—

Yes—

The proper officers will take the offspring of the good parents to the pen or fold, and there they will deposit them with certain nurses who dwell in a separate quarter; but the offspring of the inferior, or of the better when they chance to be deformed, will be put away in some mysterious, unknown place, as they should be.

Yes, he said, that must be done if the breed of the guardians is to be kept pure.

They will provide for their nurture, and will bring the mothers to the fold when they are full of milk, taking the greatest possible care that no mother recognizes her own child; and other wet-nurses may be engaged if more are required. Care will also be taken that the process of suckling shall not be protracted too long; and the mothers will have no getting up at night or other trouble, but will hand over all this sort of thing to the nurses and attendants.

You suppose the wives of our guardians to have an easy time of it when they have children.

Why, said I, and so they ought. Let us, however, proceed with our scheme. We were saying that the parents should be in the prime of life?

Very true.

And what is the prime of life? May it not be defined as a period of about twenty years in a woman's life, and thirty in a man's?

Which years do you mean to include?

A woman, I said, at twenty years of age may begin to bear children to the State, and continue to bear them until forty; a man may begin at five-and-twenty, when he has passed the point at which the pulse of life beats quickest, and continue to beget children until he be fifty-five.

Certainly, he said, both in men and women those years are the prime of physical as well as of intellectual vigor.

Any one above or below the prescribed ages who takes part in the public weddings shall be said to have done an unholy and unrighteous thing; the child of which he is the father, if it steals into life, will have been conceived under auspices very unlike the sacrifices and prayers, which at each wedding priestesses and priest and the whole city will offer, that the new generation may be better and more useful than their good and useful parents, whereas his child will be the offspring of darkness and strange lust.

Very true, he replied.

And the same law will apply to any one of those within the prescribed age who forms a connection with any woman in the prime of life without the sanction of the rulers; for we shall say that he is raising up a bastard to the State, uncertified and unconsecrated.

Very true, he replied.

This applies, however, only to those who are within the specified age: after that we allow them to range at will, except that a man may not marry his daughter or his daughter's daughter, or his mother or his mother's mother; and women, on the other hand, are prohibited from marrying their sons or fathers, or son's son or father's father, and so on in either direction. And we grant all this, accompanying the permission with strict orders to prevent any embryo which may come into being from seeing the light; and if any force a way to the birth, the parents must understand that the offspring of such a union cannot be maintained, and arrange accordingly.

That also, he said, is a reasonable proposition. But how will they know who are fathers and daughters, and so on?

They will never know. The way will be this:—dating from the day of the wedding, the bridegroom who was then married will call all the male children who are born in the seventh and tenth month afterwards his sons, and the female children his daughters, and they will call him father, and he will call their children his grandchildren, and they will call the elder generation grandfathers and grandmothers. All who were begotten at the time when their fathers and mothers came together will be called their brothers and sisters, and these, as I was saying, will be forbidden to inter-marry. This, however, is not to be understood as an absolute prohibition of the marriage of brothers and sisters; if the lot favors them, and they receive the sanction of the Pythian oracle, the law will allow them.

Quite right, he replied.

Such is the scheme, Glaucon, according to which the guardians of our State are to have their wives and families in common. And now you would have the argument show that this community is consistent with the rest of our polity, and also that nothing can be better—would you not?

Yes, certainly.

Shall we try to find a common basis by asking of ourselves what ought to be the chief aim of the legislator in making laws and in the organization of a State,—what is the greatest good, and what is the greatest evil, and then consider whether our previous description has the stamp of the good or of the evil?

By all means.

Can there be any greater evil than discord and distraction and plurality where unity ought to reign? Or any greater good than the bond of unity?

There cannot.

And there is unity where there is community of pleasures and pains—where all the citizens are glad or grieved on the same occasions of joy and sorrow?

No doubt.

Yes; and where there is no common but only private feeling a State is disorganized—when you have one half of the world triumphing and the other plunged in grief at the same events happening to the city or the citizens?

Certainly.

Such differences commonly originate in a disagreement about the use of the terms "mine" and "not mine," "his" and "not his."

Exactly so.

And is not the best-ordered State that in which the greatest number of persons apply the terms "mine" and "not mine" in the same way to the same thing?

Quite true.

Or that again which most nearly approaches to the condition of the individual—as in the body, when but a finger of one of us is hurt, the whole frame, drawn towards the soul as a center and forming one kingdom under the ruling power therein, feels the hurt and sympathizes all together with the part affected, and we say that the man has a pain in his finger; and the same expression is used about any other part of the body, which has a sensation of pain at suffering or of pleasure at the alleviation of suffering.

Very true, he replied; and I agree with you that in the best-ordered State there is the nearest approach to this common feeling which you describe.

Then when any one of the citizens experiences any good or evil, the whole State will make his case their own, and will either rejoice or sorrow with him?

Yes, he said, that is what will happen in a well-ordered State.

It will now be time, I said, for us to return to our State and see whether this or some other form is most in accordance with these fundamental principles.

Very good.

Our State like every other has rulers and subjects?

True.

All of whom will call one another citizens?

Of course.

But is there not another name which people give to their rulers in other States?

Generally they call them masters, but in democratic States they simply call them rulers.

And in our State what other name besides that of citizens do the people give the rulers?

They are called saviors and helpers, he replied.

And what do the rulers call the people?

Their maintainers and foster-fathers.

And what do they call them in other States?

Slaves.

And what do the rulers call one another in other States?

Fellow-rulers.

And what in ours?

Fellow-guardians.

Did you ever know an example in any other State of a ruler who would speak of one of his colleagues as his friend and of another as not being his friend?

Yes, very often.

And the friend he regards and describes as one in whom he has an interest, and the other as a stranger in whom he has no interest?

Exactly.

But would any of your guardians think or speak of any other guardian as a stranger?

Certainly he would not; for every one whom they meet will be regarded by them either as a brother or sister, or father or mother, or son or daughter, or as the child or parent of those who are thus connected with him.

Capital, I said; but let me ask you once more: Shall they be a family in name only; or shall they in all their actions be true to the name? For example, in the use of the word "father," would the care of a father be implied and the filial reverence and duty and obedience to him which the law commands; and is the violator of these duties to be regarded as an impious and unrighteous person who is not likely to receive much good either at the hands of God or of man? Are these to be or not to be the strains which the children will hear repeated in their ears by all the citizens about those who are intimated to them to be their parents and the rest of their kinsfolk?

These, he said, and none other; for what can be more ridiculous than for them to utter the names of family ties with the lips only and not to act in the spirit of them?

Then in our city the language of harmony and concord will be more often heard than in any other. As I was describing before, when any one is well or ill, the universal word will be with me "it is well" or "it is ill."

Most true.

And agreeably to this mode of thinking and speaking, were we not saying that they will have their pleasures and pains in common?

Yes, and so they will.

And they will have a common interest in the same thing which they will alike call "my own," and having this common interest they will have a common feeling of pleasure and pain?

Yes, far more so than in other States.

And the reason of this, over and above the general constitution of the State, will be that the guardians will have a community of women and children?

That will be the chief reason.

And this unity of feeling we admitted to be the greatest good, as was implied in our own comparison of a well-ordered State to the relation of the body and the members, when affected by pleasure or pain?

That we acknowledged, and very rightly.

Then the community of wives and children among our citizens is clearly the source of the greatest good to the State?

Certainly.

And this agrees with the other principle which we were affirming,—that the guardians were not to have houses or lands or any other property; their pay was to be their food, which they were to receive from the other citizens, and they were to have no private expenses; for we intended them to preserve their true character of guardians.

Right, he replied.

Both the community of property and the community of families, as I am saying, tend to make them more truly guardians; they will not tear the city in pieces by differing about "mine" and "not mine;" each man dragging any acquisition which he has made into a separate house of his own, where he has a separate wife and children and private pleasures and pains; but all will be affected as far as may be by the same pleasures and pains because they are all of one opinion about what is near and dear to them, and therefore they all tend towards a common end.

Certainly, he replied.

And as they have nothing but their persons which they can call their own, suits and complaints will have no existence among them; they will be delivered from all those quarrels of which money or children or relations are the occasion.

Of course they will.

Neither will trials for assault or insult ever be likely to occur among them. For that equals should defend themselves against equals we shall maintain to be honorable and right; we shall make the protection of the person a matter of necessity.

That is good, he said.

Yes; and there is a further good in the law; namely, that if a man has a quarrel with another he will satisfy his resentment then and there, and not proceed to more dangerous lengths.

Certainly.

To the elder shall be assigned the duty of ruling and chastising the younger.

Clearly.

Nor can there be a doubt that the younger will not strike or do any other violence to an elder, unless the magistrates command him; nor will he slight him in any way. For there are two guardians, shame and fear, mighty to prevent him: shame, which makes men refrain from laying hands on those who are to them in the relation of parents; fear, that the injured one will be succored by the others who are his brothers, sons, or fathers.

That is true, he replied.

Then in every way the laws will help the citizens to keep the peace with one another?

Yes, there will be no want of peace.

And as the guardians will never quarrel among themselves there will be no danger of the rest of the city being divided either against them or against one another.

None whatever.

I hardly like even to mention the little meannesses of which they will be rid, for they are beneath notice: such, for example, as the flattery of the rich by the poor, and all the pains and pangs which men experience in bringing up a family, and in finding money to buy necessaries for their household, borrowing and then repudiating, getting how they can, and giving the money into the hands of women and slaves to keep—the many evils of so many kinds which people suffer in this way are mean enough and obvious enough, and not worth speaking of.

Yes, he said, a man has no need of eyes in order to perceive that.

And from all these evils they will be delivered, and their life will be blessed as the life of Olympic victors and yet more blessed.

How so?

The Olympic victor, I said, is deemed happy in receiving a part only of the blessedness which is secured to our citizens, who have won a more glorious victory and have a more complete maintenance at the public cost. For the victory which they have won is the salvation of the whole State; and the crown with which they and their children are crowned is the fullness of all that life needs; they receive rewards from the hands of their country while living, and after death have an honorable burial.

Yes, he said, and glorious rewards they are.

Do you remember, I said, how in the course of the previous discussion some one who shall be nameless accused us of making our guardians unhappy—they had nothing and might have possessed all things—to whom we replied that, if an occasion offered, we might perhaps hereafter consider this question, but that, as at present advised, we would make our guardians truly guardians, and that we were fashioning the State with a view to the greatest happiness, not of any particular class, but of the whole?

Yes, I remember.

And what do you say, now that the life of our protectors is made out to be far better and nobler than that of Olympic victors—is the life of shoemakers, or any other artisans, or of husbandmen, to be compared with it?

Certainly not.

At the same time I ought here to repeat what I have said elsewhere, that if any of our guardians shall try to be happy in such a manner that he will cease to be a guardian, and is not content with this safe and harmonious life, which, in our judgment, is of all lives the best, but infatuated by some youthful conceit of happiness which gets up into his head shall seek to appropriate the whole State to himself, then he will have to learn how wisely Hesiod spoke, when he said, "half is more than the whole."

If he were to consult me, I should say to him: Stay where you are, when you have the offer of such a life.

You agree then, I said, that men and women are to have a common way of life such as we have described—common education, common children; and they are to watch over the citizens in common whether abiding in the city or going out to war; they are to keep watch together, and to hunt together like dogs; and always and in all things, as far as they are able, women are to share with the men? And in so doing they will do what is best, and will not violate, but preserve the natural relation of the sexes.

I agree with you, he replied.

The enquiry, I said, has yet to be made, whether such a community be found possible—as among other animals, so also among men—and if possible, in what way possible?

You have anticipated the question which I was about to suggest.[2]

* * *

2. Omitted is a discussion of warfare.

PLATO

The Republic, ca. 390–370 BCE

PART IV

Can this ideal state actually come into existence? Socrates argues that it can only happen if philosophers rule. He acknowledges that the first two "waves"—equality of women and the community of women and children—are challenging, but that this third wave—the philosopher king—will be even more difficult for people to accept. Much of Socrates' discussion of a philosophic education is omitted from these excerpts, and you are encouraged to read the famous allegory of the cave (514a–519d) elsewhere. In this simile, Socrates suggests that most of us are like prisoners chained in a cave, watching shadows on a wall which we take to be reality. Only the philosopher escapes from the cave, gazes at the sun, and sees the real objects that are casting the shadows on the cave wall.

As you read, consider the following questions:

- *How does Socrates argue that the popular notion of a philosopher is wrong?*
- *Consider carefully Socrates' analogy to piloting a ship. What criticisms of democracy are implicit in his analogy, and how might you develop or respond to them?*
- *Consider, too, his image of a powerful beast. What does this beast represent? And how do the sophists relate to this beast?*

SOURCE: *Plato,* The Republic, *trans. Benjamin Jowett (Oxford: Clarendon Press, 1894), with minor revisions for this edition. http://classics.mit.edu/Plato/republic.html (accessed February 1, 2015).*

471c But still I must say, Socrates, that if you are allowed to go on in this way you will entirely forget the other question which at the commencement of this discussion you thrust aside:—Is such an order of things possible, and how, if at all? For I am quite ready to acknowledge that the plan which you propose, if only feasible, would do all sorts of good to the State. I will add, what you have omitted, that your citizens will be the bravest of warriors, and will never leave their ranks, for they will all know one another, and each will call the other father, brother, son; and if you suppose the women to join their armies, whether in the same rank or in the rear, either as a terror to the enemy, or as auxiliaries in case of need, I know that they will then be absolutely invincible; and there are many domestic advantages which might also be mentioned and which I also fully acknowledge: but, as I admit all these advantages and as many more as you please, if only this State of yours were to come into existence, we need say no more about them. Let us now turn to the question of possibility and ways and means—the rest may be left.

If I loiter for a moment, you instantly make a raid upon me, I said, and have no mercy; I have hardly escaped the first and second waves, and you seem not to be aware that you are now bringing upon me the third, which is the greatest and heaviest. When you have seen and heard the third wave, I think you will be more considerate and will acknowledge that some fear and hesitation was natural respecting a proposal so extraordinary as that which I have now to state and investigate.

The more appeals of this sort which you make, he said, the more determined are we that you shall tell us how such a State is possible: speak out and at once.

Let me begin by reminding you that we found our way here in the search after justice and injustice.

True, he replied; but what of that?

I was only going to ask whether, if we have discovered them, we are to require that the just man should in nothing fail of absolute justice; or may we be satisfied with an approximation, and the attainment in him of a higher degree of justice than is to be found in other men?

The approximation will be enough.

We are enquiring into the nature of absolute justice and into the character of the perfectly just, and into injustice and the perfectly unjust, that we might have an ideal. We were to look at these in order that we might judge of our own happiness and unhappiness according to the standard which they exhibited and the degree in which we resembled them, but not with any view of showing that they could exist in fact.

True, he said.

Would a painter be any the worse because, after having delineated with consummate art an ideal of a perfectly beautiful man, he was unable to show that any such man could ever have existed?

He would be none the worse.

Well, and were we not creating an ideal of a perfect State?

To be sure.

And is our theory a worse theory because we are unable to prove the possibility of a city being ordered in the manner described?

Surely not, he replied.

That is the truth, I said. But if, at your request, I am to try and show how and under what conditions the possibility is highest, I must ask you to repeat your former admissions.

What admissions?

I want to know whether ideals are ever fully realized in language? Does not the word express more than the fact, and must not the actual, whatever a man may think, always, in the nature of things, fall short of the truth? What do you say?

I agree.

Then you must not insist on my proving that the actual State will in every respect coincide with the ideal: if we are only able to discover how a city may be governed nearly as we proposed, you will admit that we have discovered the possibility which you demand; and will be contented. I am sure that I should be contented—will not you?

Yes, I will.

Let me next endeavor to show what is that fault in States which is the cause of their present maladministration, and what is the least change which will enable a State to pass into the truer form; and let the change, if possible, be of one thing only, or if not, of two; at any rate, let the changes be as few and slight as possible.

Certainly, he replied.

I think, I said, that there might be a reform of the State if only one change were made, which is not a slight or easy though still a possible one.

What is it? he said.

Now then, I said, I go to meet that which I liken to the greatest of the waves; yet shall the word be spoken, even though the wave break and drown me in laughter and dishonor; and do you mark my words.

Proceed.

I said: *Until philosophers are kings, or the kings and princes of this world have the spirit and power of philosophy, and political greatness and wisdom meet in one, and those commoner natures who pursue either to the exclusion of the other are compelled to stand aside, cities will never have rest from their evils—nor the human race, as I believe—and then only will our State have a possibility of life and behold the light of day.* Such was the thought, my dear Glaucon, I would have uttered if it had not seemed too extravagant; for to be convinced that in no other State can there be happiness private or public is indeed a hard thing.

Socrates, what do you mean? I would have you consider that what you have uttered will lead numerous persons, and very respectable persons too, to pull off their coats all in a moment, and seizing any weapon that comes to hand, run at you might and main, before you know where you are, intending to do heaven knows what; and if you don't prepare an answer, and put yourself in motion, you will be skewered by their fine wits, and no mistake.

You got me into the scrape, I said.

And I was quite right. However, I will do all I can to get you out of it; but I can only give you good-will and good advice, and, perhaps, I may be able to fit answers to your questions better than another—that is all. And now, having such an auxiliary, you must do your best to show the unbelievers that you are right.

474b I ought to try, I said, since you offer me such invaluable assistance. And I think that, if there is to be a chance of our escaping, we must explain whom we mean when we say that philosophers are to rule in the State; then we shall be able to defend ourselves. We will find that there are some natures who ought to study philosophy and be leaders in the State, and others who are not born to be philosophers, and are meant to be followers rather than leaders.

Socrates must explain what he means by a "philosopher king" and why it is that the philosopher is the only possible ruler of the best state.

Then now for a definition, he said.

Follow me, I said, and I hope that I may in some way or other be able to give you a satisfactory explanation.

Proceed.

I dare say you remember, and therefore I need not remind you, that a lover, if he is worthy of the name, ought to show his love, not to some one part of that which he loves, but to the whole.

I really do not understand, and therefore beg of you to assist my memory.

Another person, I said, might fairly reply as you do; but a man of pleasure like yourself ought to know that all who are in the flower of youth do somehow or other raise a pang or emotion in a lover's breast, and are thought by him to be worthy of his affectionate regards. Is not this a way which you have with the fair: one has a snub nose, and you praise his charming face; the hook-nose of another has, you say, a royal look; while he who is neither snub nor hooked has the grace of regularity: the dark visage is manly, the fair are children of the gods; and as to the sweet "honey pale," as they are called, what is the very name but the invention of a lover who talks in diminutives, and is not adverse to paleness if appearing on the cheek of youth? In a word, there is no excuse which you will not make, and nothing which you will not say, in order not to lose a single flower that blooms in the spring-time of youth.

If you make me an authority in matters of love, for the sake of the argument, I assent.

And what do you say of lovers of wine? Do you not see them doing the same? They are glad of any pretext of drinking any wine.

Very good.

And the same is true of ambitious men; if they cannot command an army, they are willing to command a file; and if they cannot be honored by really great and important persons, they are glad to be honored by lesser and meaner people, but honor of some kind they must have.

Exactly.

Again I ask: Does he who desires any class of goods, desire the whole class or a part only?

The whole.

And is not the philosopher a lover, not of a part of wisdom only, but of the whole?

Yes, of the whole.

And he who dislikes learning, especially in youth, when he has no power of judging what is good and what is not, is one we consider not to be a philosopher or a lover of knowledge, just as he who refuses his food is not hungry, and may be said to have a bad appetite and not a good one?

Very true, he said.

Whereas he who has a taste for every sort of knowledge and who is curious to learn and is never satisfied, may be justly termed a philosopher? Am I not right?

Glaucon said: If curiosity makes a philosopher, you will find many a strange being will have a title to the name. All the lovers of sights have a delight in learning, and must therefore be included. Musical amateurs, too, are a folk strangely out of place among philosophers, for they are the last persons in the world who would come to anything like a philosophical discussion, if they could help, while they run about at the Dionysiac festivals as if they had let out their ears to hear every chorus; whether the performance is in town or country—that makes no difference—they are there. Now are we to maintain that all these and any who have similar tastes, as well as the professors of quite minor arts, are philosophers?

Certainly not, I replied; they are only an imitation.

He said: Who then are the true philosophers?

Those, I said, who are lovers of the vision of truth.

That is also good, he said; but I should like to know what you mean.[1]

* * *

Socrates observes that non-philosophers, "the multitude," do not have genuine knowledge, but only opinions about the world of appearances in which we live, a "region which is halfway between pure being and pure non-being."

Thus then we seem to have discovered that the many ideas which the multitude entertain about the beautiful and about all other things are tossing about in some region which is halfway between pure being and pure not-being?

We have.

Yes; and we had before agreed that anything of this kind which we might find was to be described as matter of opinion, and not as matter of knowledge; being the intermediate flux which is caught and detained by the intermediate faculty.

Quite true.

Then those who see the many beautiful, and who yet neither see absolute beauty, nor can follow any guide who points the way there; who see the many just, and not absolute justice, and the like,—such persons may be said to have opinion but not knowledge?

That is certain.

But those who see the absolute and eternal and immutable may be said to know, and not to have opinion only?

Neither can that be denied.

The one loves and embraces the subjects of knowledge, the other those of opinion? The latter are the same who listened to sweet sounds and gazed upon fair colors, but would not tolerate the existence of absolute beauty.

Yes, I remember.

Shall we then be guilty of any impropriety in calling them lovers of opinion rather than lovers of wisdom, and will they be very angry with us for thus describing them?

---

1. Omitted is a discussion of knowledge and opinion, in which Socrates argues that these two faculties have two different subject matters. A rudimentary idea of Plato's theory of "forms" is necessary to understand this point. Plato posits that the world of appearances—what we see and perceive—is an imperfect reflection of a more wholly real world of perfect forms and ideas. Consider, for example, that the idea of a triangle is more perfect than any triangle we might construct or come across here in the world of appearances. Plato would extend this idea beyond mathematics such that any object (e.g., a chair) or abstraction (e.g., justice) we perceive here should be understood as an imperfect reflection of a perfect chair or perfect justice. This realm of forms is the realm of true being, and the only realm about which one can have genuine *knowledge*. The world of appearances, being less perfect, cannot be known; what we think of it can be no more than *opinion*. The philosopher is the one person who seeks genuine knowledge of the forms, of genuine being, rather than a more imperfect understanding of the form's many reflections here in the world of appearances.

I shall tell them not to be angry; no man should be angry at what is true.

But those who love the truth in each thing are to be called lovers of wisdom and not lovers of opinion.

Assuredly.

And thus, Glaucon, after the argument has gone a weary way, the true and the false philosophers have at length appeared in view. Book VI

I do not think, he said, that the way could have been shortened.

I suppose not, I said; and yet I believe that we might have had a better view of both of them if the discussion could have been confined to this one subject and if there were not many other questions awaiting us, which he who desires to see in what respect the life of the just differs from that of the unjust must consider.

And what is the next question? he asked.

Surely, I said, the one which follows next in order. Inasmuch as philosophers only are able to grasp the eternal and unchangeable, and those who wander in the region of the many and variable are not philosophers, I must ask you which of the two classes should be the rulers of our State?

And how can we rightly answer that question?

Whichever of the two are best able to guard the laws and institutions of our State—let them be our guardians.

Very good.

Neither, I said, can there be any question that the guardian who is to keep anything should have eyes rather than no eyes?

There can be no question of that.

And are not those who lack the knowledge of the true being of each thing, and who have in their souls no clear pattern, and are unable as with a painter's eye to look at the absolute truth and to that original to repair, and having perfect vision of the other world to order the laws about beauty, goodness, justice in this, if not already ordered, and to guard and preserve the order of them—are not such persons, I ask, simply blind?

Truly, he replied, they are much in that condition.

And shall they be our guardians when there are others who, besides being their equals in experience and in virtue, also know the very truth of each thing?

There can be no reason, he said, for rejecting those who have this greatest of all great qualities; they must always have the first place unless they fail in some other respect.

Suppose then, I said, that we determine how far they can unite this and the other excellences.

By all means.

In the first place, as we began by observing, the nature of the philosopher has to be ascertained. We must come to an understanding about him, and, when we have done so, then, if I am not mistaken, we shall also acknowledge that such a union of qualities is possible, and that those in whom they are united, and those only, should be rulers in the State.

What do you mean?

Let us suppose that philosophical minds always love knowledge of a sort which shows them the eternal nature not varying from generation and corruption.

Agreed.

And further, I said, let us agree that they are lovers of all true being; there is no part whether greater or less, or more or less honorable, which they are willing to renounce; as we said before of the lover and the man of ambition.

True.

And if they are to be what we describe, is there not another quality they should also possess?

What quality?

Truthfulness: they will never intentionally receive into their mind falsehood, which is their detestation, and they will love the truth.

Yes, that may be safely affirmed of them.

"May be," my friend, I replied, is not the word; say rather "must be affirmed:" for he whose nature is amorous of anything cannot help loving all that belongs or is akin to the object of his affections.

Right, he said.

And is there anything more akin to wisdom than truth?

How can there be?

Can the same nature be a lover of wisdom and a lover of falsehood?

Never.

The true lover of learning then must from his earliest youth, as far as in him lies, desire all truth?

Assuredly.

But then again, as we know by experience, he whose desires are strong in one direction will have them weaker in others; they will be like a stream which has been drawn off into another channel.

True.

He whose desires are drawn towards knowledge in every form will be absorbed in the pleasures of the soul, and will hardly feel bodily pleasure—I mean, if he be a true philosopher and not a sham one.

That is most certain.

Such a one is sure to be temperate and the reverse of covetous; for the motives which make another man desirous of having and spending, have no place in his character.

Very true.

Another criterion of the philosophical nature has also to be considered.

What is that?

There should be no secret corner of illiberality; nothing can be more antagonistic than meanness to a soul which is ever longing after the whole of things both divine and human.

Most true, he replied.

Then how can he who has magnificence of mind and is the spectator of all time and all existence, think much of human life?

He cannot.

Or can such a one find death fearful?

No indeed.

Then the cowardly and mean nature has no part in true philosophy?

Certainly not.

Or again: can he who is harmoniously constituted, who is not covetous or mean, or a boaster, or a coward—can he, I say, ever be unjust or hard in his dealings?

Impossible.

Then you will soon observe whether a man is just and gentle, or rude and unsociable; these are the signs which distinguish even in youth the philosophical nature from the unphilosophical.

True.

There is another point which should be remarked.

What point?

Whether he has or has not a pleasure in learning; for no one will love that which gives him pain, and in which after much toil he makes little progress.

Certainly not.

And if he is forgetful and retains nothing of what he learns, will he not be an empty vessel?

That is certain.

Laboring in vain, he must end in hating himself and his fruitless occupation?

Yes.

Then a soul which forgets cannot be ranked among genuine philosophic natures; we must insist that the philosopher should have a good memory?

Certainly.

And once more, the inharmonious and unseemly nature can only tend to disproportion?

Undoubtedly.

And do you consider truth to be akin to proportion or to disproportion?

To proportion.

Then, besides other qualities, we must try to find a naturally well-proportioned and gracious mind, which will move spontaneously towards the true being of everything.

Certainly.

Well, and do not all these qualities, which we have been enumerating, go together, and are they not, in a manner, necessary to a soul, which is to have a full and perfect participation of being?

They are absolutely necessary, he replied.

And must not that be a blameless study which he only can pursue who has the gift of a good memory, and is quick to learn,—noble, gracious, the friend of truth, justice, courage, temperance, who are his kindred?

The god of jealousy himself, he said, could find no fault with such a study.

And to men like him, I said, when perfected by years and education, and to these only you will entrust the State.

487b Here Adeimantus interposed and said: To these statements, Socrates, no one can offer a reply; but when you talk in this way, a strange feeling passes over the minds of your hearers. They fancy that they are led astray a little at each step in the argument, owing to their own want of skill in asking and answering questions; these littles accumulate, and at the end of the discussion they are found to have sustained a mighty overthrow and all their former notions appear to be turned upside down. And as unskillful players of chess are at last shut up by their more skilful adversaries and have no piece to move, so they too find themselves shut up at last; for they have nothing to say in this new game of which words are the counters; and yet all the time they are in the right. The observation is suggested to me by what is now occurring. For any one of us might say, that although in words he is not able to meet you at each step of the argument, he sees as a fact that the votaries of philosophy, when they carry on the study, not only in youth as a part of education, but as the pursuit of their maturer years, most of them become strange monsters, not to say utter rogues, and that those who may be considered the best of them are made useless to the world by the very study which you extol.

Well, and do you think that those who say so are wrong?

I cannot tell, he replied; but I should like to know what is your opinion.

Hear my answer; I am of opinion that they are quite right.

Adeimantus objects that this picture of a philosopher does not seem true to his experience. Are not philosophers useless at best, and dangerous at worst?

Then how can you be justified in saying that cities will not cease from evil until philosophers rule in them, when philosophers are acknowledged by us to be of no use to them?

You ask a question, I said, to which a reply can only be given in a parable.

Yes, Socrates; and that is a way of speaking to which you are not at all accustomed, I suppose.

I perceive, I said, that you are vastly amused at having plunged me into such a hopeless discussion; but now hear the parable, and then you will be still more amused at the meagerness of my imagination: for the manner in which the best men are treated in their own States is so grievous that no single thing on earth is comparable to it; and therefore, if I am to plead their cause, I must have recourse to fiction, and put together a figure made up of many things, like the fabulous unions of goats and stags which are found in pictures. Imagine then a fleet or a ship in which there is a captain who is taller and stronger than any of the crew, but he is a little deaf and has a similar infirmity in sight, and his knowledge of navigation is not much better. The sailors are quarrelling with one another about the steering—every one is of opinion that he has a right to steer, though he has never learned the art of navigation and cannot tell who taught him or when he learned, and will further assert that it cannot be taught, and they are ready to cut in pieces any one who says the contrary. They throng about the captain, begging and praying him to commit the helm to them; and if at any time they do not prevail, but others are preferred to them, they kill the others or throw them overboard, and having first chained up the noble captain's senses with drink or some narcotic drug, they mutiny and take possession of the ship and make free with the stores; thus, eating and drinking, they proceed on their voyage in such a manner as might be expected of them. Him who is their partisan and cleverly aids them in their plot for getting the ship out of the captain's hands into their own whether by force or persuasion, they compliment with the name of sailor, pilot, able seaman, and abuse the other sort of man, whom they call a good-for-nothing; but that the true pilot must pay attention to the year and seasons and sky and stars and winds, and whatever else belongs to his art, if he intends to be really qualified for the command of a ship, and that he must and will be the steerer, whether other people like or not—the possibility of this union of authority with the steerer's art has never seriously entered into their thoughts or been made part of their calling. Now in vessels which are in a state of mutiny and by sailors who are mutineers, how will the true pilot be regarded? Will he not be called by them a prater, a star-gazer, a good-for-nothing?

Of course, said Adeimantus.

Then you will hardly need, I said, to hear the interpretation of the figure, which describes the true philosopher in his relation to the State; for you understand already.

Certainly.

Then suppose you now take this parable to the gentleman who is surprised at finding that philosophers have no honor in their cities; explain it to him and try to convince him that their having honor would be far more extraordinary.

I will.

Say to him, that, in considering the best philosophers to be useless to the rest of the world, he is right; but also tell him to attribute their uselessness to the fault of those who will not use them, and not to themselves. The pilot should not humbly beg the sailors to be commanded by him—that is not the order of nature; neither are "the wise to go to the doors of the rich"—the ingenious author of this saying told a lie—but the truth is, that, when a man is ill, whether he be rich or poor, to the physician he must go, and he who wants to be governed, to him who is able to govern. The ruler who is good for anything ought not to beg his subjects to be ruled by him; although the present governors of mankind are of a different stamp; they may be justly compared to the mutinous sailors, and the true helmsmen to those who are called by them good-for-nothings and star-gazers.

Precisely so, he said.

For these reasons, and among men like these, philosophy, the noblest pursuit of all, is not likely to be much esteemed by those of the opposite faction; not that the greatest and most lasting injury is done to her by her opponents, but by those who pretend to follow it, those whom your accuser has in mind when he says that the majority of them are rogues, and the best are useless; in which opinion I agreed.

Yes.

And the reason why the good are useless has now been explained?

True.

Then shall we proceed to show that the corruption of the majority is also unavoidable, and that this is not to be laid to the charge of philosophy any more than the other?

By all means.

And let us ask and answer in turn, first going back to the description of the gentle and noble nature. Truth, as you will remember, was his leader, whom he followed always and in all things; failing in this, he was an impostor, and had no part or lot in true philosophy.

Yes, that was said.

Well, and is not this one quality, to mention no others, greatly at variance with present notions of him?

Certainly, he said.

And have we not a right to say in his defense, that the true lover of knowledge is always striving after being—that is his nature; he will not rest in the multiplicity of individuals which is an appearance only, but will go on—the keen edge will not be blunted, nor the force of his desire weaken until he has attained the knowledge of the true nature of every essence by a sympathetic and kindred power in the soul, and by that power drawing near and becoming one with it, and begetting mind and truth, he will gain knowledge and will live and grow truly, and then, and not till then, will he cease from his travail.

Nothing, he said, can be more just than such a description of him.

And will the love of a lie be any part of a philosopher's nature? Will he not utterly hate a lie?

He will.

And when truth is the captain, we cannot suspect any evil of the band which he leads?

Impossible.

Justice and health of mind will be of the company, and temperance will follow after?

True, he replied.

Neither is there any reason why I should again lay out the philosopher's virtues, as you will doubtless remember that courage, magnificence, apprehension, memory, were his natural gifts. And you objected that, although no one could deny what I then said, still, if you leave words and look at facts, the persons who are thus described are some of them manifestly useless, and the greater number utterly depraved; we were then led to enquire into the grounds of these accusations, and have now arrived at the point of asking why are the majority bad, which question of necessity brought us back to the examination and definition of the true philosopher.

Exactly.

And we have next to consider the philosophic nature, why so many are spoiled—I am speaking of those who were said to be useless but not wicked—and, when we have done with them, we will speak of the imitators of philosophy, what manner of men are they who aspire after a profession which is above them and of which they are unworthy, and then, by their many mistakes, bring upon all philosophers that disrepute of which we speak. 490e

Socrates lays out how bad education and sophistry lead true philosophy into disrepute. Socratics will want to understand this section to defend Socrates against any accusation that he has trained young people to be wicked.

What are these corruptions? he said.

I will see if I can explain them to you. Every one will admit that a nature having in perfection all the qualities we required in a philosopher, is a rare plant which is seldom seen among men.

Rare indeed.

And what numberless and powerful causes tend to destroy these rare natures!

What causes?

In the first place there are their own virtues, their courage, temperance, and the rest of them, every one of which praiseworthy qualities (and this is a most singular circumstance) destroys and distracts from philosophy the soul which is the possessor of them.

That is very singular, he replied.

Then there are all the ordinary goods of life—beauty, wealth, strength, rank, and great connections in the State—you understand the sort of things—these also have a corrupting and distracting effect.

I understand; but I should like to know more precisely what you mean about them.

Grasp the truth as a whole, I said, and in the right way; you will then have no difficulty in apprehending the preceding remarks, and they will no longer appear strange to you.

And how am I to do so? he asked.

Why, I said, we know that all germs or seeds, whether vegetable or animal, when they fail to meet with proper nutriment or climate or soil, in proportion to their vigor, are all the more sensitive to the want of a suitable environment, for evil is a greater enemy to what is good than what is not.

Very true.

There is reason in supposing that the finest natures, when under alien conditions, receive more injury than the inferior, because the contrast is greater.

Certainly.

And may we not say, Adeimantus, that the most gifted minds, when they are ill-educated, become pre-eminently bad? Do not great crimes and the spirit of pure evil spring out of a fullness of nature ruined by education rather than from any inferiority, whereas weak natures are scarcely capable of any very great good or very great evil?

There I think that you are right.

And our philosopher follows the same analogy—he is like a plant which, having proper nurture, must necessarily grow and mature into all virtue, but, if sown and planted in an alien soil, becomes the most noxious of all weeds, unless he be preserved by some divine power. Do you really think, as people so often say, that our youth are corrupted by Sophists, or that private teachers of the art corrupt them in any degree worth speaking of? Are not the public who say these things the greatest of all Sophists? And do they not educate to perfection young and old, men and women alike, and fashion them after their own hearts?

When is this accomplished? he said.

When they meet together, and the world sits down at an assembly, or in a court of law, or a theater, or a camp, or in any other popular resort, and there is a great uproar, and they praise some things which are being said or done, and blame other things, equally exaggerating both, shouting and clapping their hands, and the echo of the rocks and the place in which they are assembled redoubles the sound of the praise or blame—at such a time will not a young man's heart, as they say, leap within him? Will any private training enable him to stand firm against the overwhelming flood of popular opinion? Or will he be carried away by the stream? Will he not have the notions of good and evil which the public in general have—he will do as they do, and as they are, such will he be?

Yes, Socrates; necessity will compel him.

And yet, I said, there is a still greater necessity, which has not been mentioned.

What is that?

The force of fines or confiscation or death which, as you are aware, these new Sophists and educators who are the public, apply when their words are powerless.

Indeed they do; and in right good earnest.

Now what opinion of any other Sophist, or of any private person, can be expected to overcome in such an unequal contest?

None, he replied.

No, indeed, I said, even to make the attempt is a great piece of folly; there neither is, nor has been, nor is ever likely to be, any different type of character which has had no other training in virtue but that which is supplied by public opinion—I speak, my friend, of human virtue only; what is more than human, as the proverb says, is not included: for I would not have you ignorant that, in the present evil state of governments, whatever is saved and comes to good is saved by the power of God, as we may truly say.

I quite assent, he replied.

Then let me crave your assent also to a further observation.

What are you going to say?

Why, that all those mercenary individuals, whom the many call Sophists and whom they deem to be their adversaries, do, in fact, teach nothing but the opinion of the many, that is to say, the opinions of their assemblies; and this is their wisdom. I might compare them to a man who should study the tempers and desires of a powerful beast who is fed by him—he would learn how to approach and handle him, also at what times and from what causes he is dangerous or the reverse, and what is the meaning of his several cries, and by what sounds, when another utters them, he is soothed or infuriated; and you may suppose further, that when, by continually attending upon him, he has become perfect in all this, he calls his knowledge wisdom, and makes of it a system or art, which he proceeds to teach, although he has no real notion of what he means by the principles or passions of which he is speaking, but calls this honorable and that dishonorable, or good or evil, or just or unjust, all in accordance with the tastes and tempers of the great brute. Good he pronounces to be that in which the beast delights and evil to be that which he dislikes; and he can give no other account of them except that the just and noble are the necessary, having never himself seen, and having no power of explaining to others the nature of either, or the difference between them, which is immense. By heaven, would not such a one be a rare educator?

Indeed, he would.

And in what way does he who thinks that wisdom is the discernment of the tempers and tastes of the motley multitude, whether in painting or music, or, finally, in politics, differ from him whom I have been describing? For when a man consorts with the many, and exhibits to them his poem or other work of art or the service he has done the State, making them his judges when he is not obliged, the so-called necessity of Diomede will oblige him to produce whatever they praise. And yet the reasons are utterly ludicrous which they give in confirmation of their own notions about the honorable and good. Did you ever hear any of them which were not?

No, nor am I likely to hear.

You recognize the truth of what I have been saying? Then let me ask you to consider further whether the world will ever be induced to believe in the existence of absolute beauty rather than of the many beautiful, or of the absolute in each kind rather than of the many in each kind?

Certainly not.

Then the world cannot possibly be a philosopher?

Impossible.

And therefore philosophers must inevitably fall under the censure of the world?

They must.

And of individuals who consort with the mob and seek to please them?

That is evident.

Then, do you see any way in which the philosopher can be preserved in his calling to the end? and remember what we were saying of him, that he was to have quickness and memory and courage and magnificence—these were admitted by us to be the true philosopher's gifts.

Yes.

Will not such a one from his early childhood be in all things first among all, especially if his bodily endowments are like his mental ones?

Certainly, he said.

And his friends and fellow-citizens will want to use him as he gets older for their own purposes?

No question.

Falling at his feet, they will make requests to him and do him honor and flatter him, because they want to get into their hands now, the power which he will one day possess.

That often happens, he said.

And what will a man such as he be likely to do under such circumstances, especially if he be a citizen of a great city, rich and noble, and a tall proper youth? Will he not be full of boundless aspirations, and fancy himself able to manage the affairs of Greeks and of barbarians, and having got such notions into his head will he not elevate himself in senseless pride?

To be sure he will.

Now, when he is in this state of mind, if some one gently comes to him and tells him that he is a fool and must get understanding, which can only be got by slaving for it, do you think that, under such adverse circumstances, he will be easily induced to listen?

Far otherwise.

And even if there be some one who through inherent goodness or natural reasonableness has had his eyes opened a little and is humbled and taken captive by philosophy, how will his friends behave when they think that they are likely to lose the advantage which they were hoping to reap from his companionship? Will they not do and say anything to prevent him from yielding to his better nature and to render his teacher powerless, using to this end private intrigues as well as public prosecutions?

There can be no doubt of it.

And how can one who is thus circumstanced ever become a philosopher?

Impossible.

Then were we not right in saying that even the very qualities which make a man a philosopher may, if he be ill-educated, divert him from philosophy, no less than riches and their accompaniments and the other so-called goods of life?

We were quite right.

Thus, my excellent friend, is brought about all that ruin of the natures best adapted to the best of all pursuits; they are natures which we maintain to be rare at any time; this being the class out of which come the men who are the authors of the greatest evil to States and individuals; and also of the greatest good when the tide carries them in that direction; but a small man never was the doer of any great thing either to individuals or to States.

That is most true, he said.

And so philosophy is left desolate, with her marriage rite incomplete: for her own have fallen away and forsaken her, and while they are leading a false and unbecoming life, other unworthy persons, seeing that she has no kinsmen to be her protectors, enter in and dishonor her; and fasten upon her the reproaches which, as you say, her reprovers utter, who affirm of her votaries that some are good for nothing, and that the greater number deserve the severest punishment.

That is certainly what people say.

Yes; and what else would you expect, I said, when you think of the puny creatures who, seeing this land open to them—a land well stocked with fair names and showy titles—like prisoners running out of prison into a sanctuary, take a leap out of their trades into philosophy; those who do so being probably the cleverest hands at their own miserable crafts? For, even if philosophy is in this evil case, still there remains a dignity about her not to be found in the arts. And many are thus attracted by her whose natures are imperfect and whose souls are disfigured by their meannesses, as their bodies are by their trades and crafts. Is not this unavoidable?

Yes.

Are they not exactly like a bald little tinker who has just got out of prison and come into a fortune; he takes a bath and puts on a new coat, and is decked out as a bridegroom going to marry his master's daughter, who is left poor and desolate?

A most exact parallel.

What will be the issue of such marriages? Will they not be vile and bastard?

There can be no question of it.

And when persons who are unworthy of education approach philosophy and make an alliance with her who is a rank above them what sort of ideas and opinions are likely to be generated? Will they not be sophisms captivating to the ear, having nothing in them genuine, or worthy of or akin to true wisdom?

No doubt, he said.

Then, Adeimantus, I said, the worthy disciples of philosophy will be but a small remnant: perchance some noble and well-educated person, detained by exile in her service, who in the absence of corrupting influences remains devoted to her; or some lofty soul born in a mean city, the politics of which he condemns and neglects; and there may be a gifted few who leave the arts, which they justly despise, and come to her. . . . My own case of the internal sign is hardly worth mentioning, for rarely, if ever, has such a monitor been given to any other man. Those who belong to this small class have tasted how sweet and blessed a possession philosophy is, and have also seen enough of the madness of the multitude;

and they know that no politician is honest, nor is there any champion of justice at whose side they may fight and be saved. Such a one may be compared to a man who has fallen among wild beasts—he will not join in the wickedness of his fellows, but neither is he able singly to resist all their fierce natures, and therefore seeing that he would be of no use to the State or to his friends, and reflecting that he would have to throw away his life without doing any good either to himself or others, he holds his peace, and goes his own way. He is like one who, in the storm of dust and sleet which the driving wind hurries along, retires under the shelter of a wall; and seeing the rest of mankind full of wickedness, he is content, if only he can live his own life and be pure from evil or unrighteousness, and depart in peace and good-will, with bright hopes.

Yes, he said, and he will have done a great work before he departs.

A great work—yes; but not the greatest, unless he find a State suitable to him; for in a State which is suitable to him, he will have a larger growth and be the savior of his country, as well as of himself.

* * *

497d What is there remaining?

The question how the study of philosophy may be so ordered as not to be the ruin of the State: All great attempts are attended with risk; "hard is the good," as men say.

Still, he said, let the point be cleared up, and the enquiry will then be complete.

I shall not be hindered, I said, by any want of will, but, if at all, by a want of power: my zeal you may see for yourselves; and note in what I am about to say how boldly and unhesitatingly I declare that States should pursue philosophy, not as they do now, but in a different spirit.

In what manner?

Socrates outlines how potential rulers might be instructed in philosophy, and insists that the rule of philosophers is not impossible.

At present, I said, the students of philosophy are quite young. Beginning when they are hardly past childhood, they devote only the time saved from moneymaking and housekeeping to such pursuits; and even those of them who are reputed to have most of the philosophic spirit, when they come within sight of the great difficulty of the subject—I mean dialectic—take themselves off. In after life when invited by some one else, they may, perhaps, go and hear a lecture, and about this they make much ado, for philosophy is not considered by them to be their proper business: at last, when they grow old, in most cases they are extinguished more truly than Heracleitus' sun, inasmuch as they never light up again.

But what ought to be their course?

Just the opposite. In childhood and youth their study, and what philosophy they learn, should be suited to their tender years: during this period while they are growing up towards manhood, the chief and special care should be given to their bodies that they may have them to use in the service of philosophy; as life advances and the intellect begins to mature, let them increase the gymnastics of the soul; but when the strength of our citizens fails and is past civil and military duties, then let them range at will and engage in no serious labor, as we intend them to live happily here, and to crown this life with a similar happiness in another.

How truly in earnest you are, Socrates! he said; I am sure of that; and yet most of your hearers, if I am not mistaken, are likely to be still more earnest in their opposition to you, and will never be convinced; Thrasymachus least of all.

Do not make a quarrel, I said, between Thrasymachus and me, who have recently become friends, although, indeed, we were never enemies; for I shall go on striving to the utmost until I either convert him and other men, or do something which may profit them against the day when they live again, and hold the like discourse in another state of existence.

You are speaking of a time which is not very near.

Rather, I replied, of a time which is as nothing in comparison with eternity. Nevertheless, I do not wonder that the many refuse to believe; for they have never seen that of which we are now speaking realized; they have seen only a conventional imitation of philosophy, consisting of words artificially brought together, not like these of ours having a natural unity. But a human being who in word and work is perfectly molded, as far as he can be, into the proportion and likeness of virtue—such a man ruling in a city which bears the same image, they have never yet seen, neither one nor many of them—do you think that they ever did?

No indeed.

No, my friend, and they have seldom, if ever, heard free and noble sentiments; such as men utter when they are earnestly and by every means in their power seeking after truth for the sake of knowledge, while they look coldly on the subtleties of controversy, of which the end is opinion and strife, whether they meet with them in the courts of law or in society.

They are strangers, he said, to the words of which you speak.

And this was what we foresaw, and this was the reason why truth forced us to admit, not without fear and hesitation, that neither cities nor States nor individuals will ever attain perfection until the small class of philosophers whom we termed useless but not corrupt are providentially compelled, whether they will or not, to take care of the State, and until a like necessity be laid on the State to obey them; or until kings, or if not kings, the sons of kings or princes, are divinely inspired with a true love of true philosophy. That either or both of these alternatives are impossible, I see no reason to affirm: if they were so, we might indeed be justly ridiculed as dreamers and visionaries. Am I not right?

Quite right.

If then, in the countless ages of the past, or at the present hour in some foreign clime which is far away and beyond our knowledge, the perfected philosopher is or has been or hereafter shall be compelled by a superior power to have the charge of the State, we are ready to assert to the death, that this our constitution has been, and is—yea, and will be whenever the Muse of Philosophy is queen. There is no impossibility in all this; that there is a difficulty, we acknowledge ourselves.

My opinion agrees with yours, he said.

But do you mean to say that this is not the opinion of the multitude?

I should imagine not, he replied.

O my friend, I said, do not attack the multitude. They will change their minds, if, not in an aggressive spirit, but gently and with the view of soothing them and removing their dislike of over-education, you show them your philosophers as they really are and describe as you were just now doing their character and profession, and then mankind will see that he of whom you are speaking is not such as they supposed—if they view him in this new light, they will surely change their notion of him, and answer in another strain. Who can be at enmity with one who loves them? Who that is himself gentle and free from envy will be jealous of one in whom there is no jealousy? Nay, let me answer for you, that in a few this harsh temper may be found but not in the majority of mankind.

I quite agree with you, he said.

And do you not also think, as I do, that the harsh feeling which the many entertain towards philosophy originates in the pretenders, who rush in uninvited, and are always abusing them, and finding fault with them, who make persons instead of things the theme of their conversation? and nothing can be more unbecoming in philosophers than this.

It is most unbecoming.

For he, Adeimantus, whose mind is fixed upon true being, has surely no time to look down upon the affairs of earth, or to be filled with malice and envy, contending against men; his eye is ever directed towards things fixed and immutable, which he sees neither injuring nor injured by one another, but all in order moving according to reason; these he imitates, and to these he will, as far as he can, conform himself. Can a man help imitating that with which he holds reverential converse?

Impossible.

And the philosopher holding converse with the divine order, becomes orderly and divine, as far as the nature of man allows; but like every one else, he will have his detractors.

Of course.

And if he is compelled to fashion, not only himself, but human nature generally, whether in States or individuals, into that which he beholds elsewhere, will he, think you, lack the skill to create justice, temperance, and every civil virtue?

Of course not.

And if the world perceives that what we are saying about him is the truth, will they be angry with philosophy? Will they disbelieve us, when we tell them that no State can be happy which is not designed by artists who imitate the heavenly pattern?

They will not be angry if they understand, he said. But how will they draw out the plan of which you are speaking?

They will begin by taking the State and the manners of men, from which, as from a tablet, they will rub out the picture, and leave a clean surface. This is no easy task. But whether easy or not, herein will lie the difference between them and every other legislator,—they will have nothing to do either with individual or State, and will inscribe no laws, until they have either found, or themselves made, a clean surface.

They will be very right, he said.

Having effected this, they will proceed to trace an outline of the constitution?

No doubt.

And when they are filling in the work, as I conceive, they will often turn their eyes upwards and downwards: I mean that they will first look at absolute justice and beauty and temperance, and again at the human copy; and will mingle and temper the various elements of life into the image of a man; and thus they will conceive according to that other image, which, when existing among men, Homer calls the form and likeness of God.

Very true, he said.

And one feature they will erase, and another they will put in, they have made the ways of men, as far as possible, agreeable to the ways of God?

Indeed, he said, in no way could they make a fairer picture.

And now, I said, are we beginning to persuade the attackers you mentioned, that the painter of constitutions is such a one as we are praising; at whom they were so very indignant because to his hands we committed the State; and are they growing a little calmer at what they have just heard?

Much calmer, if there is any sense in them.

Why, where can they still find any ground for objection? Will they doubt that the philosopher is a lover of truth and being?

They would not be so unreasonable.

Or that his nature, being such as we have delineated, is akin to the highest good?

Neither can they doubt this.

But again, will they tell us that such a nature, placed under favorable circumstances, will not be perfectly good and wise if any ever was? Or will they prefer those whom we have rejected?

Surely not.

Then will they still be angry at our saying, that, until philosophers bear rule, States and individuals will have no rest from evil, nor will this our imaginary State ever be realized?

I think that they will be less angry.

Shall we assume that they are not only less angry but quite gentle, and that they have been converted and for very shame, if for no other reason, cannot refuse to come to terms?

By all means, he said.

Then let us suppose that the reconciliation has been effected. Will any one deny the other point, that there may be sons of kings or princes who are by nature philosophers?

Surely no man, he said.

And when they have come into being will any one say that they must of necessity be destroyed; that they can hardly be saved is not denied even by us; but that in the whole course of ages no single one of them can escape—who will venture to affirm this?

Who indeed!

But, said I, one is enough; let there be one man who has a city obedient to his will, and he might bring into existence the ideal polity about which the world is so incredulous.

Yes, one is enough.

The ruler may impose the laws and institutions which we have been describing, and the citizens may possibly be willing to obey them?

Certainly.

And that others should approve of what we approve, is no miracle or impossibility?

I think not.

But we have sufficiently shown, in what has preceded, that all this, if only possible, is assuredly for the best.

We have.

And now we say not only that our laws, if they could be enacted, would be for the best, but also that the enactment of them, though difficult, is not impossible.

Very good.

502c And so with pain and toil we have reached the end of one subject, but more remains to be discussed;—how and by what studies and pursuits will the saviors of the constitution be created, and at what ages are they to apply themselves to their several studies?[2]

* * *

519d Then, I said, the business of us who are the founders of the State will be to compel the best minds to attain that knowledge which we have already shown to be the greatest of all—they must continue to ascend until they arrive at the good; but when they have ascended and seen enough we must not allow them to do as they do now.

What do you mean?

---

2. Omitted is most of the discussion about the education of the philosopher, including the allegory of the cave.

I mean that they remain in the upper world: but this must not be allowed; they must be made to descend again among the prisoners in the den, and partake of their labors and honors, whether they are worth having or not.

Socrates tells Glaucon that the philosopher must be forced to return to the cave to rule.

But is not this unjust? he said; ought we to give them a worse life, when they might have a better?

You have again forgotten, my friend, I said, the intention of the legislator, who did not aim at making any one class in the State happy above the rest; the happiness was to be in the whole State, and he held the citizens together by persuasion and necessity, making them benefactors of the State, and therefore benefactors of one another; to this end he created them, not to please themselves, but to be his instruments in binding up the State.

True, he said, I had forgotten.

Observe, Glaucon, that there will be no injustice in compelling our philosophers to have a care and providence of others; we shall explain to them that in other States, men of their class are not obliged to share in the toils of politics: and this is reasonable, for they grow up at their own sweet will, and the government would rather not have them. Being self-taught, they cannot be expected to show any gratitude for a culture which they have never received. But we have brought you into the world to be rulers of the hive, kings of yourselves and of the other citizens, and have educated you far better and more perfectly than they have been educated, and you are better able to share in the double duty. Wherefore each of you, when his turn comes, must go down to the general underground abode, and get the habit of seeing in the dark. When you have acquired the habit, you will see ten thousand times better than the inhabitants of the den, and you will know what the several images are, and what they represent, because you have seen the beautiful and just and good in their truth. And thus our State which is also yours will be a reality, and not a dream only, and will be administered in a spirit unlike that of other States, in which men fight with one another about shadows only and are distracted in the struggle for power, which in their eyes is a great good. Whereas the truth is that the State in which the rulers are most reluctant to govern is always the best and most quietly governed, and the State in which they are most eager, the worst.

Quite true, he replied.

And will our pupils, when they hear this, refuse to take their turn at the toils of State, when they are allowed to spend the greater part of their time with one another in the heavenly light?

Impossible, he answered; for they are just men, and the commands which we impose upon them are just; there can be no doubt that every one of them will take office as a stern necessity, and not after the fashion of our present rulers of State.

Yes, my friend, I said; and there lies the point. You must contrive for your future rulers another and a better life than that of a ruler, and then you may have a well-ordered State; for only in the State which offers this, will they rule who are truly rich, not in silver and gold, but in virtue and wisdom, which are the true blessings of life. Whereas if they go to the administration of public affairs, poor and hungering after their own private advantage, thinking that hence they are to snatch the chief good, order there can never be; for they will be fighting about office, and the civil and domestic broils which thus arise will be the ruin of the rulers themselves and of the whole State.

Most true, he replied.

And the only life which looks down upon the life of political ambition is that of true philosophy. Do you know of any other?

Indeed, I do not, he said.

And those who govern ought not to be lovers of the task? For, if they are, there will be rival lovers, and they will fight.

No question.

Who then are those whom we shall compel to be guardians? Surely they will be the men who are wisest about affairs of State, and by whom the State is best administered, and who at the same time have other honors and another and a better life than that of politics?

521b They are the men, and I will choose them, he replied.[3]

* * *

3. Omitted is further discussion of how these philosophers are to be educated.

PLATO

The Republic, ca. 390–370 BCE

PART V

In this portion of The Republic, *Socrates works through a scheme of how the best kind of state will progressively deteriorate into four inferior kinds of state—timocracy (a state like Sparta that focuses on honor and courage), oligarchy, democracy, and tyranny—and what the corresponding individual types look like. Omitted is his account of tyranny, and also of how one type deteriorates into the next.*

As you read, consider the following questions:

- *Why do you think Socrates places democracy below timocracy and oligarchy?*

- *How might you use this analysis in a critique against those who advocate a Spartan-style (timocratic), oligarchic, or democratic government?*

SOURCE: *Plato,* The Republic, *trans. Benjamin Jowett (Oxford: Clarendon Press, 1894), with minor revisions for this edition. http://classics.mit.edu/Plato/republic.html (accessed February 1, 2015).*

[Timocracy,] being in a mean between oligarchy and the perfect State, will partly follow one and partly the other, and will also have some peculiarities. Book VIII 547d

True, he said.

In the honor given to rulers, in the abstinence of the warrior class from agriculture, handicrafts, and trade in general, in the institution of common meals, and in the attention paid to gymnastics and military training—in all these respects this State will resemble the former.

True.

But in the fear of admitting philosophers to power, because they are no longer held to be simple and earnest, but are made up of mixed elements; and in turning from them to passionate and less complex characters, who are by nature fitted for war rather than peace; and in the value set by them upon military stratagems and contrivances, and in the waging of everlasting wars—this State will be for the most part peculiar.

Yes.

Yes, I said; and men of this stamp will be covetous of money, like those who live in oligarchies; they will have a fierce secret longing after gold and silver, which they will hoard in dark places, having magazines and treasuries of their own for the deposit and concealment of them; also castles which are just nests for their eggs, and in which they will spend large sums on their wives, or on any others whom they please.

That is most true, he said.

And they are miserly because they have no means of openly acquiring the money which they prize; they will spend that which is another man's on the gratification of their desires, stealing their pleasures and running away like children from the law, their father: they have been schooled not by gentle influences but by force, for they have neglected her who is the true Muse, the companion of reason and philosophy, and have honored gymnastic more than music. Undoubtedly, he said, the form of government which you describe is a mixture of good and evil. Why, there is a mixture, I said; but one thing, and one thing only, is predominantly seen,—the spirit of contention and ambition; and these are due to the prevalence of the passionate or spirited element.

Assuredly, he said.

Such is the origin and such the character of this State, which has been described in outline only; the more perfect execution was not required, for a sketch is enough to show the type of the most perfectly just and most perfectly unjust; and to go through all the States and all the characters of men, omitting none of them, would be an interminable labor.

Very true, he replied.

* * *

550c I believe that oligarchy follows next in order.

And what manner of government do you term oligarchy?

A government resting on a valuation of property, in which the rich have power and the poor man is deprived of it.

* * *

But what are the characteristics of this form of government, and what are the defects of which we were speaking?

First of all, I said, consider the nature of the qualification. Just think what would happen if pilots were to be chosen according to their property, and a poor man were refused permission to steer, even though he were a better pilot?

You mean that they would shipwreck?

Yes; and is not this true of the government of anything?

I should imagine so.

Except a city?—or would you include a city?

Nay, he said, the case of a city is the strongest of all, inasmuch as the rule of a city is the greatest and most difficult of all.

This, then, will be the first great defect of oligarchy?

Clearly.

And here is another defect which is quite as bad.

What defect?

The inevitable division: such a State is not one, but two States, the one of poor, the other of rich men; and they are living on the same spot and always conspiring against one another.

That, surely, is at least as bad.

Another discreditable feature is, that, for a like reason, they are incapable of carrying on any war. Either they arm the multitude, and then they are more afraid of them than of the enemy; or, if they do not call them out in the hour of battle, they are oligarchs indeed, few to fight as they are few to rule. And at the same time their fondness for money makes them unwilling to pay taxes.

How discreditable!

And, as we said before, under such a constitution the same persons have too many callings—they are husbandmen, tradesmen, warriors, all in one. Does that look well?

Anything but well.

There is another evil which is, perhaps, the greatest of all, and to which this State first begins to be liable.

What evil?

A man may sell all that he has, and another may acquire his property; yet after the sale he may dwell in the city of which he is no longer a part, being neither trader, nor artisan, nor horseman, nor hoplite, but only a poor, helpless creature.

Yes, that is an evil which also first begins in this State.

The evil is certainly not prevented there; for oligarchies have both the extremes of great wealth and utter poverty.

True.

But think again: In his wealthy days, while he was spending his money, was a man of this sort a whit more good to the State for the purposes of citizenship? Or did he only seem to be a member of the ruling body, although in truth he was neither ruler nor subject, but just a spendthrift?

As you say, he seemed to be a ruler, but was only a spendthrift.

May we not say that this is the drone in the house who is like the drone in the honeycomb, and that the one is the plague of the city as the other is of the hive?

Just so, Socrates.

And God has made the flying drones, Adeimantus, all without stings, whereas of the walking drones he has made some without stings but others have dreadful stings; of the stingless class are those who in their old age end as paupers; of the stingers come all the criminal class, as they are termed.

Most true, he said.

Clearly then, whenever you see paupers in a State, somewhere in that neighborhood there are hidden away thieves, and cutpurses and robbers of temples, and all sorts of malefactors.

Clearly.

Well, I said, and in oligarchical States do you not find paupers?

Yes, he said; nearly everybody is a pauper who is not a ruler.

And may we be so bold as to affirm that there are also many criminals to be found in them, rogues who have stings, and whom the authorities are careful to restrain by force?

Certainly, we may be so bold.

The existence of such persons is to be attributed to want of education, ill-training, and an evil constitution of the State?

True.

Such, then, is the form and such are the evils of oligarchy; and there may be many other evils.

Very likely.

* * *

Next comes democracy. . . . And now what is their manner of life, and what 557b
sort of a government have they? For as the government is, such will be the man.

Clearly, he said.

In the first place, are they not free; and is not the city full of freedom and frankness—a man may say and do what he likes?

'Tis said so, he replied.

And where freedom is, the individual is clearly able to order for himself his own life as he pleases?

Clearly.

Then in this kind of State there will be the greatest variety of human natures?

There will.

This, then, seems likely to be the fairest of States, being an embroidered robe which is spangled with every sort of flower. And just as women and children think a variety of colors to be of all things most charming, so there are many men to whom this State, which is spangled with the manners and characters of mankind, will appear to be the fairest of States.

Yes.

Yes, my good Sir, and there will be no better in which to look for a government.

Why?

Because of the liberty which reigns there—they have a complete assortment of constitutions; and he who has a mind to establish a State, as we have been doing, must go to a democracy as he would to a bazaar at which they sell them, and pick out the one that suits him; then, when he has made his choice, he may found his State.

He will be sure to have patterns enough.

And there being no necessity, I said, for you to govern in this State, even if you have the capacity, or to be governed, unless you like, or go to war when the rest go to war, or to be at peace when others are at peace, unless you are so disposed—there being no necessity also, because some law forbids you to hold office or be a juror, that you should not hold office or be a juror, if you have a fancy—is not this a way of life which for the moment is supremely delightful?

For the moment, yes.

And is not their humanity to the condemned in some cases quite charming? Have you not observed how, in a democracy, many persons, although they have been sentenced to death or exile, just stay where they are and walk about the world—the gentleman parades like a hero, and nobody sees or cares?

Yes, he replied, many and many a one.

See too, I said, the forgiving spirit of democracy, and the "don't care" about trifles, and the disregard which she shows of all the fine principles which we solemnly laid down at the foundation of the city—as when we said that, except in the case of some rarely gifted nature, there never will be a good man who has not from his childhood been used to play amid things of beauty and make of them a joy and a study—how grandly does she trample all these fine notions of ours under her feet, never giving a thought to the pursuits which make a statesman, and promoting to honor any one who professes to be the people's friend.

Yes, she is of a noble spirit.

These and other kindred characteristics are proper to democracy, which is a charming form of government, full of variety and disorder, and dispensing a sort of equality to equals and unequals alike.

We know her well.

Consider now, I said, what manner of man the individual is.

* * *

If he be fortunate, and is not too much disordered in his wits, when years have elapsed, and the heyday of passion is over—supposing that he then re-admits into the city some part of the exiled virtues, and does not wholly give himself up to their successors—in that case he balances his pleasures and lives in a sort of equilibrium, putting the government of himself into the hands of the one which comes first and wins the turn; and when he has had enough of that, then into the hands of another; he despises none of them but encourages them all equally. 561b

Very true, he said.

Neither does he receive or let pass into the fortress any true word of advice; if any one says to him that some pleasures are the satisfactions of good and noble desires, and others of evil desires, and that he ought to use and honor some and chastise and master the others—whenever this is repeated to him he shakes his head and says that they are all alike, and that one is as good as another.

Yes, he said; that is the way with him.

Yes, I said, he lives from day to day indulging the appetite of the hour; and sometimes he is lapped in drink and strains of the flute; then he becomes a water-drinker, and tries to get thin; then he takes a turn at gymnastics; sometimes idling and neglecting everything, then once more living the life of a philosopher; often he is busy with politics, and starts to his feet and says and does whatever comes into his head; and, if he is emulous of any one who is a warrior, off he is in that direction, or of men of business, once more in that. His life has neither law nor order; and this distracted existence he terms joy and bliss and freedom; and so he goes on.

Yes, he replied, he is all liberty and equality.

Yes, I said; his life is motley and manifold and an epitome of the lives of many. He answers to the State which we described as fair and spangled. And many a man and many a woman will take him for their pattern, and many a constitution and many an example of manners is contained in him.

Just so.

Let him then be set over against democracy; he may truly be called the democratic man. Let that be his place, he said.[1]

* * *

---

1. Omitted is the concluding book, an extended critique of the arts.

PLATO

From *Protagoras*, ca. 390–370 BCE

The Protagoras *explores the question of whether virtue can be taught. In this passage, the sophist Protagoras tells Socrates a story to explain how the gods chose to grant skill in the art of government to all men and not just a few.*

Compare Protagoras's story to the "noble lie" or "magnificent myth" that Socrates outlines in The Republic *(p. 140). Reflect on how true or how useful either story might be.*

Protagoras's argument here supports the position of the democrats in the game. You may wish to read more of the dialogue to explore further how Socrates responds to Protagoras.

SOURCE: *Plato.* Protagoras *322–324, trans. Benjamin Jowett, with minor revisions for this edition. http://classics.mit.edu/Plato/protagoras.html (accessed February 1, 2015).*

Now man, having a share of the divine attributes, was at first the only one of the animals who had any gods, because he alone was of their kindred; and he would raise altars and images of them. He was not long in inventing articulate speech and names; and he also constructed houses and clothes and shoes and beds, and drew sustenance from the earth. Thus provided, mankind at first lived dispersed, and there were no cities. But the consequence was that they were destroyed by the wild beasts, for they were utterly weak in comparison of them, and their art was only sufficient to provide them with the means of life, and did not enable them to carry on war against the animals: food they had, but not as yet the art of government, of which the art of war is a part. After a while the desire of self-preservation gathered them into cities; but when they were gathered together, having no art of government, they harmed one another unjustly, and were again in process of dispersion and destruction. Zeus feared that the entire race would be exterminated, and so he sent Hermes to them, bearing reverence and justice to be the ordering principles of cities and the bonds of friendship and conciliation.

Hermes asked Zeus how he should impart justice and reverence among men: Should he distribute them as the arts are distributed; that is to say, to a favored few only, one skilled individual having enough of medicine or of any other art for many unskilled ones? "Shall this be the manner in which I am to distribute justice and reverence among men, or shall I give them to all?"

"To all," said Zeus; "I should like them all to have a share; for cities cannot exist, if a few only share in the virtues, as in the arts. And further, make a law by my order, that he who has no part in reverence and justice shall be put to death, for he is a plague of the state."

And this is the reason, Socrates, why the Athenians and mankind in general, when the question relates to carpentering or any other mechanical art, allow but a few to share in their deliberations; and when any one else interferes, then, as you say, they object, if he be not of the favored few; which, as I reply, is very natural. But when they meet to deliberate about political virtue, which proceeds only by way of justice and wisdom, they are patient enough of any man who speaks of them, as is also natural, because they think that every man ought to share in this sort of virtue, and that states could not exist if this were otherwise. I have explained to you, Socrates, the reason of this phenomenon.

And that you may not suppose yourself to be deceived in thinking that all men regard every man as having a share of justice or honesty and of every other political virtue, let me give you a further proof, which is this. In other cases, as you are aware, if a man says that he is a good flute-player, or skilful in any other art in which he has no skill, people either laugh at him or are angry with him, and his relations think that he is mad and go and admonish him; but when honesty is in question, or some other political virtue, even if they know that he is dishonest, yet, if the man comes publicly forward and tells the truth about his dishonesty, then, what in the other case was held by them to be good sense, they now consider to be madness. They say that all men ought to profess honesty whether they are honest or not, and that a man is out of his mind who says anything else. Their notion is, that a man must have some degree of honesty; and that if he has none at all he ought not to be in the world.

Socrates often likens the virtues to the technical arts. Note here how Protagoras distinguishes justice or honesty from flute playing and the other arts.

I have been showing that they are right in admitting every man as a counselor about this sort of virtue, as they are of opinion that every man is a partaker of it. And I will now endeavor to show further that they do not conceive this virtue to be given by nature, or to grow spontaneously, but to be a thing which may be taught; and which comes to a man by taking pains. No one would instruct, no one would rebuke, or be angry with those whose calamities they suppose to be due to nature or chance; they do not try to punish or to prevent them from being what they are; they do but pity them. Who is so foolish as to chastise or instruct the ugly, or the diminutive, or the feeble? And for this reason: because he knows that good and evil of this kind is the work of nature and of chance; whereas if a man is wanting in those good qualities which are attained by study and exercise and teaching, and has only the contrary evil qualities, other men are angry with him, and punish and reprove him. Of these evil qualities one is impiety, another injustice, and they may be described generally as the very opposite of political virtue. In such cases any man will be angry with another, and reprimand him—clearly because he thinks

Note Protagoras's belief that civilized society views punishment as rehabilitation rather than retribution. What are the implications of this belief for his position that virtue can be taught to all?

that by study and learning, the virtue in which the other is deficient may be acquired.

If you will think, Socrates, of the nature of punishment, you will see at once that in the opinion of mankind virtue may be acquired; no one punishes the evil-doer under the notion, or for the reason, that he has done wrong, only the unreasonable fury of a beast acts in that manner. But he who desires to inflict rational punishment does not retaliate for a past wrong which cannot be undone; he has regard to the future, and is desirous that the man who is punished, and he who sees him punished, may be deterred from doing wrong again. He punishes for the sake of prevention, thereby clearly implying that virtue is capable of being taught. This is the notion of all who retaliate upon others either privately or publicly. And the Athenians, too, your own citizens, like other men, punish and take vengeance on all whom they regard as evil doers; and hence, we may infer them to be of the number of those who think that virtue may be acquired and taught. Thus far, Socrates, I have shown you clearly enough, if I am not mistaken, that your countrymen are right in admitting the tinker and the cobbler to advise about politics, and also that they deem virtue to be capable of being taught and acquired.

PLUTARCH

Life of Lycurgus, ca. 75–100 CE

Plutarch (46–120 CE), a Greek historian and writer, lived in Greece after it had been conquered by the Romans. His most famous work was a series of biographies of the lives of famous Greeks and Romans, The Parallel Lives. *In this excerpt, he describes the accomplishments of Lycurgus (ca. 700 BCE–630 BCE), the legendary founder of Sparta. Plutarch, like many ancient authors, was an admirer of Sparta, and you can assume that this is an idealized picture. (Note that Plutarch lived some seven hundred years after Lycurgus!)*

This text suggests why Socrates admired Sparta more than he did Athens. As you read, consider the following questions:

- *What Spartan elements does Socrates include in his ideal state? What makes his ideal state significantly different from Sparta?*

- *What Spartan institutions and attitudes would appeal to the Solonian aristocrats in Athens? What would appeal to members of the democratic factions?*

SOURCE: *Plutarch,* The Parallel Lives, *trans. John Dryden (London: J. M. Dent, 1910), edited for this edition.*

After the creation of the thirty senators, his next task was making a new division of their lands. For there was an extreme inequality amongst them, and their state was overloaded with a multitude of indigent[1] persons, while its whole wealth had centered upon a very few. To the end, therefore, that he might expel from the state arrogance and envy, luxury, and crime, and those yet more inveterate diseases of want and superfluity, he convinced them to renounce their properties, to consent to a new division of the land, and to live all together on an equal footing; merit to be their only road to eminence, and the disgrace of evil, and credit of worthy acts, their one measure of difference between man and man.

Upon their consent to these proposals, proceeding at once to put them into execution, he divided the country of Laconia in general into thirty thousand equal shares, and the part attached to the city of Sparta into nine thousand; these he distributed among the Spartans, as he did the others to the country citizens.

* * *

Not contented with this, he resolved to make a division of their movables too, that there might be no odious[2] distinction or inequality left amongst them; but finding that it would be very dangerous to go about it openly, he took another course, and defeated their avarice by the following stratagem: he commanded that all gold and silver coin should be called in, and that only a sort of money made of iron should be current, a great weight and quantity of which was worth very little; so that to lay up twenty or thirty pounds required a pretty large chest, and, to remove it, nothing less than a yoke of oxen. With the diffusion of this money, at once a number of vices were banished from Lacedaemon; for who would rob another of such a coin?

* * *

In the next place, he outlawed all needless and superfluous arts; but here he might almost have spared his proclamation; for they of themselves would have gone after the gold and silver, the money which remained being not so proper payment for curious work; for, being of iron, it was scarcely portable, neither, if

1. Indigent: poor.

2. Odious: causing hatred.

they should take the means to export it, would it pass amongst the other Greeks, who ridiculed it. So there was now no more means of purchasing foreign goods and small wares; merchants sent no shiploads into Laconian ports . . . so that luxury, deprived little by little of that which fed and fomented it, wasted to nothing and died away of itself. For the rich had no advantage here over the poor, as their wealth and abundance had no road to come abroad by but were shut up at home doing nothing. And in this way they became excellent artists in common, necessary things; bedsteads, chairs, and tables, and such like staple utensils in a family, were admirably well made there.

* * *

The third and most masterly stroke of this great lawgiver, by which he struck a yet more effectual blow against luxury and the desire of riches, was the ordinance he made, that they should all eat in common, of the same bread and same meat, and of kinds that were specified, and should not spend their lives at home, laid on costly couches at splendid tables, delivering themselves up into the hands of their tradesmen and cooks, to fatten them in corners, like greedy brutes, and to ruin not their minds only but their very bodies which, enfeebled by indulgence and excess, would stand in need of long sleep, warm bathing, freedom from work, and, in a word, of as much care and attendance as if they were continually sick.

* * *

In order to the good education of their youth he took into consideration their very conception and birth, by regulating their marriages. For Aristotle is wrong in saying that, after he had tried all ways to reduce the women to more modesty and sobriety, he was at last forced to leave them as they were, because in the absence of their husbands—who spent the best part of their lives in the wars—their wives, whom they were obliged to leave absolute mistresses at home, took great liberties and assumed the superiority; and were treated with overmuch respect and called by the title of lady or queen. The truth is, he took in their case, also, all the care that was possible; he ordered the maidens to exercise themselves with wrestling, running, throwing the discus and casting the dart, to the end that the fruit they conceived might, in strong and healthy bodies, take firmer root and find better growth, and that they, with this greater vigor, might be the more able to undergo the pains of child-bearing.

And to the end he might take away their overgreat tenderness and fear of exposure to the air, and all acquired womanishness, he ordered that the young women should go naked in the processions, as well as the young men, and dance, too, in that condition, at certain solemn feasts, singing certain songs, whilst the young men stood around, seeing and hearing them. On these occasions they now and then made, by jests, a befitting reflection upon those who had misbehaved themselves in the wars; and again sang praises upon those who had done any gallant action, and by these means inspired the younger sort with an emulation of their glory. Those that were thus commended went away proud, elated, and gratified with their honor among the maidens; and those who were teased were as touched with it as if they had been formally reprimanded; and so much the more, because the kings and the elders, as well as the rest of the city, saw and heard all that passed. Nor was there anything shameful in this nakedness of the young women; modesty attended them, and all wantonness was excluded. It taught them simplicity and a care for good health, and gave them some taste of higher feelings, admitted as they thus were to the field of noble action and glory. Hence it was natural for them to think and speak as Gorgo, for example, the wife of Leonidas, is said to have done, when some foreign lady, as it would seem, told her that the women of Lacedaemon were the only women in the world who could rule men; "With good reason," she said, "for we are the only women who bring forth men."

* * *

In their marriages, the husband carried off his bride by a sort of force; nor were their brides ever small and of tender years, but in their full bloom and ripeness. After this, she who superintended the wedding comes and clips the hair of the bride close round her head, dresses her up in man's clothes, and leaves her upon a mattress in the dark; afterwards comes the bridegroom, in his everyday clothes, sober and composed, as having supped at the common table, and, entering privately into the room where the bride lies, unties her virgin belt, and takes her to himself; and, after staying some time together, he returns composedly to his own apartment, to sleep as usual with the other young men. And so he continues to do, spending his days, and, indeed, his nights, with them, visiting his bride in fear and shame, and with circumspection, when he thought he should not be observed she, also, on her part, using her wit to help and find favorable opportunities for their meeting, when company was out of the way. In this manner they lived a long time, insomuch that they sometimes had children by their wives before ever they saw their faces by daylight. Their interviews, being thus difficult and rare, served not only for continual exercise of their self-control, but brought them together with their bodies healthy and vigorous, and their affections fresh and lively, unsated and undulled by easy access and long continuance with each other; while their partings were always early enough to leave behind unextinguished in each of them some remaining fire of longing and mutual delight. After guarding marriage with this modesty and reserve, he was equally careful to banish empty and womanish jealousy. For this object, excluding all licentious disorders, he made it, nevertheless, honorable for men to give the use of their wives to those whom they should think fit, that so they might have children by them; ridiculing those in whose opinion such favors are so unfit for participation as to fight and shed blood and go to war about it. Lycurgus allowed a man who was advanced in years and had a young wife to recommend some virtuous and approved young man, that she might have a child by him, who might inherit the good qualities of the father, and be a son to himself. On the other side, an honest man who had love for a married woman upon account of her modesty and the well-favoredness of her children, might, without formality, beg her company of her husband, that he might raise, as it were, from this plot of good ground, worthy and well-allied children for himself.

And indeed, Lycurgus was of a persuasion that children were not so much the property of their parents as of the whole commonwealth, and, therefore, would not have his citizens begot by the first-comers, but by the best men that could be found; the laws of other nations seemed to him very absurd and inconsistent, where people would be so solicitous for their dogs and horses as to exert interest and to pay money to procure fine breeding, and yet kept their wives shut up, to be made mothers only by themselves, who might be foolish, infirm, or diseased; as if it were not apparent that children of a bad breed would prove their bad qualities first upon those who kept and were rearing them, and well-born children, in like manner, their good qualities. These regulations, founded on natural and social grounds, were certainly so far from that scandalous liberty which was afterwards charged upon their women, that they knew not what adultery meant.

* * *

Nor was it lawful, indeed, for the father himself to bring up the children after his own fancy; but as soon as they were seven years old they were to be enrolled in certain companies and classes, where they all lived under the same order and discipline, doing their exercises and taking their play together. Of these, he who showed the most conduct and courage was made captain; they had their eyes always upon him, obeyed his orders, and underwent patiently whatsoever punishment he inflicted; so that the whole course of their education was one continued exercise of a ready and perfect obedience.

* * *

After they were twelve years old, they were no longer allowed to wear any undergarments, and they had one coat to serve them a year; their bodies were hard and dry, with but little acquaintance of baths and unguents; these human indulgences they were allowed only on some few particular days in the year. They lodged together in little bands upon beds made of the rushes which grew by the banks of the river Eurotas, which they were to break off with their hands without a knife; if it were winter, they mingled some thistle-down with their rushes, which it was thought had the property of giving warmth. By the time they were come to this age there was not any of the more hopeful boys who had not a lover to bear him company.

* * *

They taught them, also, to comprehend much matter of thought in few words. . . . King Agis, when some Athenian laughed at their short swords, and said that the jugglers on the stage swallowed them with ease, answered him, "We find them long enough to reach our enemies with"; and as their swords were short and sharp, so, it seems to me, were their sayings.

* * *

Nor was their instruction in music and verse less carefully attended to than their habits of grace and good-breeding in conversation. And their very songs had a life and spirit in them that inflamed and possessed men's minds with an enthusiasm and ardor for action; the style of them was plain and without affectation; the subject always serious and moral; most usually, it was in praise of such men as had died in defense of their country, or in derision of those that had been cowards; the former they declared happy and glorified; the life of the latter they described as most miserable and abject. . . . In the words of one of their own poets:

> With the iron stern and sharp,
> Comes the playing on the harp.

For, indeed, before they engaged in battle, the king first did sacrifice to the Muses, in all likelihood to put them in mind of the manner of their education, and of the judgment that would be passed upon their actions, and thereby to animate them to the performance of exploits that should deserve a record. At such times, too, the Lacedaemonians relaxed a little the severity of their manners in favor of their young men, allowing them to curl and adorn their hair, and to have costly arms and fine clothes; and were well pleased to see them, like proud horses, neighing and pressing to the course. And, therefore, as soon as they came to be well-grown, they took a great deal of care of their hair, to have it parted and trimmed, especially against a day of battle, pursuant to a saying recorded of their lawgiver, that a large head of hair added beauty to a good face, and terror to an ugly one.

When they were in the field, their exercises were generally more moderate, their fare not so hard, nor so strict a hand held over them by their officers, so that they were the only people in the world to whom war gave repose.

* * *

He filled Lacedaemon all through with proofs and examples of good conduct; with the constant sight of which from their youth up the people would hardly fail to be gradually formed and advanced in virtue.

And this was the reason why he forbade them to travel abroad, and go about acquainting themselves with foreign rules of morality, the habits of ill-educated people, and different views of government. And so he banished from Lacedaemon all strangers who would not give a very good reason for their coming there;

not because he was afraid lest they should inform themselves of and imitate his manner of government (as Thucydides says), or learn anything to their good; but rather lest they should introduce something contrary to good manners. With strange people, strange words must be admitted; these novelties produce novelties in thought; and on these follow views and feelings whose discordant character destroys the harmony of the state. He was as careful to save his city from the infection of foreign bad habits, as men usually are to prevent the introduction of a pestilence.

* * *

When he perceived that his more important institutions had taken root in the minds of his countrymen, that custom had rendered them familiar and easy, that his commonwealth was now grown up and able to go alone, then he called an extraordinary assembly of all the people, and told them that he now thought everything reasonably well established, both for the happiness and the virtue of the state; but that there was one thing still behind, of the greatest importance, which he thought not fit to impart until he had consulted the oracle; in the meantime, he wished them to observe the laws without any alteration until his return, and then he would do as the god directed him. They all consented readily, and bade him hasten his journey; but, before he departed, he administered an oath to the two kings, the senate, and the whole commons, to maintain the established form of polity until Lycurgus should be come back.

This done, he set out for Delphi, and, having sacrificed to Apollo, asked him whether the laws he had established were good, and sufficient for a people's happiness and virtue. The oracle answered that the laws were excellent, and that the people, while it observed them, should live in the height of renown. Lycurgus took the oracle in writing, and sent it over to Sparta; and, having sacrificed the second time to Apollo, and taken leave of his friends and his son, he resolved that the Spartans should not be released from the oath they had taken, and that he would, of his own act, close his life where he was. He was now about that age in which life was still tolerable, and yet might be quitted without regret. Everything, moreover, about him was in a sufficiently prosperous condition. He therefore made an end of himself by a total abstinence from food, thinking it a statesman's duty to make his very death, if possible, an act of service to the state, and even in the end of his life to give some example of virtue and effect some useful purpose. He would, on the one hand, crown and consummate his own happiness by a death suitable to so honorable a life, and on the other hand, would secure to his countrymen the enjoyment of the advantages he had spent his life in obtaining for them, since they had solemnly sworn the maintenance of his institutions until his return. Nor was he deceived in his expectations, for the city of Lacedaemon continued the chief city of all Greece for the space of five hundred years, in strict observance of Lycurgus's laws.

PLUTARCH

Life of Cimon, ca. 70–100 CE

Cimon, born into Athenian nobility, was one of the heroes of the Persian War. Plutarch contrasts him with Themistocles, another Persian war hero, throughout this passage. Themistocles was particularly admired by the poorer Athenian citizens, those who most benefitted from the growth of the Athenian navy. The navy, built at Themistocles' urging, decisively defeated the Persians at the battle of Salamis, and then enforced the laws of the Athenian empire throughout the fifth century. As you read, consider the following questions:

- *How does Plutarch's contrast of Cimon and Themistocles suggest praise for an aristocratic way of life and criticism of a democratic way of life?*
- *How might the Solonian aristocrats see Cimon's life as an argument for maintaining inequality in the political and social life of Athens? Would Socratics find anything to admire in Cimon?*

SOURCE: *From Plutarch,* The Parallel Lives, *trans. John Dryden (London: J. M. Dent, 1910), edited for this edition.*

imon was the son of Miltiades and Hegesipyle, who was by birth a Thracia, and daughter of King Olorus.

* * *

Cimon was left an orphan very young, with his sister Elpinice, who was also young and unmarried. And at first he had but an indifferent reputation, being looked upon as disorderly in his habits, fond of drinking, and resembling his grandfather, also called Cimon, in character. . . . Stesimbrotus of Thasos, who lived near about the same time with Cimon, reports of him that he had little acquaintance either with music, or any of the other liberal studies and accomplishments, then common among the Greeks; that he had nothing whatever of the quickness and the ready speech of his countrymen in Attica that he had great nobleness and candor in his disposition, and in his character in general resembled rather a native of Sparta than of Athens; as Euripides describes Hercules:

> Is this comment on his speech a criticism or a compliment?

—Rude
And unrefined, for great things well endued. . . .

They accused him, in his younger years, of cohabiting with his own sister Elpinice. . . . All the other points of Cimon's character were noble and good. He was as daring as Miltiades, and not inferior to Themistocles in judgment, and was incomparably more just and honest than either of them. Fully their equal in all military virtues, in the ordinary duties of a citizen at home he was immeasurably their superior. And this, too, when he was very young, his years not yet strengthened by any experience.

For when Themistocles, upon the Persian invasion, advised the Athenians to forsake their city and their country, and to carry all their arms on shipboard and fight the enemy by sea, in the straits of Salamis;[1] when all the people stood amazed at the confidence and rashness of this advice, Cimon was seen, the first of all men, passing with a cheerful countenance through the Ceramicus, on his way with his companions to the citadel, carrying a bridle in his hand to offer to the goddess, intimating that there was no more need of horsemen now, but of mariners. There, after he had paid his devotions to the goddess, and offered up the bridle, he took down one of the shields that hung upon the walls of the temple, and went down to the port; by this example giving confidence to many of the citizens.

He was also of a fairly handsome person, according to the poet Ion, tall and large, and let his thick and curly hair grow long. After he had acquitted himself gallantly in this battle of Salamis, he obtained great repute among the Athenians, and was regarded with affection, as well as admiration. He had many who followed after him, and bade him aspire to actions not less famous than his father's battle of Marathon. And when he came forward in political life, the people welcomed him gladly, being now weary of Themistocles; in opposition to whom, and because of the frankness and easiness of his temper, which was agreeable to every one, they advanced Cimon to the highest employments in the government. The man that contributed most to his promotion was Aristides, who early discerned in his character his natural capacity, and purposely raised him, that he might be a counterpoise to the craft and boldness of Themistocles. After the Persians had been driven out of Greece, Cimon was sent out as an admiral, when the Athenians had not yet attained their dominion by sea, but still followed Pausanias and the Spartans; and his fellow-citizens under his command were highly distinguished, both for the excellence of their discipline, and for their extraordinary zeal and readiness.[2] And further, perceiving that Pausanias was carrying on secret communications with the barbarians, and writing letters to the King of Persia to betray Greece, and

1. This refers to the decision by the Athenians to transfer the women, children, and flocks to Troezen when Xerxes attacked the city in 480 BCE (see the Historical Background section, pp. 30–31).

2. For more information on this period, see "Between the Persian and Peloponnesian Wars" in the Historical Background section, pp. 31–35.

puffed up with authority and success, was treating the allies haughtily, and committing many wanton injustices, Cimon, taking this advantage, by acts of kindness to those who were suffering wrong, and by his general humane bearing, robbed him of the command of the Greeks, before he was aware, not by arms, but by his mere language and character.

* * *

Ion relates that when he was a young man, and recently come from Chios to Athens, he chanced to sup with Cimon at Laomedon's house. After supper, when they had, according to custom, poured out wine to the honor of the gods, Cimon was desired by the company to give them a song, which he did with sufficient success, and received the commendations of the company, who remarked on his superiority to Themistocles, who, on a like occasion, had declared he had never learnt to sing, nor to play, and only knew how to make a city rich and powerful. After talking of things incident to such entertainments, they entered upon the particulars of the several actions for which Cimon had been famous. And when they were mentioning the most signal, he told them they had omitted one, upon which he valued himself most.

He gave this account of it. When the allies had taken a great number of the barbarians prisoners in Sestos and Byzantium, they gave him the preference to divide the booty; he accordingly put the prisoners in one lot, and the spoils of their rich attire and jewels in the other. This the allies complained of as an unequal division; but he gave them their choice to take which lot they would, for that the Athenians should be content with that which they refused. Herophytus of Samos advised them to take the ornaments for their share, and leave the slaves to the Athenians; and Cimon went away, and was much laughed at for his ridiculous division. For the allies carried away the golden bracelets, and armlets, and collars, and purple robes, and the Athenians had only the naked bodies of the captives, which they could make no advantage of, being unused to labor. But a little while after, the friends and kinsmen of the prisoners coming from Lydia and Phrygia, redeemed everyone his relations at a high ransom; so that by this means Cimon got so much treasure that he maintained his whole fleet with the money for four months; and yet there was some left to lay up in the treasury at Athens.

Cimon now grew rich, and what he gained from the barbarians with honor, he spent yet more honorably upon the citizens. For he pulled down all the enclosures of his gardens and grounds, that strangers, and the needy of his fellow-citizens, might gather of his fruits freely. At home he kept a table, plain, but sufficient for a considerable number; to which any poor townsman had free access, and so might support himself without labor, with his whole time left free for public duties. (Aristotle states, however, that this reception did not extend to all the Athenians, but only to his own fellow-townsmen, the Laciadae.) Besides this, he always went attended by two or three young companions, very well clad; and if he met with an elderly citizen in a poor habit, one of these would change clothes with the decayed citizen, which was looked upon as very nobly done. He enjoined them, likewise, to carry a considerable quantity of coin about them, which they were to convey silently into the hands of the better class of poor men, as they stood by them in the market-place.

* * *

Gorgias the Leontine gives him this character, that he got riches that he might use them, and used them that he might get honor by them. And Critias, one of the thirty tyrants, makes it, in his elegies, his wish to have

> The Scopads' wealth, and Cimon's nobleness,
> And King Agesilaus's success.

* * *

Cimon's generosity outdid all the old Athenian hospitality and good-nature. For though it is the city's just boast that their forefathers taught the rest of Greece to sow grain, and how to use springs of water, and to kindle fire, yet Cimon, by keeping open house for his fellow-citizens, and giving travelers liberty to eat the fruits which the several seasons produced in his land, seemed to restore to the world that community of goods, which mythology says existed in the reign of Saturn.[3]

Those who object to him, that he did this to be popular and gain the applause of the vulgar, are confuted by the constant tenor of the rest of his actions, which all tended to uphold the interests of the nobility and the Spartan policy, of which he gave instances, when together with Aristides he opposed Themistocles, who was advancing the authority of the people beyond its just limits, and resisted Ephialtes, who, to please the multitude, was for abolishing the jurisdiction of the court of Areopagus.[4] And when all of this time, except Aristides and Ephialtes, enriched themselves out of the public money, he still kept his hands clean and untainted, and to his last day never acted or spoke for his own private gain or emolument. They tell us that Rhoesaces, a Persian, who had traitorously revolted from the king his master, fled to Athens, and there, being harassed by sycophants, who were still accusing him to the people, he applied himself to Cimon for redress, and, to gain his favor, laid down in his doorway two cups, the one full of gold and the other of silver coin. Cimon smiled and asked him whether he wished to have Cimon's hired service or his friendship. He replied, his friendship. "If so," said he, "take away these pieces, for, being your friend, when I shall have occasion for them, I will send and ask for them."

* * *

---

3. The "age of Saturn" was another name for the "Golden Age," a kind of paradise.

4. For more information, see "Pericles" in the Historical Background section, pp. 33–35.

In his public life after this he continued, whilst at home, to control and restrain the common people, who would have trampled upon the nobility and drawn all the power and sovereignty to themselves. But when he afterwards was sent out to war, the multitude broke loose, as it were, and overthrew all the ancient laws and customs they had hitherto observed, and, chiefly at the instigation of Ephialtes, withdrew the jurisdiction of almost all causes from the Areopagus; so that all jurisdiction now being transferred to them, the government was reduced to a perfect democracy, and this by the help of Pericles, who was already powerful, and had pronounced in favor of the common people. Cimon, when he returned, seeing the authority of this great council so upset, was exceedingly troubled, and endeavored to remedy these disorders by bringing the courts of law to their former state, and restoring the old aristocracy of the time of Cleisthenes. This the others declaimed against with all the vehemence possible, and began to revive those stories concerning him and his sister, and cried out against him as the partisan of the Spartans. To these calumnies the famous verses of Eupolis upon Cimon refer:

> He was as good as others that one sees,
> But he was fond of drinking and of ease;
> And would at nights to Sparta often roam,
> Leaving his sister desolate at home.

But if, though slothful and a drunkard, he could capture so many towns and gain so many victories, certainly if he had been sober and minded his business, there had been no Grecian commander, either before or after him, that could have surpassed him for exploits of war. He was, indeed, a favorer of the Spartans, even from his youth, and he gave the names of Lacedaemonius and Eleus to two sons.

* * *

XENOPHON

The Economist, ca. 400–350 BCE

Xenophon (ca. 430 BCE–354 BCE) was, like Plato, a follower of Socrates and a prolific author. More a man of action than Plato, he wrote a memorable account (the Anabasis*) of his service as a mercenary in Cyrus the Younger's failed attempt to gain the Persian throne. He also wrote Socratic dialogues, all of a more practical nature than Plato's philosophical accounts of Socrates. In this work, Ischomachus, a type of Solonian aristocrat, tells Socrates how he manages his household and estate.*

In doing so, he tells us not just what it means to be a good estate manager, but also what it means to be a good person.

As you read, consider the following questions:

- *What values are most important to Ischomachus?*
- *How might these values express themselves in governing a state?*
- *How might he argue that men like himself would best govern Athens?*

SOURCE: *From* Oeconomicus, *trans. E. C. Merchant (Cambridge, MA: Harvard University Press; London: W. Heinemann, 1959), edited for this edition.*

[Ischomachus tells Socrates how he responds to his wife's realization that she has not yet learned how to put the family stores in order.]

. . . My dear, there is nothing so convenient or so good for human beings as order. Thus, a chorus is a combination of human beings; but when the members of it do as they choose, it becomes mere confusion, and there is no pleasure in watching it; but when they act and chant in an orderly fashion, then those same men at once seem worth seeing and worth hearing. Again, my dear, an army in disorder is a confused mass, an easy prey to enemies, a disgusting sight to friends and utterly useless,—donkey, trooper, carrier, light-armed, horseman, chariot, huddled together. For how are they to march in such a plight, when they hamper one another, some walking while others run, some running while others halt, chariot colliding with horseman, donkey with chariot, carrier with trooper? If there is fighting to be done, how can they fight in such a state? . . . But an army in orderly array is a noble sight to friends, and an unwelcome spectacle to the enemy. What friend would not rejoice as he watches a strong body of troopers marching in order, would not admire cavalry riding in squadrons? And what enemy would not fear troopers, horsemen, light-armed, archers, slingers disposed in serried ranks and following their officers in orderly fashion? Nay, even on the march where order is kept, though they number tens of thousands, all move steadily forward as one man; for the line behind is continually filling up the gap. . . . If I want a type of disorder, I think of a farmer who has stored barley, wheat, and pulse in one bin; and then when he wants a cake or a bread or a pudding, must pick out the grain instead of finding it separate and ready for use.

And so, my dear, if you do not want this confusion, and wish to know exactly how to manage our goods, and to find with ease whatever is wanted, and to satisfy me by giving me anything I ask for, let us choose the place that each portion should occupy; and, having put the things in their place, let us instruct the maid to take them from it and put them back again. Thus we shall know what is safe and sound and what is not; for the place itself will miss whatever is not in it, and a glance will reveal anything that wants attention.

* * *

Once I had an opportunity of looking over the great Phoenician merchantman, Socrates, and I thought I had never seen tackle so excellently and accurately arranged. For I never saw so many bits of stuff packed away separately in so small a receptacle. . . . I found that the steersman's servant, who is called the mate, knows each particular section so exactly, that he can tell even when away where everything is kept and how much there is of it, just as well as a man who knows how to spell can tell how many letters there are in Socrates and in what order they come. Now I saw this man in his spare time inspecting all the stores that are wanted, as a matter of course, in the ship. I was surprised to see him looking over them, and asked what he was doing. Sir, he answered, I am looking to see how the ship's tackle is stored, in case of accident, or whether anything is missing or mixed up with other stuff. For when God sends a storm at sea, there's no time to search about for what you want or to serve it out if it's in a muddle. For God threatens and punishes careless fellows, and you're lucky if he merely refrains from destroying the innocent; and if he saves you when you do your work well, you have much cause to thank heaven.

Now after seeing the ship's tackle in such perfect order, I told my wife: Considering that folk aboard a merchant vessel, even though it be a little one, find room for things and keep order, though tossed violently to and fro, and find what they want to get, though terror-stricken, it would be downright carelessness on our part if we, who have large storerooms in our house to keep everything separate and whose house rests on solid ground, fail to find a good and handy place for everything. Would it not be sheer stupidity on our part?

How good it is to keep one's stock of utensils in order, and how easy to find a suitable place in a house to put each set in, I have already said. And what a beautiful sight is afforded by boots of all sorts and conditions ranged in rows! How beautiful it is to see cloaks of all sorts and conditions kept separate, or blankets, or brazen vessels, or table furniture! Yes, no serious man will smile when I claim that there is beauty in the order even of pots and pans set out in neat array, however much it may move the laughter of a wit. There is nothing, in short, that does not gain in beauty when set out in order. For each set looks like a troop of utensils, and the space between the sets is beautiful to see, when each set is kept clear of it, just as a troop of dancers about the altar is a beautiful spectacle in itself, and even the free space looks beautiful and unencumbered.

* * *

In appointing the housekeeper, we chose the woman whom on consideration we judged to be the most temperate in eating and wine drinking and sleeping and the most modest with men, the one, too, who seemed to have the best memory, to be most careful not to offend us by neglecting her duties, and to think most how she could earn some reward by obliging us. We also taught her to be loyal to us by making her a partner in all our joys and calling on her to share our troubles.

Moreover, we trained her to be eager for the improvement of our estate, by making her familiar with it and by allowing her to share in our success. And further, we put justice into her, by giving more honor to the just than to the unjust, and by showing her that the just live in greater wealth and freedom than the unjust; and we placed her in that position of superiority.

When all this was done, Socrates, I told my wife that all these measures were futile, unless she saw to it herself that our arrangement was strictly adhered to in every detail. I explained that in well-ordered cities the citizens are not satisfied with passing good laws: they go further, and choose guardians of the laws, who act as overseers, commending the law-abiding and punishing law-breakers. So I charged my wife to consider herself guardian of the laws to our household. And just as the commander of a garrison inspects his guards, so must she inspect the utensils whenever she thought it well to do so; as the Council scrutinizes the cavalry and the horses, so she was to make sure that everything was in good condition: like a queen, she must reward the worthy with praise and honor, so far as in her lay, and not spare rebuke and punishment when they were called for.

* * *

[Ischomachus praises his wife's virtues.]

Well, one day, Socrates, I noticed that her face was made up: she had rubbed in white lead in order to look even whiter than she is, and alkanet[1] juice to heighten the rosy color of her cheeks; and she was wearing boots with thick soles to increase her height. So I said to her, Tell me, my dear, how should I appear more worthy of your love as a partner in our goods: by disclosing to you our belongings just as they are, without boasting of imaginary possessions or concealing any part of what we have, or by trying to trick you with an exaggerated account, showing you bad money and gilt necklaces and describing clothes that will fade as real purple?

Hush! she broke in immediately, pray don't be like that—I could not love you with all my heart if you were like that!

* * *

How then should I seem more worthy of your love in this partnership of the body—by striving to have my body hale and strong when I present it to you, and so literally to be of a good countenance in your sight, or by smearing my cheeks with red lead and painting myself under the eyes with rouge before I show myself to you and clasp you in my arms, cheating you and offering to your eyes and hands red lead instead of my real flesh?

Oh, she cried, I would sooner touch you than red lead, would sooner see your own color than rouge, would sooner see your eyes bright than smeared with grease.

---

1. A root that produces a red dye. Lead was often used as a cosmetic in the ancient world.

Then please assume, my dear, that I do not prefer white paint and dye of alkanet to your real color; but just as the gods have made horses to delight in horses, cattle in cattle, sheep in sheep, so human beings find the human body undisguised most delightful. Tricks like these may serve to gull outsiders, but people who live together are bound to be found out, if they try to deceive one another. For they are found out while they are dressing in the morning; they perspire and are lost; a tear convicts them; the bath reveals them as they are!

And, pray, what did she say to that? I asked.

Nothing, he said, only she gave up such practices from that day forward, and tried to let me see her undisguised and as she should be. Still, she did ask whether I could advise her on one point: how she might make herself really beautiful, instead of merely seeming to be so. And this was my advice, Socrates: Don't sit about forever like a slave, but try, God helping you, to behave as a mistress: stand before the loom and be ready to instruct those who know less than you, and to learn from those who know more: look after the baking-maid: stand by the housekeeper when she is serving out stores: go round and see whether everything is in its place. For I thought that would give her a walk as well as occupation. I also said it was excellent exercise to mix flour and knead dough; and to shake and fold cloaks and bedclothes; such exercise would give her a better appetite, improve her health, and add natural color to her cheeks. . . . But wives who sit about like fine ladies, expose themselves to comparison with painted and fraudulent hussies.

* * *

At this point I said, Ischomachus, I think your account of your wife's occupations is sufficient for the present—and very creditable it is to both of you. But now tell me of your own: thus you will have the satisfaction of stating the reasons why you are so highly respected, and I shall be much beholden to you for a complete account of a gentleman's[2] occupations, and if my understanding serves, for a thorough knowledge of them.

Well then, Socrates, answered Ischomachus, . . . I will tell you what principles I try my best to follow consistently in life. For I seem to realize that, while the gods have made it impossible for men to prosper without knowing and attending to the things they ought to do, to some of the wise and careful they grant prosperity, and to some deny it; and therefore I begin by worshipping the gods, and try to conduct myself in such a way that I may have health and strength in answer to my prayers, the respect of my fellow-citizens, the affection of my friends, safety with honor in war, and wealth increased by honest means.

---

2. "Gentleman" here translates a pair of Greek adjectives, *kalos* and *agathos*, which were traditionally paired to describe an honorable man. "Handsome and good" would be a more literal translation, but would not convey the aristocratic ideal this phrase implies.

What, Ischomachus, I asked on hearing that, do you really want to be rich and to have much, along with much trouble to take care of it?

The answer to your questions, said he, is, Yes, I do indeed. For I think it pleasant to honor the gods without counting the cost, Socrates, help friends in need, and look to it that the city lacks no adornment that my means can supply.

Truly noble aspirations, Ischomachus, I cried, and worthy of a man of means, no doubt! Seeing that there are many who cannot live without help from others, and many are content if they can get enough for their own needs, surely those who can maintain their own estate and yet have enough left to adorn the city and relieve their friends may well be thought high and mighty men. However, I added, praise of such men is a commonplace among us. Please return to your first statement, Ischomachus, and tell me how you take care of your health and your strength, how you make it possible to come through war with safety and honor. I shall be content to hear about your money-making afterwards.

Well, Socrates, replied Ischomachus, all these things hang together, so far as I can see. For if a man has plenty to eat, and works off the effects properly, I take it that he both insures his health and adds to his strength. By training himself in the arts of war he is more qualified to save himself honorably, and by due diligence and avoidance of loose habits, he is more likely to increase his estate.

So far, Ischomachus, I follow you, I answered. You mean that by working after meals, by diligence and by training, a man is more apt to obtain the good things of life. But now I should like you to give me details. By what kind of work do you endeavor to keep your health and strength? How do you train yourself in the arts of war? What diligence do you use to have a surplus from which to help friends and strengthen the city?

Well now, Socrates, replied Ischomachus, I rise from my bed at an hour when, if I want to call on anyone, I am sure to find him still at home. If I have any business to do in town, I make it an opportunity for getting a walk. If there is nothing pressing to be done in town, my servant leads my horse to the farm, and I make my walk by going to it on foot, with more benefit, perhaps, Socrates, than if I took a turn in the arcade. When I reach the farm, I may find planting, clearing, sowing, or harvesting in progress. I superintend all the details of the work, and make any improvements in method that I can suggest. After this, I usually mount my horse and go through exercises, imitating as closely as I can the exercises needed in warfare. . . . After I have finished, the servant gives the horse a roll and leads him home, bringing with him from the farm anything we happen to want in the city. I divide the return home between walking and running. Arrived, I clean myself with a strigil,[3] and then I have lunch, Socrates, eating just enough to get through the day neither empty-bellied nor too full.

Upon my word, Ischomachus, cried I, I am delighted with your activities. For you have methods for securing health and strength, exercises for war and specifics

3. A bronze tool for scraping dirt and sweat off the body after a workout in the gymnasium.

for getting rich, and you use them all at the same time! That does seem to me admirable! And in fact you afford convincing proofs that your method in pursuing each of these objects is sound. For we see you generally in the enjoyment of health and strength, thanks to the gods, and we know that you are considered one of our best horsemen and wealthiest citizens.

And what comes of these activities, Socrates? Not, as you perhaps expected to hear, that I am generally dubbed a gentleman, but that I am persistently slandered.[4]

Ah, said I, but I was meaning to ask you, Ischomachus, whether you include in your system ability to conduct a prosecution and defense, in case you have to appear in the courts?

Why, Socrates, he answered, do you not see that this is just what I am constantly practicing—showing my slanderers that I wrong no man and do all the good I can to many? And do you not think that I practice myself in accusing, by taking careful note of certain persons who are doing wrong to many individuals and to the state, and are doing no good to anyone?

But tell me one thing more, Ischomachus, I said; do you also practice the art of expounding these matters?

Why, Socrates, he replied, I assiduously practice the art of speaking. For I get one of the servants to act as prosecutor or defendant, and try to confute him; or I praise or blame someone before his friends; or I act as peace-maker between some of my acquaintances by trying to show them that it is to their interest to be friends rather than enemies. I assist at a court-martial and censure a soldier, or take turns in defending a man who is unjustly blamed, or in accusing one who is unjustly honored. We often sit in counsel and speak in support of the course we want to adopt and against the course we want to avoid. I have often been singled out before now, Socrates, and condemned to suffer punishment or pay damages.

By whom, Ischomachus? I asked; I am in the dark about that!

By my wife, was his answer.

And, pray, how do you plead? said I.

Pretty well, when it is to my interest to speak the truth. But when lying is called for, Socrates, I can't make the worse cause appear the better—oh no, not at all.

Perhaps, Ischomachus, I commented, you can't make the falsehood into the truth!

But perhaps I am keeping you, Ischomachus, I continued . . . For I daresay there are many things claiming your attention now; but, as you have made an appointment with those strangers, you are determined not to break it.

---

4. Ischomaschus is referring to a practice in which unscrupulous people would sue rich men in hopes of gaining a settlement out of court. The ensuing discussion on public speaking recommends role-playing with one's servants and wife, but the undertone is serious. A citizen who held an important public office would be examined and held accountable at the end of his year in office.

But I assure you, Socrates, I am not neglecting the matters you refer to, either; for I keep bailiffs[5] on my farms.

And when you want a bailiff, Ischomachus, do you look out for a man qualified for such a post . . . or do you train your bailiffs yourself?

Of course I try to train them myself, Socrates. For the man has to be capable of taking charge in my absence; so why need he know anything but what I know myself? For if I am fit to manage the farm, I presume I can teach another man what I know myself.

Then the first requirement will be that he should be loyal to you and yours, if he is to represent you in your absence. For if a steward is not loyal, what is the good of any knowledge he may possess?

None, of course; but I may tell you, loyalty to me and to mine is the first lesson I try to teach.

And how, in heaven's name, do you teach your man to be loyal to you and yours?

By rewarding him, of course, whenever the gods bestow some good thing on us in abundance.

You mean, then, that those who enjoy a share of your good things are loyal to you and want you to prosper?

Yes, Socrates, I find that is the best instrument for producing loyalty.

But, now, if he is loyal to you, Ischomachus, will that be enough to make him a competent bailiff?

* * *

Well, when I want to make bailiffs . . . I teach them also to be careful.

Pray how do you do that? I was under the impression that carefulness is a virtue that can't possibly he taught.

True, Socrates, it isn't possible to teach everyone you come across to be careful.

Very well; what sort of men can be taught? Point these out to me, at all events.

In the first place, Socrates, you can't make careful men of hard drinkers; for drink makes them forget everything they ought to do. . . . sluggards must be included; for you can't do your own business when you are asleep, nor make others do theirs. . . . I should add that in my opinion a man who falls desperately in love is incapable of giving more attention to anything than he gives to the object of his passion. For it isn't easy to find hope or occupation more delightful than devotion to the darling! Aye, and when the thing to be done presses, no harder punishment can easily be thought of than the prevention of intercourse with the beloved! Therefore I shrink from attempting to make a manager of that sort of man too.

And what about the men who have a passion for money? Are they also incapable of being trained to take charge of the work of a farm?

---

5. A bailiff was a slave in charge of running a farm.

Not at all; of course not. In fact, they very easily qualify for the work. It is merely necessary to point out to them that diligence is profitable.

And assuming that the others are free from the faults that you condemn and are covetous of gain in a moderate degree, how do you teach them to be careful in the affairs you want them to superintend?

By a very simple plan, Socrates. Whenever I notice that they are careful, I commend them and try to show them honor; but when they appear careless, I try to say and do the sort of things that will sting them.

Turn now, Ischomachus, from the subject of the men in training for the occupation, and tell me about the system: is it possible for anyone to make others careful if he is careless himself?

Of course not: an unmusical person could as soon teach music. For it is hard to learn to do a thing well when the teacher prompts you badly; and when a master prompts a servant to be careless, it is difficult for the man to become a good servant. To put it shortly, I don't think I have discovered a bad master with good servants: I have, however, come across a good master with bad servants—but they suffered for it! If you want to make men fit to take charge, you must supervise their work and examine it, and be ready to reward work well carried through, and not shrink from punishing carelessness as it deserves.

* * *

When you have impressed on a man, I resumed, the necessity of careful attention to the duties you assign to him, will he then be competent to act as bailiff, or must he learn something besides, if he is to be efficient?

Of course, answered Ischomachus, he has still to understand what he has to do, and when and how to do it. Otherwise how could a bailiff be of more use than a doctor who takes care to visit a patient early and late, but has no notion of the right way to treat his illness?

Well, but suppose he has learned how farm-work is to be done, will he want something more yet, or will your man now be a perfect bailiff?

I think he must learn to rule the laborers.

And do you train your bailiffs to be competent to rule too?

Yes, I try, anyhow.

And pray tell me how you train them to be rulers of men.

By a childishly easy method, Socrates. I daresay you'll laugh if I tell you.

Oh, but it is certainly not a laughing matter, Ischomachus. For anyone who can make men fit to rule others can also teach them to be masters of others; and if he can make them fit to be masters, he can make them fit to be kings. So anyone who can do that seems to me to deserve high praise rather than laughter.

Well now, Socrates, other creatures learn obedience in two ways—by being punished when they try to disobey, and by being rewarded when they are eager to serve you. Colts, for example, learn to obey the horsebreaker by getting something they like when they are obedient, and suffering inconvenience when they are disobedient, until they carry out the horsebreaker's intentions. Puppies, again, are much inferior to men in intelligence and power of expression; and yet they learn to run in circles and turn somersaults and do many other tricks in the same way; for when they obey they get something that they want, and when they are careless, they are punished. And men can be made more obedient by word of mouth merely, by being shown that it is good for them to obey. But in dealing with slaves the training thought suitable for wild animals is also a very effective way of teaching obedience; for you will do much with them by filling their bellies with the food they hanker after. Those of an ambitious disposition are also spurred on by praise, some natures being hungry for praise as others for meat and drink. Now these are precisely the things that I do myself with a view to making men more obedient; but they are not the only lessons I give to those whom I want to appoint my bailiffs. I have other ways of helping them on. For the clothes that I must provide for my workpeople and the shoes are not all alike. Some are better than others, some worse, in order that I may reward the better servant with the superior articles, and give the inferior things to the less deserving. For I think it is very disheartening to good servants, Socrates, when they see that they do all the work, and others who are not willing to work hard and run risks when need be, get the same as they. For my part, then, I don't choose to put the deserving on a level with the worthless, and when I know that my bailiffs have distributed the best things to the most deserving, I commend them; and if I see that flattery or any other futile service wins special favor, I don't overlook it, but reprove the bailiff, and try to show him, Socrates, that such favoritism is not even in his own interest.

Notice that Ischomachus recognizes that different motivations work for different people. Some just want their bodily needs met, but more ambitious people love praise, or honors.

Now, Ischomachus, said I, when you find your man so competent to rule that he can make them obedient, do you think him a perfect bailiff, or does he want anything else, even with the qualifications you have mentioned?

Of course, Socrates, returned Ischomachus, he must be honest and not touch his master's property. For if the man who handles the crops dares to make away with them, and doesn't leave enough to give a profit on the undertaking, what good can come of farming under his management?

Then do you take it on yourself to teach this kind of justice too?

Certainly: I don't find, however, that all readily pay heed to this lesson. Nevertheless I guide the servants into the path of justice with the aid of maxims drawn from the laws of Draco and Solon. For it seems to me that these famous men enacted many of their laws with an eye on this particular kind of justice. For it is written: thieves shall be fined for their thefts, and anyone guilty of attempt shall be imprisoned if taken in the act, and put to death. The object of these enactments was clearly to make covetousness unprofitable to the offender. By applying some of these clauses and other enactments found in the Persian king's code, I try to make my servants upright in the matters that pass through their hands. For while those laws only penalize the wrongdoer, the king's code not only punishes the guilty, but also benefits the upright. Thus, seeing that the honest grow richer than the dishonest, many, despite their love of lucre, are careful to remain free from dishonesty. And if I find any attempting to persist in dishonesty, although they are well treated, I regard them as incorrigibly greedy, and have nothing more to do with them. On the other hand, if I discover that a man is inclined to be honest not only because he gains by his honesty, but also from a desire to win my approbation, I treat him like a free man by making him rich; and not only so, but I honor him as a gentleman. For I think, Socrates, that the difference between ambition and greed consists in this, that for the sake of praise and honor the ambitious are willing to work properly, to take risks and refrain from dishonest gain.[6]

* * *

And now I asked, How is it then, Ischomachus, if the operations of husbandry are so easy to learn and all alike know what must be done, that all have not the same fortune? How is it that some farmers live in abundance and have more than they want, while others cannot get the bare necessaries of life, and even run into debt?

Oh, I will tell you, Socrates. It is not knowledge nor want of knowledge on the part of farmers that causes one to thrive while another is needy. You won't hear a story like this running about: The estate has gone to ruin because the sower sowed unevenly, or because he didn't plant the rows straight, or because someone, not knowing the right soil for vines, planted them in barren ground, or because someone didn't know that it is well to prepare the fallow for sowing, or because someone didn't know that it is well to manure the land. No, you are much more likely to hear it said: The man gets no grain from his field because he takes no trouble to see that it is sown or manured. Or, the man has got no wine, for he takes no trouble to plant vines or to make his old stock bear. . . . It is not the farmers reputed to have made some clever discovery in agriculture who differ in fortune from others: it is things of this sort that make all the difference, Socrates.

This is true of generals also: there are some branches of strategy in which one is better or worse than another, not because he differs in intelligence, but in point of carefulness, undoubtedly. For the things that all generals know, and most privates, are done by some commanders and left undone by others. For example, they all know that when marching through an enemy's country, the right way is to march in the formation in which they will fight best, if need be. Well, knowing this, some observe the rule, others break it. All know that it is right to post sentries

6. Omitted is Ischomachus's instruction to Socrates on how to farm, in which he argues that agriculture is unlike the other arts because the land itself will teach you if you have the patience to listen.

by day and night before the camp; but this too is a duty that some attend to, while others neglect it.

* * *

So, too, everyone will say that in agriculture there is nothing so good as manure, and their eyes tell them that nature produces it. All know exactly how it is produced, and it is easy to get any amount of it; and yet, while some take care to have it collected, others care nothing about it. Yet the rain is sent from heaven, and all the hollows become pools of water, and the earth yields herbage of every kind which must be cleared off the ground by the sower before sowing; and the rubbish he removes has but to be thrown into water, and time of itself will make what the soil likes. For every kind of vegetation, every kind of soil in stagnant water turns into manure.

And again, all the ways of treating the soil when it is too wet for sowing or too salty for planting are familiar to all men—how the land is drained by ditches, how the salt is corrected by being mixed with saltless substances, liquid or dry. Yet these matters, again, do not always receive attention. Suppose a man to be wholly ignorant as to what the land can produce, and to be unable to see crop or tree on it, or to hear from anyone the truth about it, yet is it not far easier for any man to test a parcel of land than to test a horse or to test a human being? For the land never plays tricks, but reveals frankly and truthfully what she can and what she cannot do. I think that just because she conceals nothing from our knowledge and understanding, the land is the surest tester of good and bad men. For the slothful cannot plead ignorance, as in other arts: land, as all men know, responds to good treatment. Husbandry is the clear accuser of the recreant[7] soul.

* * *

Farming, he added, may result in profit or in loss; it makes a great difference to the result, even when many laborers are employed, whether the farmer takes care that the men are working during the working hours or is careless about it. For one man in ten by working all the time may easily make a difference, and another by knocking off before the time; and, of course, if the men are allowed to be slack all the day long, the decrease in the work done may easily amount to one half of the whole. Just as two travelers on the road, both young and in good health, will differ so much in pace that one will cover two hundred furlongs to the other's hundred, because the one does what he set out to do, by going ahead, while the other is all for ease, now resting by a fountain or in the shade, now gazing at the view, now wooing the soft breeze; so in farm work there is a vast difference in effectiveness between the men who do the job they are put on to do and those who, instead of doing it, invent excuses for not working and are allowed to be slack.

* * *

7. Recreant: cowardly or disloyal.

These, then, are the evils that crush estates far more than sheer lack of knowledge.

* * *

Ischomachus has emphasized that running a successful farm, like other forms of leadership, requires diligence and self-discipline. In the conclusion, he acknowledges that natural talent is also required to be a successful leader of men.

But I am pondering over the skill with which you have presented the whole argument in support of your proposition, Ischomachus. For you stated that husbandry is the easiest of all arts to learn, and after hearing all that you have said, I am quite convinced that this is so.

Of course it is, cried Ischomachus; but I grant you, Socrates, that in respect of aptitude for command, which is common to all forms of business alike—agriculture, politics, estate-management, warfare—in that respect the intelligence shown by different classes of men varies greatly. For example, on a man-of-war, when the ship is on the high seas and the rowers must toil all day to reach port, some boatswains can say and do the right thing to sharpen the men's spirits and make them work with a will, while others are so unintelligent that it takes them more than twice the time to finish the same voyage. . . . Generals, too, differ from one another in this respect. For some make their men unwilling to work and to take risks, disinclined and unwilling to obey, except under compulsion, and actually proud of defying their commander: aye, and they cause them to have no sense of dishonor when something disgraceful occurs. Contrast the genius, the brave and scientific leader: let him take over the command of these same troops, or of others if you like. What effect has he on them? They are ashamed to do a disgraceful act, think it better to obey, and take a pride in obedience, working cheerfully, every man and all together, when it is necessary to work. Just as a love of work may spring up in the mind of a private soldier here and there, so a whole army under the influence of a good leader is inspired with love of work and ambition to distinguish itself under the commander's eye. Let this be the feeling of the rank and file for their commander; and I tell you, he is the strong leader, he, and not the sturdiest soldier, not the best with bow and javelin, not the man who rides the best horse and is foremost in facing danger, not the ideal of knight, but he who can make his soldiers feel that they are bound to follow him through fire and in any adventure.

* * *

So too in private industries, the man in authority—bailiff or manager—who can make the workers keen, industrious, and persevering—he is the man who gives a lift to the business and swells the surplus. But, Socrates, if the appearance of the master in the field, of the man who has the fullest power to punish the bad and reward the strenuous workmen, makes no striking impression on the men at work, I for one cannot envy him. But if at sight of him they bestir themselves, and a spirit of determination and rivalry and eagerness to excel falls on every workman, then I should say: this man has a touch of the kingly nature in him. And this, in my judgment, is the greatest thing in every operation that makes any demand on the labor of men.

* * *

XENOPHON

From *Hellenica*, ca. 400–350 BCE

Xenophon (ca. 430 BCE–354 BCE) also wrote a history of Athens, Hellenica, *that picks up where Thucydides' history left off. The following excerpts present the events leading up to the moment our game begins, in particular the reign of terror set in place by the Thirty Tyrants and the fighting of the democratic exiles to regain Athens. The excerpts begin with the conflict between two of the Thirty—Critias (a relative of Plato) and Theramenes—which ends with Theramenes' execution.*

Solonian Aristocrats in the game may find Theramenes an appealing figure: a man who opposed both democracy and the excesses of the Thirty. Democrats may find inspiration in the leadership of Thrasybulus. All should note that the fighting described here is a civil war, one that pitted fellow citizens, relatives, and friends against one another.

SOURCE: *Xenophon,* Hellenica, *trans. H. G. Dakyns (New York: Macmillan & Co, 1897), edited for this edition.*

The Thirty had been chosen almost immediately after the long walls and the fortifications round Piraeus had been razed [following Athens's defeat by Sparta in 404 BCE during the Peloponnesian War]. They were chosen to compile a code of laws for the future constitution of the State. These laws were never published, and the Thirty appointed a Council and other magistrates as suited them. They then turned their attention to those who were known to have made their living as informers under the democracy, particularly those who had attacked aristocrats. These they seized and condemned to death.

* * *

But the Thirty did not stop there. Soon they began to consider how they might gain absolute control. They sent Aeschines and Aristoteles to Sparta, and persuaded

Lysander[1] to support them in having a Spartan garrison sent to Athens—just until they had the "malignants" out of the way, and had established the constitution; and they would maintain these troops at their own cost. Lysander agreed, and a bodyguard, with Callibius as governor, was sent.

Once they had got the garrison, they began to flatter Callibius in order that he might support their doings. Thus he allowed some of the Spartan garrison to accompany the Thirty while they proceeded to seize whomever they wanted. They no longer confined themselves to criminals and those of no importance, but seized those they thought would oppose them or could command the largest number of supporters.

At first, Critias was of one mind with Theramenes, and the two were friends. But when Critias began to rush headlong into wholesale carnage, like one who thirsted for the blood of the democracy which had banished him, Theramenes opposed him. It was barely reasonable, he argued, to put to death people who had done nothing wrong, simply because they had enjoyed influence and honor under the democracy.

* * *

Critias would retort (for they were still friends), "We have no choice, since we intend to take power, but to get rid of those who are best able to stop us. If you think because we are Thirty instead of one our government requires any less careful guarding than an actual tyranny, you must be very innocent."

So things went on. Day after day the number of persons put to death grew longer. Day after day resentment grew till Theramenes spoke again, protesting that they must bring more persons into the conduct of affairs or the oligarchy would certainly come to an end.

Critias and the rest of the Thirty, alarmed that Theramenes might become a dangerous popular leader, drew up a list of three thousand citizens, fit and proper persons to have a share in the government. But Theramenes objected, seeing it as ridiculous that in their effort to bring the best men into the government, they should fix on just that particular number—three thousand—as if that figure had some necessary connection with the exact number of good men in the State.

* * *

So he spoke, but his colleagues instituted a military inspection. The Three Thousand were drawn up in the Agora, and the rest of the citizens—those not included in the list—elsewhere in the city. The order to take arms was given; but while the men's backs were turned, the Thirty sent the Spartan guards to take

---

1. Lysander was the Spartan general commanding the soldiers who eventually occupied Athens.

away the arms of all except the Three Thousand, carry the arms to the Acropolis, and deposit them in the temple.

Once this was done, they felt they could do what they pleased, and began to kill people in great numbers, whether because they were disliked or because they were rich. Soon the question rose: How were they to get money to pay the garrison? To meet this difficulty they decided that each should seize one of the metics, put him to death, and confiscate his property. Theramenes was told to seize one of them, to which he replied that it was hardly honorable for "the best men" to behave more badly than the informers. "At least the victims of the informers were allowed to live; our innocents must die that we may get their wealth. Their method was innocent compared with ours."

The Thirty now regarded Theramenes as an obstacle to any course they might wish to adopt and proceeded to plot against him. They spoke to members of the Council in private and denounced him as an opponent of the government. Then they issued an order to the young men, picking out the most unscrupulous characters they could find, to be present, each with a dagger hidden under his arm, and called a meeting of the Council. When Theramenes had taken his place, Critias rose and addressed the meeting:

"If," said he, "any member of this council imagines that too much blood has been shed, let me remind him that in periods of revolution such things cannot be avoided. It is inevitable that we should find many sworn foes toward oligarchy in Athens, for two reasons. First, because the population of this city is the largest in Greece; and also, because the people have grown fat on liberty for such a long time.

"We are clear on two points. The first is that democracy is an oppressive form of government for persons like ourselves and like you; the next is that Athenian democracy could never be friends with our saviors, the Spartans. But the Spartans can count on the loyalty of the better classes. And so we are establishing an oligarchical constitution with their approval. That is why we do our best to rid us of anyone opposed to the oligarchy; and, in our opinion, if one of ourselves should undermine this government of ours, he would deserve punishment.

"And the case," he continued, "is no imaginary one. The offender is here present—Theramenes. He is intent on destroying you and us by every means in his power. These are not baseless charges, but are amply shown by his criticism of our present state, and by his persistent opposition to us, his colleagues. . . . This is the very man who originated our friendly and confidential relations with Sparta. This is the very man who authorized the abolition of the democracy, who urged us on to inflict punishment on the earliest batch of prisoners brought before us. But today all is changed; now you and we are unpopular with the people, and he accordingly has ceased to support our proceedings. The explanation is obvious. In case of a catastrophe, how much pleasanter for him to run free, and leave us to render account for our past performances.

"This man is not just an ordinary enemy, but a traitor to you and to us. And treason is far more dangerous than open war, since it is harder to guard against a hidden assassin than an open foe. . . . There he stands unmasked. He has forfeited our confidence forever. But to show you that these are no new tactics of his, to prove to you that he is a traitor in essence, I will recall some points in his past history.

"He began by being held in high honor by the democracy; but taking a leaf out of his father's book, he next showed a most headlong anxiety to transform the democracy into the Four Hundred [in 411], and, in fact, for a time held the first place in that body. But soon, detecting the formation of rival power to the oligarchs, round he shifted; and we find him next a ringleader of the popular party in attacking them.

* * *

"The case is clear. We therefore cite this man before you as a conspirator and traitor against yourselves and us. Consider one further point. No one, I think, will dispute the perfection of the Spartan constitution. Imagine one of the ephors[2] there in Sparta, instead of devoted obedience to the majority, finding fault with the government and opposing all measures. Do you not think that the ephors themselves, and the whole state besides, would hold him worthy of punishment? So, too, by the same token, if you are wise, show no mercy to Theramenes. His preservation would cause the courage of your opponents to rise; his destruction will cut off the last hopes of all your enemies, both within and without the city."

With these words he sat down, but Theramenes rose and said: "Sirs . . . I must say, I do agree with Critias on one point. Whoever wishes to end your government or strengthen your enemies should be severely punished; but who is actually doing this? You will best discover that, I think, by looking more closely into the past and the present conduct of each of us.

"Up to the time when you became members of the Council, when the magistrates were appointed, and certain notorious informers were brought to trial, we all held the same views. But later on, when our friends began to arrest respectable honest men, I began to differ from them. From the moment when Leon of Salamis, a man of well-deserved reputation, was put to death, though he had committed no crime, I knew that all his equals must tremble for themselves, and, so trembling, turn against the government. And when Niceratus, son of Nicias, was arrested—a wealthy man, who, no more than his father, was in any way a leader of the democrats—it did not require much insight to discover that his friends would become our enemies. When it came to Antiphon being put to death—Antiphon, who during the war contributed two triremes out of his own resources—it was

2. Ephors were members of the ruling elite in Sparta.

then clear that all who had ever been enthusiastically patriotic must eye us with suspicion.

"Once more I could not help speaking out in opposition to my colleagues when they suggested that each of us ought to seize some metic. For what could be more certain than that their death-warrant would turn all the metics into enemies of the government? I spoke out again when they deprived the people of their arms, since I did not think we should remove the strength of the city.

* * *

"I might prove the truth of what I say in many ways, but consider this. Which condition of affairs here in Athens will make Thrasybulus and Anytus and the other exiles happier? That which I recommend, or that which my colleagues are producing? As things now are, they [the exiles] must be saying to themselves, 'Our allies are growing quickly.' But if the best people in the city supported us, our enemies could scarcely gain any foothold.

"Then, with regard to what he said of me and my tendency to change sides. . . . So I have tried to please both parties. But what of the man who pleases neither? What in heaven's name are we to call him? You—Critias—under the democracy were the greatest hater of the people, and now under the aristocracy you are the bitterest enemy of everything respectable. I have always been opposed to those who think a democracy cannot reach perfection until slaves and those who must get their drachma a day take part in the government. But I am no less an opponent of those who think a perfect oligarchy demands the despotism of a few. On the contrary, my own ambition has been to combine with those who are rich enough to possess a horse and shield, and to use them for the benefit of the State. That was my ideal in the old days, and I hold to it still. Name any time I have connived with either despots or demagogues to deprive decent people of their citizenship. If you can convict me of such crimes in the present or the past, I admit that I deserve to die."

Theramenes expresses support for a moderate oligarchy as opposed to democracy.

Theramenes ceased, and the applause that followed revealed the Council's support. Critias realized that if the Council voted, Theramenes would escape, and this was intolerable to him. And so, he stepped forward and spoke a word or two in the ears of the Thirty. He then went out and gave an order to the attendants with the daggers to stand close to the bar separating the Council from the public. Again he entered and addressed the Council: "A good president, when he sees his friends deluded, will intervene, and that is what I propose to do. Indeed our friends standing here by the bar say that if we acquit a man openly doing harm to the oligarchy, they will not let us do so. There is a clause in the new code forbidding any of the Three Thousand to be put to death without your vote; but the Thirty have power of life and death over all outside that list. Thus, with the approval of the Thirty, I strike this man, Theramenes, off the list. And now," he continued, "we condemn him to death."

Hearing these words Theramenes sprang to the altar, shouting: "I ask only for justice. Let it not be in the power of Critias to strike from the list anyone he wishes. But in my case—in what may be your case as well—if we are tried, let our trial be in accordance with the law. I know," he added, "that this altar will not protect me, but I will make it plain that these men respect the gods no more than they do men. Yet I wonder, gentlemen, that you will not help yourselves, when you must see that each of your names may be erased as easily as mine."

At this point the herald gave the order to the Eleven[3] to seize Theramenes. They entered with their attendants—at their head Satyrus, the boldest and most shameless of the body—and Critias exclaimed, "We hand over to you Theramenes there, who has been condemned according to the law. Take him away to the proper place, and do what is necessary." As Critias spoke, Satyrus dragged Theramenes from the altar, who called upon gods and men to witness what was happening. The Council members meanwhile kept silence, seeing the companions of Satyrus at the bar, who they knew were armed with daggers, and the whole front of the Council house was crowded with foreign guards.

And so Theramenes was dragged through the Agora, as he shouted out the wrongs he was suffering. One notable thing he said. When Satyrus told him, "Be silent, or you will regret the day," he answered, "And if I be silent, shall I not regret it?" Also, when the time was come to drink the hemlock, they tell how he playfully threw the dregs from the bottom of the cup, like one who plays cottabos, with the words, "This to the lovely Critias."[4] These are sayings too trivial, it may be thought, to find a place in history. Yet I think it admirable that when death was near, neither his wits nor his playfulness abandoned him.

So Theramenes met his death, and the Thirty, feeling they could exercise power without fear, issued an order forbidding all whose names were not on the list [of the Three Thousand] to enter the city. Retirement in the country districts was no protection, since the prosecutor followed them there and evicted them, so that the Thirty and their friends might gain those farms and properties.

* * *

Soon Thrasybulus, with about seventy followers, marched out from Thebes, and seized the fortress of Phyle.[5] The weather was brilliant, and the Thirty marched out against them with the Three Thousand and the cavalry. When they reached the place, some overconfident young men attacked the fortress, but without effect.

---

3. The Eleven were a group of men who carried out punishments under the Thirty.

4. Executions were carried out by forcing the condemned man to drink hemlock, a poison. Cottabos was a drinking game in which men would toss the dregs of wine from their cup towards a target and dedicate it to their boy love.

5. Phyle was a fortress on the northern border of Athenian territory (see map on page 24).

The Thirty now intended to blockade the place. By shutting off all avenues of supply, they thought to force the garrison to capitulate. But a heavy snowfall that night and the following day halted their plans, and they retreated to the city—but not without the loss of many of their camp-followers, who fell prey to the men in Phyle. The government in Athens realized they must now secure the farms and country houses from plundering, and so they sent out most of the Spartan garrison and two divisions of cavalry to protect the boundary estates, about two miles south of Phyle.

But by this time there were now about 700 men collected in Phyle; and Thrasybulus descended with them one night. When he was not quite half a mile from the enemy's encampment he grounded arms, and they waited in silence until the enemy were beginning to rise at dawn. At this moment Thrasybulus and his men grabbed their arms and charged the enemy. They killed some on the spot and routed the whole body, pursuing them for nearly a mile, and killing some 120 hoplites.

* * *

After this the Thirty, who had begun to realize the insecurity of their position, were anxious to take over Eleusis,[6] as a refuge for them should they need it. They ordered out the cavalry; and Critias and the rest of the Thirty visited Eleusis. There they held a review of the townspeople in the presence of the cavalry; and, on the pretext of wishing to learn how many they were and how large a garrison they would need, they ordered the townsfolk to enter their names. As each man did so he went out by a gate leading to the sea. But there were lines of cavalry drawn up in waiting, and as each man appeared he was seized by the accomplices of the Thirty. When all were seized, Lysimachus, the commander of the cavalry, took them off to the city to deliver them over to the Eleven.

Next day they summoned to the theater the hoplites and cavalry who were on the list. Critias rose and addressed them, saying: "Sirs, we are organizing this government in your interests as well as ours. You, too, must participate in its dangers, even as you benefit from its honors. We expect you therefore to vote for the death of these men of Eleusis, so that our hopes and fears may be identical." Then, pointing to a particular spot, he said, "You will please deposit your votes there within sight of all." Armed Spartan guards were present at the time, filling one-half of the theater. These proceedings pleased those members of the State (besides the Thirty) who thought only of their advantage.

But Thrasybulus at the head of his followers (by now 1000 strong) descended from Phyle and reached Piraeus in the night. The Thirty, when they learned this, hurried to the rescue with the Spartan garrison and their own cavalry and hoplites, advancing along the carriage road leading into Piraeus. The men from Phyle at first

---

6. Eleusis was a town to the west of Athens (see map on page 24).

tried to prevent their passage, but as the wide circuit of the walls needed a larger defense force, they retreated to Munychia.[7] The troops from the city poured into the Agora of Hippodamus. Here they formed in line, stretching along and filling the street leading to the temple of Artemis. This line was at least fifty shields deep; and in this formation they at once began to march up.

The men of Phyle also blocked the street at the opposite end but they presented a thin line, not more than ten deep, though behind them were light-armed javelin men, supported by stone-throwers—a great number from the people of the port. While the enemy was advancing, Thrasybulus gave the order to ground their heavy shields, and he stood among them, saying: "Men and fellow-citizens, of the men advancing beneath us there, the right division are the very men we routed only five days ago; while on the extreme left there you see the Thirty. These are the men who have robbed us of our city, though we did no wrong; who have driven us from our homes; who have killed and confiscated the property of our dearest friends. But now what they never expected, and what we have prayed for, has come about. Here we stand with our swords in our hands, face to face with our foes, and the gods themselves are with us, seeing that we were arrested in the midst of our peaceful pursuits. At any moment, while we supped, or slept, or marketed, sentence of banishment was passed upon us: we had done no wrong and many of us were not even in the city.

"Today, the gods clearly fight on our side, the great gods, who raised a snowstorm even in the midst of calm for our benefit, and when we begin to fight, will enable our little company to set up the trophy of victory over our many foes. Today they have brought us to a place where the steep climb will prevent our enemies from reaching with lance or arrow further than our foremost ranks; but we with our volley of spears and arrows and stones cannot fail to inflict casualties. Had we been forced to meet them vanguard to vanguard, on an equal footing, who could have been surprised? But as it is, let fly your missiles with a will. No one can miss his mark when the road is full of our enemies. To avoid our darts they must hide beneath their shields; but we will rain blows upon them in their blindness; we will leap upon them and cut them down.

"Now, friends let me call on you to act so that each knows that victory was won by him and him alone. Victory, God willing, shall this day restore to us the land of our fathers, our homes, our freedom, and the rewards of civic life. Thrice happy will be those among us who as conquerors look upon this gladdest of all days. Nor less fortunate the man who falls today. Not all the wealth in the world will purchase him a monument so glorious. At the right moment I will strike the battle cry; then, with an invocation to the God of battle, let us avenge ourselves for the wrongs these men have inflicted on us."

---

7. Munychia was the citadel of Piraeus, Athens's port. The marketplace in Piraeus was often called the "agora of Hippodamus."

Having spoken, he turned round, facing the enemy, and kept quiet, for the seer had told them not to charge before one of their side was slain or wounded. "As soon as that happens," said the seer, "the victory shall be yours; but for myself, I see that death is waiting." He spoke truly, for they had barely taken up their arms when he himself, as though driven by fate, fell upon the enemy and was slain, and lies now buried at the passage of the Cephisus. But the rest were victorious, and pursued the enemy down to the level ground. Two of the Thirty, Critias himself and Hippomachus, fell, and with them Charmides, the son of Glaucon, one of the ten archons in Piraeus, and another seventy men. The arms of the slain were taken; but, as fellow-citizens, the conquerors did not despoil them of their coats. And afterward, they gave back the dead under cover of a truce, when the men on either side stepped forward and conversed with one another.

Then Cleocritus (a truly sweet-voiced herald), called for silence, and addressed the combatants as follows: "Fellow-citizens—Why do you drive us forth? Why would you slay us? What evil have we done to you? or is it a crime that we have shared with you in the most solemn rites and sacrifices and festivals? We have been companions in the chorus, the school, the army. We have braved a thousand dangers with you by land and sea in behalf of our common safety, our common liberty. By the gods of our fathers and mothers, by the hallowed names of kinship and marriage and comradeship, those three bonds which knit the hearts of so many of us, bow in reverence before God and man, and cease to sin against the land of our fathers. Cease to obey these most wicked Thirty, who for the sake of private gain have in eight months slain almost more men than the Spartans did in ten years of warfare. We can live as citizens in peace; it is only these men who bring upon us this horror of fratricidal war, loathed of God and man. Be well assured, that we as well as you have wept for many of your men fallen today."

So he spoke, but the surviving officers of the defeated army, not wanting their troops to listen, led them back to the city. The next day, the Thirty, down-hearted and desolate, sat in the Council chamber. The Three Thousand began to quarrel with one another. Those who were frightened because of the crimes they had committed objected to yielding to the party in Piraeus. Those who had faith in their own innocence tried to convince their neighbors that they should end their present evils. "Why give obedience to these Thirty?" they asked, "Why give them the power of destroying the State?" In the end they voted to depose the government and elect another. This was a Board of Ten, elected one from each tribe.

The Thirty now retired to Eleusis; but the Ten, assisted by the cavalry officers, had enough to do to keep watch over the men in the city, whose anarchy and mutual distrust were rampant. The cavalry did not return to quarters at night, but slept out in the theater, keeping their horses and shields close beside them. Indeed the distrust was so great that from evening onwards they patrolled the walls on foot with their shields, and at break of day mounted their horses, at every moment fearing some sudden attack upon them by the men in Piraeus. The Piraeus men were now so numerous that it was difficult to find arms for all, and some had to be content with shields of wood or wicker-work.

Within ten days, the men at Piraeus gave oaths that all fighting with them would secure full citizenship, with equality of taxation and tribute to all, even foreigners. Thus they soon took the field with large numbers of hoplites and light-armed troops, and about 70 cavalry. They would send foraging parties for wood and provisions, returning at nightfall to Piraeus. No one from the city ventured to take the field under arms; except the cavalry, who would capture stray pillagers from Piraeus or inflict some damage on their opponents.

* * *

But it was to Sparta that men's eyes now turned. The Thirty sent ambassadors from Eleusis, as did the men on the list of Three Thousand in the city, asking the Spartans for aid, on the grounds that the democrats had revolted from Sparta. Lysander, thinking he could force the democrats in Piraeus to terms through a blockade, supported their application. . . . And so proceeding to the scene of action at Eleusis, he got together a large body of Spartan hoplites, while his brother, the admiral, kept watch by sea to prevent provisioning of Piraeus by water. Thus the men in Piraeus were soon again in difficulty, while the hopes of the city folk rose.

At this stage, Pausanias[8] intervened. Jealous of Lysander—who seemed about to achieve fame *and* Athens as his own property—the king persuaded three of the ephors to support him, and called out the army. With him marched contingents of all the allied States, except the Boeotians and Corinthians.[9]

* * *

Still, his feelings were not embittered against his adversary. On the contrary he sent secretly and instructed the men of Piraeus what sort of terms they should propose to himself and the ephors in attendance. They followed his advice, while Pausanias also fostered a division in the party within the city. He advised men in the city to approach him and the ephors, and to say they had no wish to make war on the men of Piraeus, and that they would prefer a general reconciliation and the friendship of both sides with Sparta.

---

8. At that time, Pausanias was one of the kings of Sparta. Sparta was unusual in having two kings of equal importance and with equal responsibilities.

9. Omitted is a skirmish between Pausanias's troops and the democrats in Piraeus.

SELECTED BIBLIOGRAPHY

GENERAL HISTORIES OF ATHENS

Camp, J. M. *The Archaeology of Athens*. New Haven: Yale University Press, 2001.

Coldstream, J. N. *The Formation of the Greek Polis: Aristotle and Archaeology*. Opladen: Westdeutscher Verlag, 1984.

Green, P. *The Greco-Persian Wars*. Berkeley: University of California Press, 1996.

Hanson, V. D. *Hoplites: The Classical Greek Battle Experience*. London: Routledge, 1993.

Hansen, M. H., ed. *The Ancient Greek City-State*. Copenhagen: Royal Danish Academy of Sciences and Letters, 1993. See especially K. Raaflaub, "Homer to Solon: the Rise of the Polis, the Written Sources," 41–105.

Krentz, P. *The Thirty at Athens*. Ithaca: Cornell University Press, 1982.

Meiggs, R. *The Athenian Empire*. Oxford: Clarendon Press, 197.

Ober, J. *Mass and Elite in Democratic Athens: Rhetoric, Ideology, and the Power of the People*. Princeton: Princeton University Press, 1989.

Ober, J. *Political Dissent in Democratic Athens: Intellectual Critics of Popular Rule*. Princeton: Princeton University Press, 1998.

Raaflaub, K., J. Ober, and R. Wallace. *The Origins of Democracy in Ancient Greece*. Berkeley: University of California Press, 2007.

Miller, M. C. *Athens and Persia in the Fifth Century B.C.* Cambridge: Cambridge University Press, 1997.

Rhodes, P. J. *A Commentary on the Aristotelian "Athenaion politeia."* Oxford: Clarendon Press, 1981.

Rhodes, P. J. "The Athenian Revolution." In D. M. Lewis et al., eds., *The Cambridge Ancient History*, Vol. V. 2nd ed. Cambridge: Cambridge University Press: 1991.

Travlos, J. *Pictorial Dictionary of Ancient Athens*. New York: Praeger, 1971. (Also available on Perseus.)

WOMEN

Brock, R. "The Labour of Women." *Classical Quarterly* 44 (1994): 336–346.

Cohen, D. "Seclusion, Separation and the Status of Women in Classical Athens." *Greece & Rome* 36 (1989): 3–15.

Connelly, J. B. *Portrait of a Priestess: Women and Ritual in Ancient Greece*. Princeton: Princeton University Press, 2007.

Dillon, M. *Girls and Women in Classical Greek Religion*. London and New York: Routledge, 2002.

Kennedy, R. F. *Immigrant Women in Athens: Gender, Ethnicity, and Citizenship in the Classical City*. London and New York: Routledge, 2014.

Lewis, S. *The Athenian Woman: An Iconographic Handbook*. London and New York: Routledge, 2002.

Llewellyn-Jones, L. "Domestic Abuse and Violence against Women in Ancient Greece." In S. Lambert, ed., *Sociable Man: Essays in Social History in Honor of Nick Fisher*, pp. 231–266. Swansea: Classical Press of Wales, 2011.

Nevett, L. "Towards a Female Topography of the Athenian Greek City: Case Studies from Late Archaic and Early Classical Athens (c. 520–400 BCE)." *Gender and History* 23 (2011): 576–596.

Patterson, C. *The Family in Greek History*. Cambridge, MA: Harvard University Press, 1998.

Rotroff, S., and R. Lamberton. *Women in the Athenian Agora*. Princeton: ASCSA, 2006.

Schaps, D. "The Woman Least Mentioned: Etiquette and Women's Names." *Classical Quarterly* 27 (1977): 323–330.

Schaps, D. M. *Economic Rights of Women in Ancient Greece*. Edinburgh: Edinburgh University Press, 1981.

METICS

Akrigg, B. "Demography and Classical Athens." In C. Holleran and A. Pudsey, eds., *Demography and the Graeco-Roman World. New Insights and Approaches*, pp. 37–59. Cambridge: Cambridge University Press, 2011.

Bakewell, G. "Lysias 12 and Lysias 31: Metics and Athenian Citizenship in the Aftermath of the Thirty." *Greek, Roman, and Byzantine Studies* 40 (1999): 5–22.

Duncan-Jones, R. "Metic Numbers in Periclean Athens." *Chiron* 10 (1981): 101–109.

Kamen, D. *Status in Classical Athens*. Princeton: Princeton University Press, 2013.

Kennedy, R. *Immigrant Women in Athens: Gender, Ethnicity, and the City in the Classical City*. New York: Routledge, 2014.

Patterson, C. *Pericles' Citizenship Law of 451–50 BC*. New York: Arno Press, 1981.

Patterson, C. "The Hospitality of Athenian Justice: The Metic in Court." In J. C. Edmondson and V. J. Hunter, eds., *Law and Social Status in Classical Athens*, pp. 93–112. Oxford: Oxford University Press, 2000.

Whitehead, D. *The Ideology of the Athenian Metic*. Cambridge: Cambridge Philological Society, 1977.

SLAVES

Braund, D. "The Slave Supply in Classical Greece." In K. Bradley and P. Cartledge, eds., *The Cambridge World History of Slavery, Vol. 1: The Ancient Mediterranean World*, pp. 112–33. Cambridge: Cambridge University Press, 2011.

duBois, P. *Slaves and Other Objects*. Chicago: University of Chicago Press, 2003.

Finley, M. *Economy and Society in Ancient Greece*. London: Chatto and Windus, 1981.

Gagarin, M. "The Torture of Slaves in Athenian Law." *Classical Philology* 91 (1996): 1–18.

Golden, M. "Slavery and the Greek Family." In K. Bradley and P. Cartledge, eds., *The Cambridge World History of Slavery, Vol. 1: The Ancient Mediterranean World*, pp. 134–52. Cambridge: Cambridge University Press, 2011.

Kamen, D. *Status in Classical Athens*. Princeton: Princeton University Press, 2013.

Lewis, D. "Near Eastern Slaves in Classical Attica and the Slave Trade with Persian Territory." *Classical Quarterly* 61 (2011): 91–113.

Vlassopoulos, K. "Greek Slavery From Domination to Property and Back Again." *Journal of Hellenic Studies* 131 (2011): 115–130.

Wrenhaven, K. *Reconstructing the Slave: The Image of the Slave in Ancient Greece*. London: Bloomsbury Academic Press 2012.

Zelnick-Abramovitz, R. *Not Wholly Free: The Concept of Manumission and the Status of Manumitted Slaves in the Ancient Greek World*. Leiden: Brill Academic Publishers, 2005.

FINANCES

Amemiya, T. *Economy and Economics of Ancient Greece*. New York: Routledge, 2007.

Davies, J. K. *Athenian Propertied Families, 600–300 B.C.* Oxford: Oxford University Press, 1971.

Hanson, V. D. *Warfare and Agriculture in Ancient Greece*. Los Angeles: University of California Press, 1998.

Jordan, B. "The Athenian Navy in the Classical Period: A Study of Athenian Naval Administration and Military Organization in the Fifth and

Fourth Centuries B.C." In *University of California Publications: Classical Studies, Vol. 13*. Berkeley: University of California Press, 1975.

Osborne, R. *Classical landscape with figures. The ancient Greek city and its countryside*. London: George Philip and New York: Sheridan House, 1987.

Osborne R., ed. *The World of Athens: An Introduction to Classical Athenian Culture*. Cambridge: Cambridge Univerisity Press, 2008.

PRONUNCIATION GUIDE, GREEK NAMES AND TERMS

This is a basic pronunciation guide for important Greek words and names. According to accentuation rules in Greek, the accent may fall only on the last syllable, the next to last syllable, or the second to last syllable of any Greek word.

Aegospotami (ē-jus-POT-a-mē)

Aeschylus (ES-ku-lus)

Alcibiades (al-si-BI-a-dēz)

Alcmeonid (alk-ME-o-nid)

Areopagus (air-ē-AH-pa-gus)

Arginusae (ar-gi-NU-si)

Aristides (a-ris-TI-dēz)

Aristogeiton (a-ris-tō-GUY-ton)

Boeotia (bē-O-shah)

Cimon (KEE-mon)

Cleisthenes (KLIS-then-ēz)

Critias (KRIT- ē-as)

Darius (da-RI-us)

Deceleia (deck-i-LAY-a)

Demos (DE-mōs); demokratia (dē-mō-kra-TE-a)

Ephialtes (ef-e-AL-tēz)

Eunomia (ū-nō-ME-a)

Gylippos (gil-LIP-pōs)

Isonomia (ē-sō-nō-ME-a)

Lamachus (LAH-mah-kōs)

Marathonomachoi (mair-ah-thō-nō-MAH-kōy)

Miltiades (mil-TI-a-dēz)

Mycale (mi-KA-lē)

Nicias (NICK-ē-as)

Pausanias (pow-SAY-nē-as)

Peisistratus: (pī-SIS-tra-tus)

Peloponnese (pe-lō-pō-NEZ)

Pericles (PER-i-klēz)

Phalanx (FA-lanx)

Pheidippides (phī-DIP-pi-dēz)

Piraeus (pie-RAY-us)

Solon (SO-lon)

Strategos (STRAH-tē-gōs)

Themistocles (the-MIS-tō-klēz)

Theramenes (the-RAH-men-ēz)

Thermopylae (therm-MOP-i-lē)

Thetes (THEE-tēz)

Trittys (TRI-tēz)

Xerxes (ZERK-sēz)

NOTES

Part Two: Historical Background

1. This section of the Historical Background narrative was contributed by Rebecca Kennedy.
2. This section of the Historical Background narrative was drafted by Bret Mulligan.

ACKNOWLEDGMENTS

This game, which has been in continuous development for nearly eighteen years, has been a collaborative endeavor of the richest kind. Over that time, scores of professors and thousands of students have raised provocative questions, unearthed revelatory sources, and offered ingenious enhancements. We cannot possibly begin to list everyone by name. Indeed, it is some measure of the extent of this collaboration that the authors have donated their share of the royalties to the Reacting Consortium.

For this particular edition, however, we especially acknowledge Lisa Cox (Greenfield Community College), who edited the primary sources and drafted many of the teaching materials; Rebecca Futo Kennedy (Denison University), who wrote the section on women, slaves and metics; and Bret Mulligan (Haverford College), who drafted the materials on demography and economics. We also cite David Worthington (DePauw University), who proposed the special section on rhetoric; and Kenny Morrell (Rhodes College), who shared his thoughts on indeterminate roles. And we thank Justin Cahill, editor and creative force behind the Norton RTTP project. This edition reflects his wise insistence on clarity.

We further acknowledge the guidance of the Board of the Reacting Consortium, expertly chaired by John Burney since its inception, and the sustained work of Nicolas Proctor, chair of the Editorial Board of the Reacting Consortium. We are especially grateful to Dana Johnson of Barnard College, Administrative Director of the Reacting Consortium. She is largely responsible for building the Reacting community that has collectively created this game.